CONTEMPORARY HUNGARIAN COMPOSERS

EDITIO MUSICA BUDAPEST 1979

Fourth, revised, enlarged edition

© 1967 Editio Musica, Budapest
ISBN 963 330 275 7

Responsible for publishing: The Director of Editio Musica, Budapest.
Responsible editor: Gyula Czigány.
Typography: László Ginács.
Technical execution by Vera Izsák.
Technical manager: Nándor Blaskó.

Z 4728/4

Printed in Hungary

LIST OF COMPOSERS

ÁDÁM, JENŐ
BALASSA, SÁNDOR
BALÁZS, ÁRPÁD
BÁRDOS, LAJOS
BARTÓK, BÉLA
BORGULYA, ANDRÁS
BOZAY, ATTILA
DARVAS, GÁBOR
DÁVID, GYULA
DECSÉNYI, JÁNOS
DOBOS, KÁLMÁN
DUBROVAY, LÁSZLÓ
DURKÓ, ZSOLT
FARKAS, FERENC
FEKETE GYŐR, ISTVÁN
GAÁL, JENŐ
GÁRDONYI, ZOLTÁN
GESZLER, GYÖRGY
GRABÓCZ, MIKLÓS
GULYÁS, LÁSZLÓ
HAJDÚ, LÓRÁNT
HAJDU, MIHÁLY
HARMAT, ARTUR
HIDAS, FRIGYES
HORUSITZKY, ZOLTÁN
HUSZÁR, LAJOS
HUZELLA, ELEK
JÁRDÁNYI, PÁL
JEMNITZ, SÁNDOR

JENEY, ZOLTÁN
JUHÁSZ, FRIGYES
KADOSA, PÁL
KALMÁR, LÁSZLÓ
KARAI, JÓZSEF
KARDOS, ISTVÁN
KÁROLYI, PÁL
KAZACSAY, TIBOR
KELEN, HUGÓ
KENESSEY, JENŐ
KOCSÁR, MIKLÓS
KODÁLY, ZOLTÁN
KÓKAI, REZSŐ
KÓSA, GYÖRGY
KURTÁG, GYÖRGY
LAJTHA, LÁSZLÓ
LÁNG, ISTVÁN
LENDVAY, KAMILLÓ
LORÁND, ISTVÁN
MADARÁSZ, IVÁN
MAROS, RUDOLF
MEZŐ, IMRE
MIHÁLY, ANDRÁS
MOLNÁR, ANTAL
PAPP, LAJOS
PATACHICH, IVÁN
PETROVICS, EMIL
PONGRÁCZ, ZOLTÁN

RÁNKI, GYÖRGY
RIBÁRI, ANTAL
SÁRAI, TIBOR
SÁRI, JÓZSEF
SÁRKÖZY, ISTVÁN
SÁRY, LÁSZLÓ
SOPRONI, JÓZSEF
SUGÁR, REZSŐ
SULYOK, IMRE
SZABÓ, FERENC
SZÉKELY, ENDRE
SZÉKELY, IVÁN
SZELÉNYI, ISTVÁN
SZERVÁNSZKY, ENDRE
SZOKOLAY, SÁNDOR
SZŐLLŐSY, ANDRÁS
SZŐNYI, ERZSÉBET
SZUNYOGH, BALÁZS
TARDOS, BÉLA
VAJDA, JÁNOS
VÁNTUS, ISTVÁN
VÁRY, FERENC
VASS, LAJOS
VAVRINECZ, BÉLA
VÉCSEY, JENŐ
VIDOVSZKY, LÁSZLÓ
VINCZE, IMRE
VISKI, JÁNOS
WEINER, LEÓ

ABBREVIATIONS OF PUBLISHING HOUSES REFERRED TO IN THE LIST OF COMPOSITIONS:

AMP	=	Associated Music Publishers, N. Y.
BH	=	Boosey & Hawkes, London, New York, Bonn
BM	=	Belwin-Mills, Melville, N. Y.
Cs	=	Cserépfalvi, Budapest
D	=	Doblinger A. G., Vienna
EMB	=	Editio Musica, Budapest
EMB+BH	=	Co-production
EMM	=	Edition Modern, Munich
GMP	=	General Music Publisher, N. Y.,
KÓTA	=	Kórusok Országos Tanácsa (National Council of Choruses), Budapest
L	=	Alphonse Leduc, Paris
MK	=	Magyar Kórus (Hungarian Chorus), Budapest
NI	=	Népművelési Intézet (Institute of Popular Culture), Budapest
NPI	=	Népművelési Propaganda Intézet (Information Bureau of Public Education), Budapest
OPI	=	Országos Pedagógiai Intézet (National Pedagogical Institute), Budapest
OUP	=	Oxford University Press
Püski	=	Püski Sándor, Budapest
R	=	Rózsavölgyi & Co., Budapest
S	=	Simrock
UE	=	Universal Edition A. G., Vienna

The unpublished works appear in the list only with their date of composition. The dates refer always to the year of composition and not to the date of publication.
If not marked differently the discography refers to records produced by the Hungarian Record Company Hungaroton.

Closing of the Almanac: 31st January, 1978.

JENŐ ÁDÁM

(b. Szigetszentmiklós, 13 Dec. 1896). He studied composition under Zoltán Kodály and graduated in 1925 simultaneously also in Hungarian literature. During the first World War he was taken P.O.W. in Russia, thus he saw Western Siberia and Turkestan, subsequently he continued his musical profession. In 1933 he studied conducting under Felix Weingartner. From 1929 to 1959 he was professor at the Academy of Music, Budapest (faculty: training courses of singing, and education of secondary school music teachers). He was a member of the Board of Directors of ISME (International Society for Musical Edication), and secretary of the Hungarian Section of the International Folk Music Council. In 1955 he was awarded the title of "Merited Artist of the Hungarian People's Republic", and in 1957 the Kossuth Prize.

STAGE WORKS: *Ez a mi földünk* (That is Our Country), 1923; *Magyar karácsony* (Hungarian Christmas), 1930; *Mária Veronika* (Mary Veronica), 1936–37.

CHORAL WORKS: *Falu végén kurta kocsma* (Village Inn), 1927; *Two Mixed Choruses,* 1930; *Hej, rózsa, rózsa* (Hey, Rose, Rose), Foetisch Frères S. A., Lausanne; *Cinegemadár* (You Little Bird), 1939, MK; *Szegény juhász nótái* (Songs of the Poor Shepherd) 1939, MK; *Somogy-balatoni nóták* (Folk Songs from the Somogy-Balaton Re-

7

gion), 1939, MK, EMB., *A farkas és a szúnyogok* (The Wolf and the Mosquitos), for three children's voices, 1950; *Geneva Psalms No. 8 and No. 130* for mixed voices, 1968; *Geneva Psalms No. 77 and No. 134* for mixed voices, 1970; *Régi magyar énekek* (Early Hungarian Songs), for mixed voices, 1960; *Three Easy Songs* for mixed voices, 1955, EMB; *Three Peasant Songs* for mixed voices, 1963, EMB.

ORCHESTRAL MUSIC: *Dominica Suite,* 1925, transcription: *Az én falum* (My Village), 1963; *Meditation from "Mary Veronica",* 1938; *Europa 1939,* variations for orchestra, 1947; *Ábel siratása* (Lament for Abel), symphonic fresco.

WORKS FOR CHORUS AND ORCHESTRA: *Lacrima Sonata* – orchestral songs, 1927; *Suite* from the opera "Hungarian Christmas", 1940; *Lament and Rejoicing Song* from "Mary Veronica", 1941; *Ember az úton* (Man on the Way), a transcribed version of "Mary Veronica", 1945.

CHAMBER MUSIC: *String Quartet* No. 1, 1924, EMB; *Sonata* for Violoncello and Piano, 1926; *String Quartet* No. 2, 1930.

WORKS FOR CHAMBER ORCHESTRA, MIXED CHOIR AND SOLO VOICES: *Thirty-five Folk Songs,* 1941–46, EMB; *Két szál pünkösdrózsa* (Two Peonies), 1948, EMB; *Tulipán* (Tulip), *Folk Song Suite,* 1954; *Songs of János Arany,* 1951; *Songs of Pista Dankó,* 1934; *Songs of Béni Egressy,* 1957.

SONGS: *Thirty-five Hungarian Soldiers' Songs,* 1924; *Twelve Russian Folk Songs,* 1927; *Hungarian Folk Songs* – in various collections, EMB.

Numerous choral arrangements of folk songs, smaller choral works and incidental music to six films.

WRITINGS: *Módszeres énektanítás a relatív szolmizáció alapján* (Methodical Teaching of Singing, Based upon the Movable Do System, the so called: Kodály-Method), 1943; *Szó-mi* I-VIII, 1943-46; *Song-books for Schools* I-VIII, 1947-48, and I-II, 1958; *A skálától a szimfóniáig* (From the Scale to the Symphony), 1943; *A muzsikáról* (On Music), 1953–55. He delivered numerous educational lectures in the Hungarian Radio and the Television.

DISCOGRAPHY:
Folk song arrangements – Songs of János Arany
Margit László, Júlia Hamari, Sándor Tekeres (soloists), Tibor Ney (violin).
Choir and Orchestra of the Hungarian Radio and Television, conductor: Jenő Ádám
LPX 1291
Két szál pünkösdrózsa (Folksong suite in four parts)
Szilvia Geszty, Sándor Tekeres.
Choir and Orchestra of the Hungarian Radio and Television, conductor: Jenő Ádám
LP 10028 MM 758

SÁNDOR BALASSA

(b. Budapest, 20 Jan. 1935). He began studying music at seventeen. At first he took up choral leadership at the Béla Bartók Conservatory, then transferred to the Academy of Music, Budapest to study composition. He graduated as a pupil of Endre Szervánszky in 1965. Preceding his music studies, but also during his courses of study, he worked as an engine fitter. Since 1964 he has been on the staff of the Hungarian Radio, from 1966 as music producer.

STAGE WORK: *Az ajtón kívül* (The Man Outside), opera in five movements. Based on W. Borchert's play, libretto by Géza Fodor, 1973–1977.

CHORAL WORKS: *Five Children's Choruses,* 1965, EMB; *Legend* (Poem by J. Dsida) for mixed voices, 1967, EMB; *Summer Night,* hymn for female choir, 1968, EMB; *Motetta* (Poem by G. Trakl) for mixed voices, 1973. *Nádi csibe* (Little Chicken of the Reedy), (Poem by S. Weöres) for female choir, 1977.

WORKS FOR CHORUS AND ORCHESTRA: *Golden Age* (Poem by R. Tagore), cantata for soprano solo, choir and symphonic orchestra, 1965; *Zenith* (Poem by G. Apollinaire), for contralto solo and full orchestra, 1967; *Requiem for Lajos Kassák* (Kassák: Poemcollage), for soprano, tenor, bass solo, mixed voices and full orchestra, 1969, EMB; *Cantata Y,* for soprano solo and symphonic orchestra, 1970, EMB.

ORCHESTRAL MUSIC: *Concerto* for violin and orchestra, 1964; *Iris,* for symphonic orchestra, 1971, EMB; *Lupercalia,* concerto in memoriam Igor Stravinsky, for wind and brass instruments, 1972, EMB; *Chant of Glarus,* for symphonic orchestra, 1978.

CHAMBER MUSIC: *Locks,* monologue for soprano and chamber ensemble, to the poem of Vildrac, 1963; *Dimensioni* per flauto e viola, 1966, EMB + BH; *Wind Quintet,* 1966, EMB; *Antinomia* (Poems by Leckins and J. Dsida), trio for soprano, clarinet and violoncello, 1968, EMB; *Quartetto per percussioni,* 1969, EMB; *Trio* per violino, viola e arpa, 1970, EMB + BM; *Xénia,* nonet, 1970, EMB + BM; *Intermezzo* for flute and piano, in Wind Music, 1971, EMB; *Tabulae* for chamber ensemble, 1972, EMB.

INSTRUMENTAL MUSIC: *Bagatelles and Sequences* for piano, 1957–1969, EMB.

SONGS: *Two Songs* (Poems by D. Kosztolányi), 1957–1969, EMB.

DISCOGRAPHY:

Antinomia
Erika Sziklay (soprano), Béla Kovács (clarinet), Árpád Szász (violoncello)
conductor: András Mihály
LPX 11494

Requiem for Lajos Kassák
Erika Sziklay (soprano), Sándor Palcsó (tenor), Endre Ütő (bass)
Choir and Orchestra of the Hungarian Radio and Television, conductor: György Lehel.

Cantata Y
Erika Sziklay
Orchestra of the Hungarian Radio and Television, conductor: György Lehel.

Legend
Choir of the Hungarian Radio and Television, conductor: Ferenc Sapszon
SLPX–11681

Iris; Lupercalia
Orchestra of Hungarian Radio and Television, conductor: György Lehel

Tabulae; Xenia
Budapest Chamber Orchestra, conductor András Mihály.
SLPX–11732

ÁRPÁD BALÁZS

(b. Szentes, 1 Oct. 1937). First he studied music at the Conservatory in Szeged, then took up composition at the Budapest Academy of Music as a pupil of Ferenc Farkas. He graduated in 1964. He had several successful world premières and concerts as composer in the USA in 1970 and 1973, and in several European towns (Rome, London, the Hague). He was awarded the Erkel Prize in 1970, and won first prize at the composer's competition of the OIRT in 1972 and 1974, the Gold Medal of the Order of Labour, in 1975.

STAGE WORKS: *Varjak* (Crows), ("in memoriam abreptorum"), Miniature ballet, 1972; *A fehéringes* (The Man in White Shirt), ("in memoriam S. Petőfi"), ballet in 6 parts, 1973; *Engedetlen szeretők* (Disobedient Lovers), musical comedy. Text by M. Padisák—I. Hajnal, 1974; *Mi, szemüvegesek* (We, Bespectacled), musical comedy. Text by K. Fehér—E. Tarbay, 1974; *II. Rákóczi Ferenc* (Ferenc Rákóczi II), text by Gy. Száraz—F. Baranyi, 1975.

CHORAL WORKS FOR MIXED VOICES: *Two Mixed Choirs* (Poems by F. Lődi), 1964, NI, Musikaltelno Isdatelstvo, Sofia (Bulgarian text), EMB; *Memento* – suite in five movements, 1967, EMB (with Hungarian, Latin, English, French and German references to the text); *Two Amorous Madrigals,* 1967, NI; *Csillagzene* (Music of the Stars),

11

four choruses (Poems by S. Weöres), 1968, EMB, Edition "Muzika", Moscow (Russian text), Musikaltelno Izdatelstvo, Sofia (Bulgarian text); *Napigéző* (Enchantment of the Sun), 1969, NI; *Three mixed choruses* (Poems by Gy. Juhász), 1971, EMB, (Hungarian and German text); *Fáklya* (Torch) canon for mixed choir, 1971, EMB; *Budapest* – a tribute to the centenary of the unification of Pest and Buda, 1972, EMB; *Szavak a könyvhöz* (Words to the Book), to a poem by M. Vörösmarty, 1973, EMB; *Négy őszi vázlat* (Four Autumn Sketches) (Poems by J. Arany, M. Váci, I. Vasvári and I. Simon), 1973, EMB; *Clamor pro Béla Bartók,* cum verbis Horatii, 1973; *Két pasztellkép* (Two Pictures in Crayon) (Poems by Shelley), 1973, EMB; *Éneklő Európa* (Singing Europe), seven pieces for mixed voices, (Poems by F. Villon, R. Burns, H. Heine, J. W. Goethe, T. Shevtchenko, P. Verlaine), 1973, NPI; *Virágim, virágim,* rev. 1975, EMB; *Két tájkép vegyeskarra* (Two Landscapes for Mixed Voices) (Poems by I. Vasvári), 1977, EMB.

CHORAL WORKS FOR EQUAL VOICES: *Hajnali köszöntő* (Greeting at Daybreak) 1958, NI, EMB, Musikhojskolens Forlag, Denmark (Danish text), Edition "Musika", Moscow (Russian text), *Két leánykar* (Two Works for Female Voices), 1964, NI, EMB, Edition Liesmas, Riga (Lettish text), Musikaltelno Izdatelstvo, Sofia (Bulgarian text); *Madrigaleszk,* for female choir with chamber ensemble accompaniment, 1967, EMB, and Musikhojskolens Forlag, Denmark; *Két rózsaének* (Two Songs on the Rose), 1967, NI and Edition Liesmas, Riga; *Ének a dalról* (Song on the Song), 1967, EMB; *Carmina Pannoniae* (Poems by J. Pannonius), lyrical suite for female choir and harp, Latin text, 1968; *Ugratós* (Banter), jocular folk song for male choir, 1970, EMB; *Borsodi ének* (Song from Borsod) suite for female choir, 1971, EMB; *Varázslások* (Witchcraft), ancient supertitions for girls' choir in ten movements, 1971–72; *Tavaszébresztő* (The Awakening of Spring), 1971, EMB; *Kikeleti napköszöntő* (Springtime Sun Greeting), 1972, EMB; *Röptető* (Let Fly), 1973, EMB; *Csúfoló* (Mocking), for children's voices, 1974, EMB, Edition "Muzika", Moscow (Russian text); *Rózsatánc* (Dance of Roses), suite for girls' choir, rev. 1975, EMB; *Kis zenei ABC* (Small Musical ABC), for children's voices, 1976, EMB; Three Children's Choruses to poems by J. Pinczési, 1977; *Szabadságkánon* (Liberty Canon) for female voices to text by F. Jankovich and K. Nádas, 1977; *Készülődés* (Preparation), suite to poems by I. Vasvári, rev. 1977, EMB.

WORKS FOR CHORUS AND ORCHESTRA: *Tüzek* (Fires), oratorio, 1969; *Tavaszlesen* (Waiting for Spring), cantata for children to poems by twentieth century Hungarian poets, 1965, NI, EMB; *Ének Budapestről* (Song on Budapest), miniature cantata for soprano solo, male choir, orchestra on the centenary of the unification of Pest and Buda, 1972; *A Tél lebírása* (Winter is defeated), cantata to poems by Gy. Illyés, for baritone solo, male choir and orchestra 1974, EMB; *Viharban született* (Born in Storm), cantata for tenor and bass solo, male choir and orchestra, 1975.

ORCHESTRAL MUSIC: *Musica piccola per orchestra da fiati* – suite 1966, NI; *Lyrical Suite,* 1966; *Overture,* 1967, NI; *Three Sketches for Orchestra,* 1971–72; *Varjak* (Crows), ballet music, 1972; *A fehéringes* (The Man in White Shirt), ballet suite in 6 movements in memoriam S. Petőfi, 1972–73.

CHAMBER MUSIC: *Serenade* for wind quintet, 1961, EMB; *Burlesca* – for flute and piano, 1970, EMB + BH; *Three Little Pieces* – for two flutes, 1970; *Tánc* (Dance) for two trumpets, 1972, EMB; *Danza umorastica* for flute and cimbalom, 1977, EMB; *Three miniatures* for flute and cimbalom, 1977, EMB.

INSTRUMENTAL SOLO PIECES: *33 Piano Pieces for Children,* 1967–69; *Improvisation for Solo Trumpet,* 1972; *14 Easy Piano Pieces,* 1972, EMB + BH; *Toccata* for piano, rev. 1976; *Táncpár* (Dance Pair) for cimbalom, 1976, EMB.

DISCOGRAPHY:
Song on Budapest – Carry the May Flag – Memento
HVDSZ Male Choir, Vándor Choir, Choir of the Iron Workers' Art Ensemble
LPX 15039
Viharban született (Born in Storm)
Dénes Gulyás, Péter Kovács
Central Male Choir of the Labour Guard, Hungarian State Orchestra, conductor:
László Révész
SLPX 15051

LAJOS BÁRDOS

(b. Budapest, 1 Oct. 1899). He studied music under Albert Siklós and Zoltán Kodály. Having finished his studies in 1925, he taught in a high school and in a teacher's college until 1928, then he was appointed professor to the Academy of Music, Budapest (harmony, theory and history of music, seminars in musical style etc.) until 1968. From 1925 to 1941 he was also conductor of the Cecilia Chorus, from 1929 to 1933 of the Palestrina Chorus; these two ensembles were then united under the name of Budapest Chorus. He was Regens-chori of the Városmajor Church, and of the Matthias Coronation Church from 1942 to 1947, from 1925 to 1942, and from 1942 to 1962, respectively. He is an outstanding Hungarian choral conductor. In 1931 (with Gyula Kertész) he founded the Magyar Kórus publishing company which played an important part in the revival of Hungarian choral singing. He was director of this company and of the musical periodical of the same title, up to 1950. In 1934 he organized the Singing Youth movement. He was one of the leaders of the National Association of Hungarian Choirs from 1936, – of the Béla Bartók Association from 1949 to 1950. In 1953 he was awarded the Erkel Prize, in 1954 the title of "Merited Artist of the Hungarian People's Republic", in 1955 the Kossuth Prize, in 1964 the Viennese Gold Medal; and the Gold Medal of the Order of Labour, in 1969.

STAGE WORKS (mystery-plays): *Nyolc boldogság* (The Eight Beatitudes), 1927; *Hajnalvárás* (Waiting for Dawn), 1927; *Advent*, 1928; *Rózsák szentje* (The Saint of Roses), 1932; *A gyermek útja* (The Way of the Child), 1935; *Szent Imre* (Saint Emeric), 1937; *Árpádházi Szent Margit* (Saint Margaret of the House of Árpád), 1939; *Alexius*, 1946.

WORKS FOR CHORUS AND ORCHESTRA: *Körtánc* (Roundelay), 1953; *Fújd a sípot* (Blow the Pipe), 1953; *Somogyi kalászok* (Spikes in Somogy County), 1955; *Csángó leánytánc* (Tshango Girls' Dance), 1956, Educational Publishers; *Kis kacsa* (The Little Duckling), 1959; *Cantate!* for mixed voices and guitar orchestra, 1977.

VOCAL COMPOSITIONS

SACRED MUSIC: three *Masses*, 1933, 1934, 1944; *Ave Maris Stella*, for female voices, BH; numerous *Motets, Offertories, Psalms* and arrangements of *Folk Hymns*.

WORKS FOR MIXED CHOIRS: *Ungaresca*, 1931, MK, EMB; *Folk Song Choruses* I–IV, 1933, MK, EMB; *Spártai gyermek* (Spartan Child), 1935, MK, EMB; *Széles a Duna* (Wide is the Danube), 1937, MK, EMB; *Szeged felől* (From Szeged), 1938, MK; *A nyúl éneke* (Song of the Rabbit), 1944; *Patkóéknál* (At the Patkós'), 1948, EMB; *Régi táncdal* (Old Dance Song), 1948; *Tilinkós* (The Shepherd's Pipe), 1951; *A földhez* (To Earth), 1951, EMB; *Hetven év* (Seventy Years), 1952; *Zászlódal* (To the Flying Colours), 1952; *Csokonaidalok* (Csokonai Songs), 1953; *Becskereki menyecske* (Young Wife at Becskerek), 1953, EMB; *Baranyai vasárnap* (Sunday at Baranya County), 1953, EMB; *I. népdalrapszódia* (Folk Song Rhapsody No. 1), 1953, EMB; *Elmúlt a tél* (Winter is Gone), 1953, EMB; *Kossuth Suite*, 1953, EMB; *Small Suite*, 1954, EMB; Seven Two-part Mixed Choirs, 1953, EMB; *Az nem lehet* (It Can't Be), 1955, EMB; *Lakodalmas rondo* (Wedding Rondo), 1955, EMB; *Jeremiás siralma* (Lament of Jeremiah), 1956; *Éjféli órán* (At Midnight), 1956; *Ének a dalról* (Song on the Song), 1956, EMB; *Szakcsi dalcsokor* (Songs from Szakcs), 1956; *Távoli álom* (Faraway Dream), 1957, EMB; *Veszprémi jelhang* (Signal for Veszprém), 1958; *Szabad kunok népe* (People of Free Cumanians), 1959; *Miénk az élet* (Life is Ours), 1961; *II. népdalrapszódia* (Folk Song Rhapsody No. 2), 1961, EMB; *A munka* (Work), 1962; *Tűzszivárvány* (Fire-Rainbow), 1963; *Dalol a gyár* (The Factory is Singing), 1963; *Küzdeni!* (Fight!), 1964, EMB; *Még nem elég* (Not Enough!), 1965; *Eger*, 1965; *Ünnepi zászlók* (Decked with Banners), 1966; *Kőszegi ének* (Song of Kőszeg), 1966; *Énekeljetek* (Sing!), 1967; *Esztergom sorsáról* (On the Fate of Esztergom), 1967; *Ezékiel látomása* (Ezekiel's Vision), 1967; *Ének a bányáról* (Song on the Mine), 1968; *Nárcisz-dal* (Narcissus Song), 1968, NPI; *Béke-himnusz* (Hymn of Peace), 1969; *Szól a doromb* (Ributhe Music), 1970; *Csillagvirág* (Blue-Bell), 1970; *G. Thury emlékezete* (In Memoriam G. Thury), 1970; *Hazaváró* (Song of the Home), 1971; *Szabadságban élni!* (Living in Freedom), 1971; *A dal titka* (Secret of Song), 1972; *Zrínyi-ének* (Zrínyi Song), 1972; *Bartók*, 1975, NPI; *Cantemus!* 1977, EMB; *Candida rosa*, 1977, Ed. Zanibon; *Libera me*, 1978, EMB.

WORKS FOR EQUAL VOICES: *Négy földrész* (Four Continents), 1933; *Kicsinyek kórusa* I–III (Chorus for the Little Ones I–III), 1934–52, MK, EMB; *Megütik a dobot*

(The Drum is Sounded), for male voices, 1936, MK; *Liszt Ferenchez* (To Ferenc Liszt), for male voices, 1936; *Húzd rá, te cigány* (Play Up, You Gipsy), for male voices, 1939, MK; *Kossuth Songs,* for male voices, 1940, EMB; *Dana-dana* (Sing-Song), for male voices, 1940, MK, Gwinn, Llangollen; *Magos a rutafa* (High is the Rue Tree), for female voices, 1941, MK, EMB; *Etudes,* for male voices, 1942; *Jókedvű dallamok* (Merry Melodies), for male voices, 1943, MK; *Gyászének* (Dirge), for male voices, 1947, MK; *Napfényes utakon* (On Sunny Ways), 1948, MK, EMB; *Négy szó* (Four Words), 1948, MK; *Tavaszi induló* (Spring March), 1948; *Hangképek férfikarra* (Musical Sketches for Male Choir), 1948; *Gazdadicsérő* (Praise of the Farmer), 1952, EMB; *Huszár toborzó* (Recruiting Song of the Hussars), 1952; *Zászlódal* (To the Flying Colours), 1952, EMB; *Old Dance Song,* for male choir, 1952; *Two Kuruc Songs,* for male choir, 1953; *Tettrehívó* (Alert!), for male choir, 1953; *Katonák bordala* (Drinking Song of Soldiers), for male choir, 1954; *Száraz ágon* (Upon those Dry Branches), for male choir, 1956; *A márciusi ifjak* (The Youth of March), 1956; *A madár fiaihoz* (A Bird to his Small Ones), for male choir, 1957, EMB; *Csengő-bongó karácsony* (Tinkling Christmas), for children's choir, 1963, EMB; *Twenty Choruses for Equal Voices,* 1963, EMB; *Csillag az égen* (Star in the Sky), for female voices, 1963; *Himnusz a naphoz* (Hymn to the Sun), 1964; *Tavunga,* for female choir, 1964, EMB; *Tanzmelodie* (Dance Melody), for children's choir, 1964; Bärenreiter; *Bartók emlékére* (To the Memory of Béla Bartók), 1965; *Ne félj!* (Don't Fear!), 1967; *Európa peremén* (On the Edge of Europe), 1970; *Serkenj, ifjúság!* (Spur on, Youth!), 1971; *Hellasz* (Eight biciniums), 1977, EMB; numerous canons and folk song arrangements.

INSTRUMENTAL WORKS: *String Quartet* — 1925; *Three Hungarian Folk Songs,* 1927, OUP; several small pieces for violoncello, piano or organ. *Hungarica antiqua,* 1971.

SONGS: to the poems of Petőfi, Ady and Móra, folk song arrangements, singing exercises, etc.

PUBLICATIONS: *Hundred and one Hungarian Folk Songs,* 1928, MK; *Harmonia Sacra,* 1934, MK; *Magyar Cantuale,* 1935, MK; *Gyöngyvirág* (Lily-of-the-Valley – 92 Hungarian Folk Songs), 1952, EMB; *Százszorszép* (Daisy – Hundred Hungarian Folk Songs), 1957, EMB; *70 kánon* (70 Canons), 1970, EMB.

LITERARY ACTIVITY: *Hangzat-gyakorló* (Exercise Book of Harmony), 1954; *Modális harmóniák* (Modal Harmonies), 1961, EMB; *Harminc írás* (The Theory and Practice of Music, Essays.), 1969; *Zenei prozódia* (Musical Prosody), 1972; *Tíz írás* (The Theory and Practice of Music, Essays.), 1974, EMB; *A lokriszi skála Kodály műveiben* (The Locris Scale in Kodály's Works), 1976, Magyar Zene; *Bartók-dallamok és a népzene* (Bartók Melodies and the Folk Music), 1977, OPI.

DISCOGRAPHY:
To the Earth; Two biciniums from the series: "Chorus for the Little Ones"; Blow the Pipe;

In the Autumn; Sing-Song; Folk Song Rhapsody No. 2; Ave Maris Stella; Tünde Song;
High is the Rue Tree; Tavunga; Song of the Rabbit; Winter is Gone; Old Dance Song
György Melis, Zsuzsa Németh (soloists)
Mixed Choir and Children's Choir of the Hungarian Radio and Television, Male Choir
of the Honvéd Art Ensemble, conductors: Ferenc Sapszon, István Kiss.
LPX 11538

BÉLA BARTÓK

(b. Nagyszentmiklós, 25 March 1881; d. New York 26 Sept. 1945). Studied composition with János Koessler, piano with István Thomán at the Academy of Music, Budapest. In his early years he was influenced by Brahms, Wagner, Liszt and Richard Strauss. A turning point of his musical style was his acquaintance with folk music. From 1906 he systematically collected folk songs in Hungary and in the neighbouring countries, in North-Africa and in Turkey. In 1907 he was appointed professor at the Academy of Music, Budapest. As a composer and pianist, he played his own works first and foremost on his European and American concert tours. Protesting against Nazism he left Hungary in 1940 and went to the USA to await the end of the war and Nazism. His return home was made impossible by his grave illness which also caused his early death in 1945.

STAGE WORKS: *A kékszakállú herceg vára* (Duke Bluebeard's Castle), Op. 11, opera in one act, 1911, UE; *A fából faragott királyfi* (The Wooden Prince), Op. 13, ballet in one act, 1914–16, Suite version, 1931, UE; *A csodálatos mandarin* (The Miraculous Mandarin), Op. 19, pantomime in one act, 1918–19, Suite version, 1919, UE.

WORKS FOR SOLO VOICE, CHORUS AND ORCHESTRA: *Tiefblaue Veilchen* (Song for Soprano and Orchestra), 1899; *Falun* (Village Scenes), for four or eight fe-

18

male voices and chamber orchestra, 1926, transcription of *Five Village Scenes* Nos. 3, 4, 5, UE; *Cantata profana* for double mixed chorus, tenor and baritone solo and orchestra, 1930, UE; *Five Hungarian Folk Songs* for voice and orchestra, 1933, transcription; *Five Choruses for Female Choir and Orchestra* (from the 27 Choruses, 1935), BH; *Five Choruses for Children's Choir and School Orchestra* (from the 27 Choruses, 1935), MK, EMB.

ORCHESTRAL MUSIC

CONCERTOS: *Rhapsody for Piano and Orchestra,* 1904, R, EMB; *Scherzo for Piano and Orchestra,* Op. 2, 1904, EMB; *Piano Concerto* No. 1, 1926, UE; *Piano Concerto* No. 2, 1930–31, UE; *Piano Concerto* No. 3, last 17 measures completed by Tibor Serly, 1945, BH; *Concerto for two Pianos and Orchestra* (transcription of the *Sonata for two Pianos and Percussion*), 1940, BH; *Violin Concerto,* 1907–08, BH; *Rhapsody No. 1 and No. 2 for Violin and Orchestra* (transcription of the violin and piano version), 1928, No. 2 rev. 1944, UE, BH; *Violin Concerto,* 1937–38, BH; *Viola Concerto,* unfinished, reconstructed and orchestrated by Tibor Serly, 1945, BH.

SYMPHONIC WORKS: *Symphony* in E flat major (only the *Scherzo* scored), 1902; *Kossuth,* symphonic poem in ten tableaux, 1903, EMB; *SuiteNo. 1,* Op. 3, 1905, R, rev. c. 1920, EMB; *Suite No. 2,* Op. 4, 1905–07, rev. 1920 and 1943, UE, BH; *Két portré* (Two Portraits), Op. 5, 1907–11, Rozsnyai, EMB, BH; *Két kép* (Two Pictures, Deux Images), Op. 10, 1910, R, UE, EMB; *Rumanian Dance* for orchestra (transcription of No. 1 of the *Two Rumanian Dances* for Piano), 1911, EMB; *Four Orchestral Pieces* Op. 12, 1912, orchestration 1921, UE; *Rumanian Folk Dances* for orchestra (from the piano version), 1917, R, UE; *Tánc-suite* (Dance Suite), 1923, UE, transcription for piano, 1923, UE; *Erdélyi táncok* (Transylvanian Dances) for orchestra, transcription of the *Sonatina* for piano, 1931, R, EMB; *Magyar képek* (Hungarian Sketches), transcription of earlier piano pieces, 1931, Rozsnyai, R, EMB; *Magyar parasztdalok* (Hungarian Peasant Songs) for orchestra, transcriptions of Nos. 6–12, 14, 15 of *Fifteen Hungarian Peasant Songs,* 1933, UE; *Zene húroshangszerekre, ütőkre és celestára* (Music for Strings, Percussion and Celesta), 1936, UE; *Divertimento* for string orchestra, 1939, BH; *Concerto* for orchestra, 1943, BH.

CHAMBER MUSIC: *Sonata for Violin and Piano,* 1895; *Sonata for Violin and Piano,* 1897; *Quartet for Piano and Strings* in E flat major, 1898; *String Quartet* in F major, 1898; *Duo* for two violins, 1902; *Albumblatt* for violin and piano, 1902; *Sonata for Violin and Piano,* 1903, EMB; *Quintet for Piano and Strings,* 1904, EMB; *String Quartet* No. 1, Op. 7, 1908, R, EMB; *String Quartet* No. 2, Op. 17, 1915–17, UE; *Sonata for Violin and Piano* No. 1, 1921, UE; *Sonata for Violin and Piano* No. 2, 1922, UE; *String Quartet* No. 3, 1927, UE; *Rhapsody No. 1* for violin and piano, or for violoncello and piano, 1928, UE, BH; *Rhapsody No. 2* for violin and piano, 1928, rev. vers. 1944, UE, BH; *String Quartet* No. 4, 1928, UE; *Forty-four Duos* for two violins, 1931, UE; *Magyar népdalok* (Hungarian Folk Songs) for violin and piano (Nine pieces from *For Children* arranged by Tivadar Országh and Bartók); 1934, R, EMB; *String Quartet* No. 5, 1934, UE; *Sonata for two Pianos and Percussion,* 1937, BH; *Contrasts* for violin, clarinet and piano, 1938, BH; *String Quartet* No. 6, 1939, BH; *Sonata for Violin Solo,* 1944, BH.

PIANO PIECES: "Op. 1 – Op. 31" (first set of Opus-numbers:) small pieces (Valse, Mazurka, Polka, March, Ländler, Sonatina etc., among them *A Duna folyása* [The Flow of the Danube], Op. 20), 1890–94; "Op. 1 – Op. 21" (second set of Opus-numbers, from 1894–98:) sonatas, Fantasy, Capriccio, etc. a selection published by Denijs Dille in the volume *Az ifjú Bartók II* (The Young Bartók II) EMB, containing No. 1 of *Three Piano Pieces* Op. 13, 1897, *Scherzo or Fantasy* Op. 18, 1897, No. 1 and 2 of *Three Piano Pieces* Op. 21, 1898; (further pieces:) *Scherzo* in B minor, 1898; *Scherzo in Sonata Form,* 1900?; *Scherzo* in B flat minor, 1900; *Scherzo,* 1900; *Variations* on a theme by F. F., 1900, EMB (in The Young Bartók II); *Tempo di Minuetto,* 1901; *Four Piano Pieces,* 1903, Bárd, EMB; *Rhapsody* Op. 1, 1904, R, UE, EMB; *Petits morceaux* for piano, c. 1905, EMB (in The Young Bartók II); *Három csíkmegyei népdal* (Three Hungarian Folk Songs from the Csík District), 1907, Rozsnyai, EMB; *Tizennégy bagatell* (Fourteen Bagatelles), Op. 6, 1908, Rozsnyai, UE, EMB; *Tíz könnyű zongoradarab* (Ten Easy Piano Pieces), 1908, Rozsnyai, UE, EMB; *Két elégia* (Two Elegies), Op. 8/b, 1908–09, Rozsnyai, UE, EMB; *Gyermekeknek* (For Children), original version, 85 pieces in four volumes, based on Hungarian and Slovakian folk songs, 1908–09, Rozsnyai, UE, EMB, rev. vers. 1945, BH; *Két román tánc* (Two Rumanian Dances), Op. 8/a, 1910, R, EMB; *Vázlatok* (Seven Sketches), Op. 9/b, 1908–10, Rozsnyai, UE, EMB; *Négy siratóének* (Four Dirges), Op. 9/a, 1910, Rozsnyai, UE, EMB; *Három burleszk* (Three Burlesques), Op. 8/c, 1908–11, R, UE, EMB; *Allegro barbaro,* 1911, UE; *Kezdők zongoramuzsikája* (First Term at the Piano), eighteen elementary pieces for the piano method of Sándor Reschofsky, 1913, R, EMB; *Sonatina,* based on Rumanian folk tunes, 1915, R, UE, EMB; transcribed: *Erdélyi táncok* (Transylvanian Dances), 1931, R, EMB; *Rumanian Folk Dances,* 1915, UE; *Román kolinda-dallamok* (Rumanian Christmas Carols – Colinde), 1915, UE; Suite, Op. 14, 1916, UE; *Leszállott a páva* (The Peacock has Alighted), 1914–17(?); *Három magyar népdal* (Three Hungarian Folk Tunes, c. 1914–17, No. 1 in 1925 as *Leszállott a páva* [The Peacock has Alighted] in an early version reproduced, Nos. 1-3 published in "Homage to Paderewski" 1942, BH); *Tizenöt magyar parasztdal* (Fifteen Hungarian Peasant Songs), 1914–18, UE; *Studies* Op. 18, 1918, UE, BH; *Improvizációk magyar parasztdalokra* (Eight Improvisations on Hungarian Peasant Songs), Op. 20, 1920, UE; *Sonata* for piano, 1926, UE; *Szabadban* (Out of Doors), 1926, UE; *Kilenc kis zongoradarab* (Nine Little Piano Pieces), 1926, UE, BH; *Három rondó népi dallamokkal* (Three Rondos on Folk Tunes), I: 1916, II–III: 1927, UE; *Kis szvit* (Petite Suite), transcriptions of Nos. 28, 38, 43, 16, 36 of *Forty-Four Duos* for two violins, 1936, UE; *Mikrokosmos,* 153 progressive piano pieces in six volumes, 1926–39, BH, EMB; *Seven Pieces from Mikrokosmos* for two pianos, 1939 (?), BH; *Suite for two Pianos* (free transcription of the *Suite No. 2* for orchestra), Op. 4/b, 1941, BH.

SONGS WITH PIANO ACCOMPANIMENT: *Three Songs,* 1898; *Liebeslieder* (Love Songs), 1900:(No. 2 and No. 4 of the six songs in The Young Bartók I), edited by

Denijs Dille, EMB; *Négy dal Pósa Lajos verseire* (Four Songs to poems by L. Pósa), 1902, Bárd; *Est* (Evening, text by K. Harsányi), 1903 (in The Young Bartók I), EMB; *Four Hungarian Songs and Folk Songs,* 1904–05 (No. 1 in The Young Bartók I, No. 4 in Documenta Bartókiana IV, Publishing House of the Hungarian Academy of Sciences); *Székely népdal* (Székely Folk Song), 1905, in Documenta Bartókiana V; *A kicsi "Tót"-nak* (To the Little "Slovak"), five songs for a child, 1905; *Magyar népdalok* (Twenty Hungarian Folk Songs, Nos. 1–10 by Bartók, Nos. 11–20 by Zoltán Kodály), 1906. rev. 1938, Rozsnyai, R, EMB (a different version of Nos. 1, 2, 4a, 9 and 8, as *Öt magyar népdal* [Five Hungarian Folk Songs], edited by Denijs Dille, EMB); *Magyar népdalok* (Hungarian Folk Songs), 2nd series, No. 1–10, 1906 (Nos. 3–4 and 6–8 in The Young Bartók I); *Two Hungarian Folk Songs,* 1906? (No. 1 in The Young Bartók I, No. 2 in Documenta Bartókiana IV); *Négy szlovák népdal* (Four Slovak Folk Songs), c. 1907 (Nos. 1, 3–4 in The Young Bartók I); *Nine Rumanian Folk Songs,* 1915; *Five Songs,* Op. 15, 1916, BH; *Slovak Folk Song* (in The Young Bartók I); *Five Songs* to poems by E. Ady, Op. 16, 1969, UE, BH; *Nyolc magyar népdal* (Eight Hungarian Folk Songs), 1907–17, UE, BH:; *Négy szlovák népdal* (Four Slovak Folk Songs), for mixed choir and piano, 1917, UE, BH, EMB; *Falun* (Five Village Scenes), for voice and piano, 1924, UE; *Húsz magyar népdal* (Twenty Hungarian Folk Songs), in four volumes, 1929, UE, BH; *Debrecennek van egy vize* (Debrecen has a River), 1927, transcription of *For Children* No. 16; *A férj keserve* (The Husband's Grief), Ukranian folk song, for voice and piano, 1945.

UNACCOMPANIED CHORAL WORKS: *Est* (Evening), text by K. Harsányi, 1903, Documenta Bartókiana I; *Négy régi magyar népdal* (Four Old Hungarian Folk Songs), for male choir, 1910–12, UE; *Two Rumanian Folk Songs* for female choir, 1915; *Five Slovak Folk Songs* for male choir, 1917, UE, BH; *Magyar népdalok* (Four Hungarian Folk Songs), for mixed choir, 1930, UE, BH; *Székely dalok* (Székely Songs), for male choir, 1932, MK, EMB; *Twenty-seven Choruses* for two- and three-part children's or female choir, on folk words, 1935, MK, EMB; *Elmúlt időkből* (From Olden Times), from revised texts of folk songs and other old songs, for three-part male choir, 1935, MK, EMB.

DISCOGRAPHY:
Rhapsody for Piano and Orchestra, Op. 1 – Concertos for Piano Nos. 1, 2, 3
Gábor Gabos (piano)
Hungarian State Concert Orchestra, conductor: György Lehel
LPX 12501

Rhapsodies for Violin and Piano No. 1, 2
József Szigeti (violin), Béla Bartók (piano)
(archive recording)
LPX 11373/4

Rhapsody for Violin and Piano No. 1
Albert Kocsis (violin), Csilla Szabó (piano)
LPX 11484

Cantata profana
József Réti, András Faragó (soloists)
Choir and Orchestra of the Hungarian Radio and Television, conductor: György Lehel
LPX 1162

BARTÓK BÉLA — COMPLETE EDITION ON HUNGAROTON.

Orchestral Music

Music for Strings, Percussion and Celesta
The Miraculous Mandarin — concert suite
Budapest Symphony Orchestra
Cond.: György Lehel
SLPX 1301

Two Portraits, Op. 5
Two Pictures, Op. 10
Four Pieces for Orchestra Op. 12
Budapest Philharmonic Orchestra
Cond.: Miklós Erdélyi
SLPX 1302

The Miraculous Mandarin — Pantomime Op. 19
Dance Suite
Hungarian Peasant Songs
Budapest Philharmonic Orchestra
Cond.: András Kórodi
SLPX 11319

Suite No. 2., Op. 4
Hungarian Sketches for Orchestra
Transylvanian Dances for Orchestra
Rumanian Folk Dances for Orchestra
Budapest Symphony Orchestra
Cond.: Miklós Erdélyi
SLPX 11355

Violin Concerto (1937–1938)
Rhapsody Nos. 1., and 2. for Violin and Orchestra
Dénes Kovács (violin)
Budapest Symphony Orchestra
Cond.: János Ferencsik, Ervin Lukács
SLPX 11350

Violin Concerto (1907–1908)
Rumanian Dance No. 1
The Wooden Prince — suite
Dénes Kovács (violin)
Budapest Philharmonic Orchestra
Cond.: András Kórodi
SLPX 11314

Rhapsody for Piano and Orchestra Op. 1
Suite No. 1, Op. 3
Erzsébet Tusa (piano)
Budapest Symphony Orchestra
Hungarian State Orchestra
Cond.: Gyula Németh, János Ferencsik
SLPX 11480

Concerto for Piano and Orchestra Nos. 1, and 2.
Zoltán Kocsis (piano)
Budapest Symphony Orchestra
Cond.: György Lehel
SLPX 11516

Kossuth — Symphonic Poem
Scherzo from the Symphony in E flat major
Scherzo for Piano and Orchestra Op. 4
Erzsébet Tusa (piano)
Budapest Symphony Orchestra
Cond.: György Lehel
SLPX 11517

The Wooden Prince — ballet in one act
Budapest Philharmonic Orchestra
Cond.: András Kórodi
SLPX 11403

Concerto for two Pianos, Percussion and Orchestra
Suite for two Pianos, Op. 4b
Erzsébet Tusa, Ditta Pásztory-Bartók, Maria Comensoli (piano)
Ferenc Petz, József Marton (percussion)
Budapest Symphony Orchestra
Cond.: János Sándor
SLPX 11398

Concerto
Divertimento
Hungarian State Orchestra
Cond.: Antal Doráti
SLPX 114537

Piano Concerto No. 3
Viola Concerto
Dezső Ránki (piano), Géza Németh (viola)
Hungarian State Orchestra
Budapest Philharmonic Orchestra
Cond.: János Ferencsik, András Kórodi
SLPX 11421

CHAMBER MUSIC

Quartets Nos. 1–6.
Tátrai Quartet
SLPX 1294–6

44 Duos, for two violins
7 Pieces from Mikrokosmos, for two pianos
Wanda Wilkomirska, Mihály Szücs (violin)
Ditta Pásztory-Bartók, Erzsébet Tusa (piano)
SLPX 11320

Quintet for String Quartet and Piano
Csilla Szabó (piano)
Tátrai Quartet
SLPX 11518

Sonata for Violin and Piano Nos. 1. and 2.
Gidon Kremer (violin), Yuri Smirnov (piano)
SLPX 11655

Rhapsodies Nos. 1. and 2., for violin and piano
Hungarian Folk Songs, for violin and piano
Rhapsody No. 1., for violoncello and piano
Contrasts
Zoltán Székely, Mihály Szücs, Miklós Szenthelyi (violin), László Mező (violoncello),
Kálmán Berkes (clarinet), Isobel Roston Moore, Erzsébet Tusa, Zoltán Kocsis (piano)
SLPX 11357

Sonata for Two Pianos and Percussion
Sonata for Violin Solo
Dezső Ránki, Zoltán Kocsis (piano),
Ferenc Petz, József Marton (percussion),
Dénes Kovács (violin)
SLPX 11479

PIANO MUSIC

Ten Easy Pieces
Three Hungarian Folk Songs from the Csik District
Fourteen Bagatelles Op. 6
Kornél Zempléni (piano)
SLPX 1299

Four Piano Pieces
Rhapsody for Piano Op. 1
Gábor Gabos (piano)
SLPX 1300

Two Elegies Op. 8b
Two Rumanian Dances Op. 8a
Sketches Op. 9
Four Dirges Op. 9a
Loránt Szűcs
SLPX 11335

Fifteen Hungarian Peasant Songs
Three Rondos on Folk Tunes
Three Studies Op. 18
Improvisations on Hungarian Peasant Songs Op. 20
Dance Suite
Gábor Gabos (piano)
SLPX 11337

Sonata for Piano
Nine Little Piano Pieces
Out of Doors
Petite Suite
Erzsébet Tusa (piano)
SLPX 11338

For Children
Kornél Zempléni (piano)
SLPX 11394–5

Mikrokosmos
Kornél Zempléni, Loránt Szűcs (piano)
SLPX 11405–7

Three Burlesques Op. 9c
Allegro Barbaro
The First Term at the Piano
Sonatina
Rumanian folk Dances
Rumanian Christmas Carols
Three Hungarian Folk Tunes
Suite Op. 14
Dezső Ránki (piano)
SLPX 11336

VOCAL MUSIC

27 Children's and Women's Choruses
Female Choir of the High School of Music, Győr
Cond.: Miklós Szabó
SLPX 1290

Bluebeard's Castle — opera in one act. Op. 11
Katalin Kasza, György Melis
Budapest Philharmonic Orchestra
Cond.: János Ferencsik
SLPX 11486

Four Old Hungarian Folk Songs
Slovak Folk Songs
Four Slovak Folk Songs
Hungarian Folk Songs

26

Székely Songs
From Olden Times
Male Choir of the Hungarian Peoples Army
Slovak Philharmonic Choir
Cond.: Zoltán Vásárhelyi, Miklós Szabó
SLPX 11519

Cantata Profana
Five Hungarian Folk Songs
Village Scenes
Seven Choruses
Girl's Choir of Győr
Chamber Chorus of the Liszt Ferenc Academy of Music
Budapest Chorus
Budapest Chamber Ensemble
Budapest Symphony Orchestra
Hungarian State Orchestra
Cond.: Antal Doráti, János Ferencsik, András Kórodi
SLPX 11510

Twenty Hungarian Folk Songs
Village Scenes
Four Songs from the Mikrokosmos
Erika Sziklay (soprano), István Lantos (piano)
SLPX 11610

Five Songs, Op. 15
Five Ady-Songs
Eight Hungarian Folk Songs
Ten Hungarian Folk Songs
Eszter Kovács (soprano), Ádám Fellegi (piano)
SLPX 11603

SUPPLEMENT

Violin Concerto (1937–1938)
Zoltán Székely (violin)
Amsterdam Concertgebouw Orchestra
Cond.: Willem Mengelberg
(Recording of the first performance in 1939)
LPX 11573

ANDRÁS BORGULYA

(b. Szarvas, 15 Sept. 1931). Studied composition (1950–1958) at the Academy of Music, Budapest, first under János Viski, later under Ferenc Szabó. He worked at the Institute of Popular Culture for a period. From 19163 to 1967 he was active exclusively as composer. Between 1967 and 1974 he worked with Editio Musica, and since 1976 he has been active at the State Opera House while teaching at the Academy of Music. He has won prizes at several competitions for his works.

STAGE WORKS: *Johanna,* musical in two acts to a libreto by Imre Györe, 1974; *Légy jó mindhalálig* (Be Faithful Unto Death), the completion of Ferenc Szabó's unfinished 3-act opera based on the novel of Zsigmond Móricz, libretto by Ferenc Szabó and József Romhányi — the closing scenes for Acts II and III, orchestration of the whole work, 1975.

WORKS FOR CHORUS AND ORCHESTRA: *A hajnal hősei* (Heroes of Dawn), 1960; several popular songs.

CHORAL WORKS: *Falusi hangverseny* (Village Concert), 1962, NI; *A kiskakas rézgarasa* (The Brass Farthing of the Little Cock), 1962, NI; *Hajnalban* (At Dawn), 1963, NI, EMB; *Április* (April), 1963, NI; *Körúti hajnal* (Dawn on the Boulevard), *Áprilisi capriccio* (April Capriccio), two works for mixed choir to poems by Árpád

28

Tóth, 1964, EMB; *Nem én kiáltok* (It is Not Me Whom You Hear), canon for 4 parts to the poem by Attila József, 1966; *Még nem elég* (Not Enough Yet) (Poem by M. Váci), a cappella, for equal voices, 1966, NPI; *Építs tetőt* (Build a Roof) (Poem by M. Váci), a cappella for male voices, 1971; *Buzdítás* (Encouragement) (Poem by P. Vajda), for female voices, string orchestra and piano, 1972.

CHORAL WORKS: *Ballada 1888* (Ballad 1888), folk song arrangement for mixed choir, 1973; *Zuhogj csak, ár* (Gush Forth, Stream) (poem by Imre Györe), a cappella for mixed voices, 1974; *Mind magasabbra* (Higher and Higher) (poem by Imre Györe), micro-cantata for baritone solo, mixed voices and wind instruments, 1975; *Papírsárkány 21* (Paper Kite 21), a cappella for male voices to poems by Imre Szücs, 1975; *A mesebeli János* (John of the Fairy Tale), a cappella for male voices to a poem by Endre Ady, 1975; *Vajda Péter halálára* (On the Death of Péter Vajda) (poem by Sándor Petőfi) a cappella for mixed or equal voices, 1977; *Ének a forradalomról* (Song on the Revolution) (poem by Imre Györe), choral song for baritone solo, mixed voices, symphony orchestra, 1977.

SYMPHONIC WORKS: *Symphony,* 1958; *Concerto breve,* for violoncello and orchestra, 1962, EMB; *Viola Concerto,* 1965; *Piano Concerto,* 1968; *Buffo Serenade* for wind instruments, 1965, NI; *Suite* for wind orchestra, 1966; *Burlesque* (A vén gavallér - The Old Cavalier), for E flat alto saxophone and brass orchestra, 1964; *Scherzando; Three Pieces* for Young Pioneers' woodwind orchestra, 1976.

CHAMBER MUSIC: *String Trio,* 1962, EMB; *Rhapsody* for two pianos, 1963; *Duos per flauto dolce e viola,* 1964–65, EMB; *Trio* for violin, clarinet and piano, 1965, EMB; *5 Canons* for two violins, 1966, EMB; *Postludium* for organ, 1966; *String Quartet,* 1970, EMB; *Trio* for flute, bassoon and piano, 1970, GMP.

INCIDENTAL MUSIC TO PUPPET PLAYS: *Az engedetlen kiskacsa* (The Disobedient Little Duck); *Az elvarázsolt egérkisasszony* (The Enchanted Lady Mouse).

SONGS: *Verebek* (Sparrows), 1961, EMB; numerous chansons.

ATTILA BOZAY

(b. Balatonfűzfő, 11 Aug. 1939). He studied composition at the Békéstarhos Conservatory (Zoltán Pongrácz), then at the Béla Bartók Conservatory, Budapest (István Szelényi), and finally at the Academy of Music, Budapest where he obtained his diploma as a pupil of Ferenc Farkas in 1962. In 1962 he was teaching composition and harmony at the Szeged Conservatory; from 1963 up to 1966 he was editor of the Hungarian Radio. In 1967 he visited Paris, on a UNESCO scholarship. Since 1967 he has devoted himself to composition as his main activity. In 1968 he was awarded the Erkel Prize. Significant festivals, where his works were performed: ISCM (Prague, London), IRCAM (Brussels, Grenoble, Paris), Holland Festival (Amsterdam, the Hague), Cheltenham, Witten, Warsaw Autumn, Steirischer Herbst (Graz), Musikbiennale Zagreb, NMC Toronto, and Budapest Music Weeks. Since 1973 he has performed his own works as zither and recorder player in Switzerland, Holland, Belgium, France, the German Federal Republic, Austria, Canada, the German Democratic Republic, Poland, Czehoslovakia and Jugoslavia.

VOCAL MUSIC: *Papírszeletek* (Paperslips), cycle of songs for soprano solo, clarinet and violoncello, to poems by M. Radnóti, 1962, EMB; *Kiáltások* (Outcries), cycle of songs for tenor solo and chamber ensemble, to poems by A. József, 1963, MS;

Trapéz és korlát (Trapeze and Bars), cantata for soprano and tenor solo, mixed choir and orchestra, to poems by J. Pilinszky, 1966, MS; *Lux perpetua* motet for mixed choir, to poems by A. Károlyi, 1969, EMB; *Két tájkép* (Two Landscapes), for baritone solo, flute and zither, to poems by Á. Fodor, 1970–71, EMB.

ORCHESTRAL MUSIC: *Pezzo concertato No. 1* for viola and orchestra, 1965, EMB + BH; *Pezzo sinfonico No. 1* for orchestra, 1967, EMB; *Pezzo d'archi* for string orchestra, 1968, 1974, EMB; *Pezzo concertato No. 2* for zither and orchestra, 1974–75, EMB; *Pezzo sinfonico No. 2* for orchestra, 1975–76; *Gyermekdalok* (Children's Songs), for eighteen strings, 1976; *Variazioni* for orchestra, 1977, EMB.

CHAMBER MUSIC: *Duo* for two violins, 1958, EMB; *Trio per archi* (String Trio), 1960, 1966, EMB + BH; *Quintetto per fiati* (Quintet for Wind Instruments), 1962, EMB; *Quartetto per archi No. 1* (String Quartet No. 1), 1964, EMB; *Sorozat* (Series), for chamber ensemble, 1970, EMB + BH; *Quartetto per archi No. 2* (String Quartet No. 2), 1971, EMB + BH; *Malom* (Mill), for chamber ensemble, 1972–73, EMB; *Improvisations* II, for recorders and string trio, 1976, EMB; *Tükör* (Mirror), for zither and dulcimer, 1977, EMB.

INSTRUMENTAL MUSIC: *Episodi* for bassoon and piano, 1959, EMB + BH; *Bagatelles* for piano, 1961, EMB; *Ritornelli* for violin solo, 1963, EMB + BH; *Variazioni* for piano, 1964, EMB; *Intervalli* for piano, 1969, EMB + BH; *Formazioni* for violoncello solo, 1969, EMB + BH; *Tételpár* (Two Movements), for oboe and piano, 1970, EMB + BH; *Postlude* for piano, 1970, EMB; *Improvisations I* for zither solo, 1971–72, EMB.

EDUCATIONAL MUSIC: *Medáliák* (Medals), thirty-six small piano pieces, 1956, EMB + BH; *Öt kis zongoradarab* (Five Small Piano Pieces), 1975, EMB.

DISCOGRAPHY:
Quartetto per archi No. 1, op. 9; Variazioni per pianoforte op. 10; Paperslips op. 5; Pezzo concertato No. 1, op. 11; Pezzo sinfonico No. 1, op. 13
Bartók String Quartet, Loránt Szűcs (piano), Erika Sziklay (soprano), Tibor Dittrich (clarinet), László Mező (violoncello), Géza Németh (viola)
Symphony Orchestra of the Hungarian Radio and Television, Hungarian State Orchestra, conductor: János Ferencsik
LPX 11412

Quartetto per archi No. 1, op. 9.
Bartók String Quartet
LPX 11525

Wind Quintet op. 6
Hungarian Wind Quintet
LPX 11630

31

Intervalli op. 15; Formazioni op. 16; Lux perpetua op. 17; Two Movements op. 18; Improvisations I. op. 22; Series op. 19

Klára Körmendi (piano), László Mező (violoncello), Heinz Holliger (oboe), Attila Bozay (zither)

Chamber Chorus of the Hungarian Radio and Television, conductor: Ferenc Sapszon

Chamber Ensemble, conductor: Péter Eötvös

LPX 117142

GÁBOR DARVAS

(b. Szatmárnémeti, 18 Jan. 1911). He studied composition at the Academy of Music, Budapest, as a pupil of Zoltán Kodály. From 1939 to 1948 he lived in Chile where he was assistant-conductor to Erich Kleiber; later he devoted himself to musicology. In 1948 he returned to Hungary and has been active since as consultant at various institutions (Hungarian Radio, Editio Musica, Hungarian Gramophone-Record Manufacturing Co., Artisjus). In 1955 he was awarded the Erkel Prize.

ORCHESTRAL AND CHAMBER MUSIC: *Improvisations symphoniques* pour piano et orchestre, 1963; *Sectio Aurea,* for orchestra, 1964, EMB; *Medaille,* for soprano solo, percussion, keyboard instruments and two loudspeakers, 1965, EMB; *The Tower,* 1967; *Rotation for 5,* 1968, EMB; *Children Music,* 1969; *Antiphon,* for tape, 1970; *Cell* for percussion and tape, 1973; *Passion Music* for voices and tape, 1977.

EDITIONS AND ORCHESTRATIONS: Bálint Bakfark: *Three Fantasies,* 1951, EMB; Liszt: *Spanish Rhapsody,* 1952; *Concerto Pathétique,* 1953, EMB; *Csárdás macabre,* 1954, EMB; *Second Hungarian Rhapsody,* 1959, EMB; Bartók: *Vier kleine Tanzstücke und sechs ungarische Volkslieder* (Four Small Dance Pieces and Six Hungarian Folk Songs), 1961, Schott and BH; *Tänze aus Siebenbürgen* (Dances from Transylvania), 1962, Schott and BH; *Skizzen and Bagatellen* (Sketches and Bagatelles), 1965,

Schott and BH; C. Ph. E. Bach: *Concerto* for two pianos, 1969, Eulenburg; Liszt: *Requiem,* 1969, Eulenburg; C. Ph. E. Bach: *Piano Concerto* Re minore, 1968, BH; Muffat: *Florilegium,* 1968–71, Doblinger; C. Ph. E. Bach: *Magnificat,* 1971, Eulenburg; C. Ph. E. Bach: *Die Israeliten in der Wüste,* 1971, Eulenburg; Dufay: *Missa Caput,* 1971, Eulenburg; Dufay: *Missa L'homme armé,* 1971, BH; Des Prés: *Missa Sexti Toni,* 1971, BH; Ockeghem: *Missa L'homme armé,* 1972, BH; Obrecht: *Missa L'homme armé,* 1972, BH; Ockeghem: *Missa Caput,* 1972, Eulenburg; Stölzel: *Concerto grosso in D,* 1972, Litolff - Peters; Carver: *Missa L'homme armé,* 1975, BH; Ockeghem: *Requiem,* 1977, Eulenburg.

WRITINGS: *A zenekari muzsika műhelytitkai* (Workshop-Secrets of Orchestral Music), 1960; *Évezredek hangszerei* (Instruments of Thousand Years), 1961; *Zenei ABC* (Musical ABC), 1963; *Bevezető a zene világába* (Introduction to the World of Music), I–V, 1965–68, all these works: EMB; *A zene anatómiája* (Anatomy of Music), 1974, EMB; *A totem-zenétől a hegedűversenyig* (The History of Music until 1700), 1977, EMB.

DISCOGRAPHY:
Ferenc Liszt—Gábor Darvas: *Spanish Rhapsody*
Hungarian State Concert Orchestra, conductor: Gyula Németh
LPX 11341

Ferenc Liszt—Gábor Darvas: *Csárdás Macabre*
Symphony Orchestra of the Hungarian Radio and Television, conductor: László Somogyi
EP 1564

Johannes Brahms — Gábor Darvas: *Hungarian Dances*
Philharmonic Orchestra of Győr, conductor: János Sándor
LPX 11566

Music Life in Old Hungary — edited by Gábor Darvas.
SLPX 11491–93

GYULA DÁVID

(b. Budapest, 6 May 1913; d. Budapest, 14 March 1977.) He studied composition at the Academy of Music, Budapest, as a pupil of Zoltán Kodály. He played the viola in the Municipal Orchestra up to 1945, was conductor at the National Theatre up to 1949. Between 1950 and 1964 he was professor of chamber music (wind instruments) at the Academy of Music, in 1964 he was appointed professor of chamber music at the Béla Bartók Conservatory. He was also organizer and director of several ensembles. He won the Erkel Prize in 1952 and 1955, and was awarded the Kossuth Prize in 1957. From 1967 until his death professor of chamber music at the teachers' training college of the Ferenc Liszt Academy of Music.

STAGE WORKS: *Nádasban* (Among the Reeds), ballet, 1961; incidental music to the following plays: Shakespeare: *King Richard III, Hamlet;* Molière: *Le bourgeois gentilhomme, Le malade imaginaire;* Lope de Vega: *The Gardener's Dog;* García Lorca: *Blood Wedding;* Madách: *The Tragedy of Man;* Csokonai: *Özvegy Karnyóné* (two variants), *Tempefői;* and several to other plays.

WORKS FOR CHORUS AND ORCHESTRA: *Three Orchestral Songs,* 1949; *Five Csokonai Songs,* 1955, arrangement with piano accompaniment, EMB; *Lakjatok vígan* (Be Merry), orchestral songs, 1956, arrangement with piano accompaniment, EMB;

Dob és tánc (Drumming and Dancing), 1961, EMB; *Felhőtlen ég* (Cloudless Skies), cantata, 1964; *Égő szavakkal* (With Flaming Words), cantata for mixed choir and symphonic orchestra, 1969.

A CAPPELLA CHORAL WORKS: *Tavaszi szeretők verse* (Poem of Spring Lovers), (Poem by M. Radnóti), for mixed voices, 1959; *Five Choruses to a poem* by A. József for equal voices, 1959; *Változások* (Changes), four madrigals to poems by I. Raics, for mixed voices, 1964; *A rózsa lángolás* (The Rose is Flaming) (Poem by I. Vas), 1967.

SYMPHONIC WORKS: *Symphony No. 1,* 1948; *Symphony No. 2,* 1958, EMB; *Symphony No. 3,* 1960, EMB; *Sinfonietta,* 1960, EMB; *Ballet Music,* 1948; *Dance Music,* 1950, EMB; *Theatrical Music,* 1955, EMB; *Symphony No. 4,* 1970, EMB; *Fest Overture,* 1972, EMB.

CONCERTOS: *Viola Concerto,* 1950, EMB; *Concerto Grosso* for viola and string orchestra, 1963; *Concerto for Violin,* 1966; *Concerto for Horn,* 1971, EMB.

CHAMBER MUSIC: *Quintet for Wind Instruments* No. 1, 1949, EMB; *Quintet for Wind Instruments,* No. 2, (Serenade), 1955, Mills, London; *Quintet for Wind Instruments* No. 3, 1964, EMB; *String Quartet,* 1962, EMB; *Study for Three Wind Instruments,* 1959; *A rózsa lángolás* (The Rose is Flaming), chamber music for female voice, flute and viola, 1966, EMB; *Miniatűrök* (Miniatures), for brass sextet, 1968; *Wind Quintet,* 1967; *Quintet for Wind Instruments,* 1968; *Trio,* for violin, violoncello and piano, 1972, EMB; *String Quartet No. 2,* 1973, EMB; *Pezzo* per viola con accompagnamento di pianoforte, 1974, EMB.

DISCOGRAPHY:
Sonata for Flute and Piano
Zoltán Jeney — Hédy Schneider
HLP SZK 3505

String Quartet No. 1
Tátrai Quartet
LPX 1227

Viola Concerto
Pál Lukács
Hungarian State Orchestra, conductor: János Ferencsik
LPX 1058

Festival Ouverture
Hungarian State Orchestra, conductor: János Ferencsik

Horn Concerto
Ferenc Tarjáni
Symphony Orchestra of the Hungarian Radio and Television,
conductor: György Lehel
SLPX 11699

JÁNOS DECSÉNYI

(b. Budapest, 24 March 1927). He studied composition with Rezső Sugár at the Béla Bartók Conservatory, and with Endre Szervánszky at the Academy of Music, Budapest. He has been working at the Music Department of the Hungarian Radio since 1951, at present he is acting manager of the Symphonic and Dramatic Section. He was prize winner at the World Youth Festival in Warsaw in 1955 and at the Vercelli Competition of Composers in 1956. In 1975 he was awarded the Erkel Prize.

STAGE WORKS: *Képtelen történet* (An Absurd Story), ballet, 1962.

CHORAL WORKS: *Three Madrigals,* 1956; *Five Children's Choruses,* 1958; *Augusztusi köszöntő* (August Toast), 1959, NI, EMB; *Three Small Chorus Works* for children's choir, 1961, EMB; *Three Elegies* to poems by Quasimodo, 1962; *Chanson,* to a poem by L. Áprily, 1968; *Újévi ablak* (New Year's Window), to a poem by Gy. Illyés, 1968.

ORCHESTRAL WORKS: *Szerelem* (Love), orchestral songs, 1957; *Divertimento per Clavicembalo e Orchestra da Camera,* 1959, EMB; *Öt Csontváry kép* (Five Csontváry Pictures), 1967, EMB + BH; *Melodiae hominis,* for chamber orchestra, 1969, EMB; *Gondolatok* (Thoughts), triptych:

1. *Gondolatok – nappal, éjszaka.* Válasz Th. W. A.-nak. (Thoughts – by Day, by Night. Reply to Th. W. A.), for full orchestra, 1971, EMB;
2. *A gondolat játékai* (The Play of Thought), cantata for soprano solo and chamber orchestra, to poems by the composer, 1972.
3. *Kommentárok Marcus Aureliushoz* (Comments on Marc Aurel), for strings, 1973, EMB;

Double for chamber orchestra, 1974; *Variations* for full orchestra with piano obbligato, 1976; *Concerto boèmo,* 1976; *Concerto grosso* for chamber orchestra, 1978.

CHAMBER MUSIC: *String Trio,* 1955; *Sonatina Pastorale,* for flute and piano, 1956, EMB; *Metamorfosi per soprano e pianoforte,* 1964; *Shakespeare Monologues,* for bass, baritone solo and piano, 1968.

EDUCATIONAL MUSIC: *Concertino* for violin and youth string orchestra, 1958; *Suite* for youth string orchestra, 1960, EMB; *Piano Sonatina,* 1962, EMB; *Sinfonietta* for youth string orchestra, 1962, EMB; *Ten Etudes* for youth string orchestra, 1964, EMB + BH; *Kati dalai* (Kate's Songs), arrangements of European folk songs for children's choir and youth orchestra, EMB; *Concertino* for violoncello and youth string orchestra with piano accompaniment, 1976.

Songs, choral works and incidental music to theatre and radio plays.

KÁLMÁN DOBOS

(b. Szolnok, 22 July 1931). In 1945 he lost his eyesight and started studying music; then took up composition at the Academy of Music, Budapest as a pupil of János Viski. He left the Academy in 1957. He won several prizes at various competitions. At present he works at the Music Department of the Hungarian Radio. Since 1952 he has given piano concerts in several countries of Europe, Asia and Africa and made recordings at more than 50 radio and television stations.

CHURCH MUSIC: *Missa brevis* for mixed choir a cappella, 1957; *Missa brevis* for a cappella mixed voices, 1957, Schola Cantorum Paris; *Ad Mariam* for mixed choir a cappella, 1963; *Missa aperta* for female choir or children's choir a cappella, 1967; *46. genfi zsoltár* (Psalm 46. of Geneva), for mixed choir, a cappella, 1971; *Ave maria*, canon for equal voices, 1972; *Missa '76* for mixed voices a cappella, 1976; *Three Christmas Antiphons* for male a cappella choir, 1976.

ORCHESTRAL MUSIC: *Symphony,* 1957; *Three Hungarian dances,* 1964; *Sound Phenomena,* 1968, EMM.

CHAMBER MUSIC: *Sonata* for violoncello and piano, 1956, EMB; *Adagio and Fugue* for string quartet, 1959; *Two Movements* for violin, violoncello and piano, 1960; *Musica da camera* per violino e pianoforte, 1962, EMB; *String Trio,* 1963; *Villanások*

(Flashes), for soprano and piano trio, 1963, EMB; *Manifestations,* for string quartet, piano and percussion, 1969, EMB; *Belső mozdulatok* (Inner Movements), for clarinet, piano and percussion, 1970, EMB; *Vetületek* (Projections) for four percussion instruments, 1975, EMB; *Sonatina* for two horns, 1976.

PIANO PIECES: *Sonata* for piano, 1957; *Meditation,* 1964; *Változatok egy magyar népdalra* (Variations on a Hungarian Folk Song), for piano, 1972; *Ringató* (Rocking), for piano, 1972.

ORGAN PIECE: *Variations and fugue* on a Hungarian melody of the 16th century, for organ, 1974.

SONGS: *Four Songs* (Poems by S. Weöres), 1952; *Emlékezés* (Remembrance), with orchestral accompaniment (K. Kótzián), 1969; *Úton* (On the Way) (S. Weöres), 1957; *Hungarian Folk Songs from Moldavia,* for mezzosoprano solo and chamber ensemble, 1974.

A CAPPELLA CHORAL WORKS: *Three Madrigals* for female voices (Poems by S. Weöres), 1956, EMB; *Autumnal Rondo* for mixed voices (Poem by. S. Weöres), 1964, NI; *After us...* for mixed voices (Poem by I. Kormos), 1968; *Deák Ferenc* for male voices (Poem by M. Vörösmarty), 1975; *Under the North Star,* for children's voices (Text by Finnish poets), 1976.

Pieces for wind orchestra, music accompaniment to radio plays and some film music.

WRITING: *János Viski,* monograph, 1968, EMB and articles.

ERNŐ DOHNÁNYI

(b. Pozsony, 27 July 1877; d. New York, 9 Febr. 1960). He studied composition with János Koessler, piano with István Thomán at the Academy of Music, Budapest. He started to compose early, his compositions are performed all over the world. He played piano from 1899 in Europe and America with great success. In 1908 was appointed professor at the Berlin High School of Music, from 1916 at the Academy of Music, Budapest. In 1928–1934 was director-general of this institution, later honorary president. In 1919 he became conductor of the Budapest Philharmonic Society. From 1945 he lived in Austria, then settled from 1948 on in Argentina. From 1949 until his death was professor at Tallahasee University, Florida (USA).

STAGE WORKS: *Pierrette fátyola* (Pierrettes's Veil), pantomime in three parts, (text by A. Schnitzler), Op. 18, 1908–1909, D; *Tante Simona* (Aunt Simona), comic opera in one act, libretto by V. Heindl. Op. 20, 1911–1912, S; *A vajda tornya* (The Tower of the Voivod), romantic opera in three acts, from H. H. Ewerss and M. Henry. Op. 30, 1915–1922, R; *A Tenor* (The Tenor), comic opera in three acts, based on the comedy "Citizen Schippel" by K. Sternheim, libretto by E. Goth and K. Sternheim, Op. 34, 1920–1927, Alberti.

WORKS FOR CHORUS AND ORCHESTRA: *Missa in Dedicatione Ecclesiae* (Szegedi mise – Mass of Szeged). Op. 35, 1930, R; *Cantus Vitae,* symphonic cantata, (Words taken from the dramatic poem: Tragedy of Man by I. Madách), Op. 38, 1939–1941, unpubl.; *Stabat Mater,* Op. 46, 1952–1953, AMP.

ORCHESTRAL WORKS

CONCERTOS: *Concerto* for piano and orchestra, in E minor, Op. 5, 1897–1898, D; *Konzertstück* concert-piece for violoncello with orchestra, in D major, Op. 12, 1903–1904, D; *Variations on a Nursery Song,* for full orchestra with piano, Op. 25, 1914, S; *Concerto* for violin with orchestra, D minor, Op. 27, 1914–1915, Alberti; *Valses Nobles* for piano by Fr. Schubert. For concert usage arranged, 1920, R; *Pianoforte Concerto* No. 2 in B minor, Op. 42, 1946–1947, Lengnick; *Violin Concerto* No. 2 in C minor, Op. 43, 1949–1950, AMP; *Concertino* for harp and chamber orchestra, Op. 45, 1952, AMP.

SYMPHONIC MUSIC: *Symphony* in D major for full orchestra, Op. 9, 1900-1901, Schott; *Suite* for orchestra in four movements, F sharp minor, Op. 19, 1908–1909, D; *Hitvallás* (Confession), (Text by Mrs. E. Papp-Váry), 1920, R; *Ünnepi nyitány nagyzenekarra* (Festive Overture for Full Orchestra), Op. 31, 1923, unpubl.; *Ruralia Hungarica,* (Five pieces for orchestra), Op. 32/b, 1924, R; *Szimfonikus percek zenekarra* (Symphonic Minutes for Orchestra), Op. 36, 1933, R; *Suite en Valse* (Waltz Suite), Op. 39, 1942–1943, Lengnick; *Symphony* No. 2, E major, Op. 40. 1st version 1943–1944, 2nd version 1953–1956, Lengnick; *American Rhapsody for Orchestra,* Op. 47, 1953, AMP.

CHAMBER MUSIC: *Quintet* for piano, two violins, viola and violoncello, C minor, Op. 1, 1895, D; *Quartet* No. 1, A major, Op. 7, 1899, D; *Sonata* for violoncello and piano in B flat minor, Op. 8, 1899, Schott; *Serenade* for violin, viola and violoncello, C-major, Op. 10, 1902, D; *Quartet* No. 2 in D flat major, Op. 15, 1906, S; *Sonata* for violin and piano in C sharp minor, Op. 21, 1912, S; *Quintet* No. 2, in E flat minor, Op. 26, 1914, S; *Ruralia Hungarica,* three pieces for violin and piano, Op. 32/c, 1924, R; *Ruralia Hungarica:* Andante rubato for violoncello or violin and piano, Op. 32/d, 1924, EMB; *Quartet* No. 3, in A minor, Op. 33, 1926, R; *Sextet* for piano, violin, viola, violoncello, clarinet and horn, in C major, Op. 37, 1935, Lengnick; *Aria for Flute and Piano,* Op. 48 No. 1, 1958, AMP; *Passacaglia for Flute Solo,* Op. 48, No. 2, 1959, Broude Brothers.

PIANO PIECES: *Four Pieces* for piano, Op. 2, 1896–1897, D; Waltz. *Piano for four hands* in F sharp minor, Op. 3, 1897, D; *Variations and Fugue* on a theme of E. G. for piano, in G major, Op. 4, 1897, D; *Two Waltzes* from L. Delibes's ballet "Naila", arranged for piano, 1897; *Gavotte and Musette* for piano, in B flat major, 1898, D; *Passacaglia* for piano, in E flat minor, Op. 6, 1899, D; *Four Rhapsodies* for piano, Op. 11, 1902–1903, D; *Winterreigen* (Winter Roundelay), ten bagatelles for piano, Op. 13. 1905, D; *Humoresques* in form of a suite for piano, Op. 17, 1907, S; *Three Pieces* for piano, Op. 23, 1912, S; *Fugue* for piano, for left hand, D minor, 1913, AMP; *Suite* in old style for piano, Op. 24, 1913, S; *Cadenzas* to Beethoven's piano concerto No. 4 in G major, Op. 58, 1897, D; *Cadenzas* to Beethoven's piano concertos, No. 1, C major, Op.

15, No. 2, B flat major, Op. 19, No. 3, C minor, Op. 37, 1900–1915, Arcadia; *Six Concert-Etudes* for piano, Op. 28, 1916, R; *Variations on a Hungarian Folksong* for piano, Op. 29, 1917, R; *Pastorale.* Hungarian Christmas Song: An Angel from Heaven... for piano, 1920, R; *Ruralia Hungarica,* Seven pieces for piano, Op. 32/a, 1923–1924, R; Leo Delibes: Valse "Coppelia" arranged for piano, 1925, R; Johann Strauss: Two waltzes "Treasure-waltz" from Gipsy baron and "Thou and Thou" from Bat, arranged for piano, 1928, R; *Essential Finger Exercises* for obtaining a sure piano technique, 1929, R; *Cadenzas* to all (27) piano concertos and to the concerto for 2 pianos, E flat major (K 365) of W. A. Mozart. 1906–1941, D (K 453), R (K 271, K 365); *Suite en Valse* (Waltz Suite). Arrangement for piano duet, four hands, Op. 39/a, 1945, Lengnick; *Six Pieces for the Piano,* Op. 41, 1945, Lengnick; *Twelve Short Studies for the Advanced Pianist,* 1950, AMP; *Three Singular pieces,* Op. 44, 1951, AMP; *Daily Finger Exercises for the Advanced Pianist.* (In three volumes), 1960, Mills.

SONGS WITH PIANO ACCOMPANIMENT: *Six Poems* by V. Heindl, Op. 14, 1905–1906, D; *Im Lebenslenz* (In the Prime of Life), Six poems by W. C. Gomoll, Op. 16, 1906–1907, D; *Magyar népdalok énekhangra zongorakísérettel* (Hungarian folksongs for voice with piano acc.), 1922, R.

WORK FOR SOLO VOICE WITH ORCHESTRAL ACCOMPANIMENT: *Three songs* with orchestra from W. C. Gomoll's poems, Op. 22, 1912, unpubl.

DISCOGRAPHY:

Quintet in E flat minor for piano, violins, viola and cello, Op. 26
Sextet in C major for piano, violin, viola, cello, clarinet and horn
Ernő Szegedi (piano), Béla Kovács (clarinet), Ferenc Tarjáni (horn)
Tátrai Quartet
SLPX 11624

String Quartet in A major Op. 7
String Quartet in D flat major, Op. 15 No. 2
Kodály Quartet
SLPX 11853

LÁSZLÓ DUBROVAY

(b. Budapest, 23 March 1943). He received his musical education at the Béla Bartók Conservatory, then at the Academy of Music, Budapest graduating with distinction in 1966. In 1972–1974 he studied composition under Karlheinz Stockhausen and electronic music with Hans Ulrich Humpert on a Deutscher Akademischer Austauschdienst scholarship. Since 1976 he is professor at the Academy of Music, Budapest.

CHORAL WORKS: *Tél* (Winter), for mixed voices (Poem by A. József), 1967; *A halál félelmei* (Fears of Death) for mixed voices, 1968; *Zenepalota* (Music Palace) for female voices, 1968; *Cuatro angeles, Abril* for female voices and piano, (Poems by D'Ors and Jiménez), 1970; *Numberplay No. 2* for mixed voices and tape, 1976; *Alleluja* for mixed voices 1977; *Caput* for mixed voices, electronic organ and phase shifter, 1977.

ORCHESTRAL WORKS: *Verificazione,* 1970; *Succesion,* 1974.

INSTRUMENTAL MUSIC: *Five piano pieces,* 1970; *Felhangok* (Harmonics) for piano, 1977, EMB; *Interferences No. 2* for piano, 1978; *Delivrance* for organ, 1972, EMB.

CHAMBER MUSIC: *Cinque pezzi* per fagotto e pianoforte, 1967, EMB + BH; *Sei duo* per violino e percussioni, 1969, EMB + BH; *Streichquartett,* 1970; *Quintetto per ottoni,* 1971; *Quintetto per fiati,* 1972; *Stigmák* (Stigmata), for tenor solo and piano, to poems by L. Nagy, 1969; *Középkori örmény szerzetes énekei* (Songs of an Armenian Monk of the Middle Ages), (Poems by S. Weöres), for tenor solo and piano 1971; *Magic Square* for violin and cimbalom, 1975, EMB; *Matuziada No. 1, No. 2, No. 3* for four flutes, 1977; *Geometrum II* (String Quartet), 1976, EMB; *Numberplay No. 1* for twenty performers, 1976; *Interferences No. 1* for two cimbaloms, 1976, EMB; *Music* for two cimbaloms, 1977, EMB.

TAPE MUSIC: *Mutations,* 1972; *Kyrie,* 1973; *Sóhaj* (Sigh), 1974; *Geometrum I,* 1975, Bosse Verlag; *Endless Rest,* 1975; *Endless Dance,* 1976; *Endless Movement,* 1976.

LIVE ELECTRONIC: *E-Trio* for violin, percussion and synthesizer, 1974; *Sequence* for recorder or for woodwind instrument and synthesizer, 1975, EMB; A^2 for violin, violoncello, percussion, piano and synthesizer, 1975, EMB; *Oscillations No. 1* for electronic organ and synthesizer, 1975; *Oscillations No. 2* for electronic organ, violoncello, cimbalom and synthesizer, 1976; *Oscillations No. 3* for piano and synthesizer, 1977.

DISCOGRAPHY:
Streichquartett
Kodály String Quartet
SLPX 11754

A^2
Gyula Stuller (violin), Katalin Vas (violoncello), Gábor Kósa (percussion), László Dubrovay (piano), Zsuzsanna Kiss (synthesizer)
Oscillations Nos. 1 and 3
László Dubrovay (piano), Zsuzsanna Kiss (synthesizer)
Oscillations No. 2
Ilona Szeverényi (cimbalom), Katalin Vas (violoncello), László Dubrovay (electric organ), Zsuzsanna Kiss (synthesizer)
SLPX 12030

Matuziada No. 2
István Matuz (flute)
SLPX 11920

ZSOLT DURKÓ

(b. Szeged, 10 Apr. 1934). He studied composition at the Budapest Academy under Ferenc Farkas. Then he attended Goffredo Petrassi's master course at the Santa Cecilia Academy in Rome for two years, graduating in 1963.

He has written several orchestral and chamber music works which have been performed all over Europe, America and Australia and at festivals such as Warsaw Autumn, Zagreb Biennale, Darmstadt, Montreal, Paris Tribune Internationale, Festival du Royan, ISCM, Basel, as well as Budapest Art Weeks. He has commissions from music centers, like the Hungarian Radio, BBC and Koussewitzky Foundation.

His work Episods on theme B—A—C—H was awarded the d'Atri prize at the Accademia di Santa Cecilia in Rome, 1963; String Quartet No. 1 third prize at International Composer Competition of the "Jeunesses Musicales" in Montreal, 1967; Una Rapsodia Ungherese Erkel Prize second degree in Budapest, 1968; String Quartet No. 2 second prize at the International Composer Contest "Béla Bartók" in Budapest, 1970; Fioriture for Orchestra on his disc was awarded Special Citation of International Koussevitzky Award in New York, 1971; Burial Prayer for tenor and baritone solo, choir and orchestra won the first prize of the "Tribune Internationale des Compositeurs" Paris in 1975.

VOCAL MUSIC: *Altamira* for chamber choir and orchestra, 1967–68, EMB + BH; *Cantata No. 1* for baritone solo, mixed choir and orchestra, to poems by E. Ady, 1971, EMB + BH; *Cantata No. 2* for double mixed choir and orchestra, to poem by E. Ady, 1972, EMB; *Six Studies* for choir a cappella, to poems by Á. Tóth and A. József, 1970–1972; *Halotti beszéd* (Burial Prayer), oratorio, 1972; *Moses,* opera in three acts, 1973–1977, EMB.

ORCHESTRAL MUSIC: *Episodi sul tema B—A—C—H,* for orchestra, 1962–63, EMB, 1967, 1968; *Organismi,* for violin solo and orchestra, 1964, EMB, 1965, 1968; *Una Rapsodia Ungherese* for two clarinets and orchestra, 1964–65, EMB 1968, EMB + BH 1969; *Fioriture,* for orchestra, 1966, EMB + BH 1969; *Cantilene,* for piano solo and orchestra, 1968.

CHAMBER MUSIC: *11 pezzi per quartetto d'archi,* 1962, EMB 1966, EMB + BH 1968; *Psicogramma,* for piano solo, 1964, EMB 1966, EMB + BH 1968; *Improvvisazioni,* for wind quintet, 1965, EMB + BH; *Dartmouth concerto,* for soprano solo and chamber orchestra, to a poem by J. Masefield, 1966, EMB; *String Quartet* No. 1, 1966, EMB + BH; *Symbols,* for horn and piano, 1968–69, EMB + BH; *Colloïdes,* for flute, piccolo, bassoon, string quartet and five alto voices, 1969, EMB + BH; *String Quartet* No. 2, 1969, EMB + BH; *Quartetto d'Ottoni,* 1970, EMB + BH; *Iconography No. 1,* for two cellos and harpsichord, 1970, EMB + BH; *Iconography No. 2,* for horn solo and chamber ensemble, 1971, EMB + BH; *Fire Music* for flute, clarinet, piano and string trio, 1971, EMB + BH; *Assonance* for organ, 1972, EMB + BH; *Turner Illustrations* for violin and 14 instruments, 1976, EMB + BH.

DISCOGRAPHY:
Organismi per violino solo e orchestra
Mihály Szűcs (violin)
Symphony Orchestra of the Hungarian Radio and Television,
conductor: György Lehel
LPX 1298

Fioriture per orchestra – *Una rapsodia ungherese* per due clarinetti soli e orchestra – *String Quartet* No. 1 – *Symbols* for horn and piano – *Psicogramma* per pianoforte solo
Béla Kovács, Tibor Dittrich (clarinet), Péter Solymos (piano), Ferenc Tarjáni (horn), Ádám Fellegi (piano), Bartók String Quartet, Choir and Orchestra of the Hungarian Radio and Television, conductor: György Lehel
LPX 11363

Una rapsodia ungherese per due clarinetti soli e orchestra
Béla Kovács, Tibor Dittrich (clarinet)
Symphony Orchestra of the Hungarian Radio and Television,
conductor: György Lehel
LPX 11525

String Quartet No. 2
Kodály String Quartet
LPX 11546

Psicogramma
Elsbeth Heim (piano)
Duchesne
Liège Belgium
DD 6064

Iconographies I–II; Fire Music; Altamira
Budapest Chamber Ensemble, conductor: András Mihály
Choir and Orchestra of the Hungarian Radio and Television,
conductor: György Lehel
SLPX 11607

Halotti beszéd (Burial Prayer)
Choir and Orchestra of the Hungarian Radio and Television,
conductor: György Lehel
SLPX 11803

FERENC FARKAS

(b. Nagykanizsa, 1905). He studied composition at the Academy of Music, Budapest, under Leo Weiner and Albert Siklós. From 1928 he was coach and conductor at the Municipal Theatre, Budapest, then as holder of a state-scholarship he was studying with Ottorino Respighi at the Conservatorio Santa Cecilia, Rome. Subsequently for some years he was engaged in composing incidental music to films in Vienna and Copenhagen. When he returned to Hungary he commenced his pedagogical activity at the Budapest Municipal Superior Music School. In 1941 he was appointed professor, later director of the Conservatory in Kolozsvár. In 1946 he organized the State Conservatory at Székesfehérvár, as director of same. Since 1949 he has been active as professor of composition at the Academy of Music, Budapest. In 1950 he was awarded the Kossuth Prize, in 1960 the Erkel Prize and in 1965 the "Merited Artist of the Hungarian People's Republic" title. In 1970 he received the distinction "Outstanding Artist". Since his retirement in 1975 he has devoted himself exclusively to composition.

STAGE WORKS: *A bűvös szekrény* (The Magic Cupboard), two-act opera, 1938–1942, UE, EMB; *Furfangos diákok* (The Sly Students), one-act ballet, 1949, EMB; *Csínom Palkó,* musical play, 1950, new version: 1960, EMB, Henschel Verlag, Berlin; *Vidróczki,* three-act opera, 1964, EMB; *Piroschka,* musical comedy in two parts, with

German text, 1967, UE; *A Noszty fiú esete Tóth Marival* (The Story of Noszty, Junior with Mary Tóth) musical comedy in 3 acts, 1971; *Panegyricus,* 3-act ballet with choirs (Latin and Italian texts) and dialogues, 1972.

WORKS FOR CHORUS AND ORCHESTRA: *Szent János kútja* (Cantata Lirica), 1945, EMB (Hungarian and German texts); *Tisza partján* (On the Banks of the Tisza), 1950, EMB; *Tinódi históriája Eger várának viadaláról* (Tinódi's Chronicle about the Siege of Eger), 1952; Version for baritone solo and male choir, 1970; *Cantus Pannonicus,* 1959, EMB (Latin text); *Missa in honorem Sancti Andreae,* 1962; *Szigetvár dicsérete* (Laudatio Szigethiana), oratorio, 1966, EMB; *Tavaszvárás* (Waiting for the Spring), 1967, EMB; *Kőröshegyi Betlehemes Kantáta* (Praesepe Keuresheghiense), for choir, organ and chamber ensemble (Latin and Hungarian texts), 1970; (*Jeu de crèche*–French text, *Ein Krippenspiel* – German text, Ed. Cantate Domino), version for choir, organ and orch.: 1975; *Bontott zászlók* (Flying Flags) for soprano and baritone solo, male choir and orchestra, 1973, EMB; *Vita Poetae* (Latin and Italian texts), soli, mixed choir and chamber ensemble, 1976, EMB; *Psaumes de Fête,* for tenor, baritone solo, male choir and orchestra (French text), 1977; *La cigale et la fourmi,* a little cantata for solo, mixed choir and piano, French text, 1977/ *Aspirationes Principis,* cantata for tenor, baritone solo and orchestra (Latin and Hungarian texts), 1974–1975.

SYMPHONIC WORKS: *Divertimento,* 1930; *Finnish Popular Dances* (String-Orchestra) 1935, Sidem; *Asztali muzsika* (Dinner Music), 1938, Sidem; *Rhapsodia Carpathiana,* 1940, Sidem; *Two Hungarian Dances,* 1940, Sidem; *Bábtáncoltató szvit* (The Marionette's Dance Suite) 1941, EMB; *Musica Pentatonica* (String Orchestra) 1945, Sidem; *Márciusi szvit* (March Suite), 1947, EMB; *Prelude and Fugue,* 1947, Mills; *Furfangos diákok,* szvit (The Sly Students, Suite), 1950, EMB; *Lavotta,* Suite, 1951, Sikorsky Verlag; *Concert Overture* to the "Magic Cupboard", 1952, EMB, UE; *Symphonic Overture,* 1952, EMB; *Bükki vázlatok* (Sketches from the Bükk), 1955, Mills; *Gyász és vígasz* (Planctus et Consolationes), 1965, EMB; *Ünnepi nyitány* (Festive Overture, Commemoratio Agriae), 1969, EMB; *Piccola Musica di Concerto,* for string orchestra, 1961, EMB, Schott; *Scherzo sinfonico,* 1952, new version 1970; *Variációk* soproni zenélőóra dallamokra (Variazioni classiche) 1976; *Jelky András Suite* 1974, EMB; *Partita all'ungaresca* 1974, EMB, Schott.

CONCERTOS: *Fantasy* for piano and orchestra, 1929; *Concertino* for harp and orchestra, 1937, revised version: 1956, UE; *Concertino* for piano and orchestra, 1948, EMB, transcribed for harpsichord and string orchestra, 1949, UE; *Trittico Concertato* for violoncello and string orchestra, 1964, EMB; *Concerto all'Antica* for baryton (or viola da gamba) and string orchestra, 1965, EMB, UE; *Serenata concertante* for flute and string orchestra, 1967, EMB; *Concertino rustico* for Alpine horn and string orchestra, 1977.

CHAMBER MUSIC: *Arioso,* for violoncello or viola and piano, 1926, EMB; *Notturno* for string trio, 1929, EMB; *Two Sonatinas* for violin and piano, 1930–31, EMB; *Alla Danza Ungherese* (Hétfalusi boricza-tánc) for violin or violoncello and piano, 1934, EMB; *Serenade* for flute and two violins, 1940, MK, revised version: 1965, EMB;

Six Hungarian Folk Songs for recorder, violin and violoncello, 1947, MK; *Rumanian Dances from Bihar* for violin, or viola, or flute, or clarinet and piano, 1950, EMB; *Serenade* for woodwind-quintet, 1951, EMB; *Old Hungarian Dances from the 17th Century,* for woodwind-quintet, 1953, EMB; *Folk Song Sonatina,* for double bass, or bassoon, or violoncello and piano, 1955, EMB; *Rondo Capriccio,* for violin and piano, or violin and woodwind-quintet, 1957, Mills; *Burattinata,* for violin and piano, 1957, EMB; *Third Sonatina,* for violin and piano, 1959, EMB; transcribed for flute and piano, EMB; *Sonata a Due,* for viola and violoncello, 1961, EMB; *All'Antica,* for viola da gamba and harpsichord, or violoncello vand piano, 1962, EMB; *Ballade,* for violoncello and piano, 1963, EMB, BH; *Quattro pezzi,* for double bass and piano, or for double bass and woodwind-quintet, 1965, EMB, transcribed for violoncello and piano, EMB; *Lavottiana,* Divertissement for wind quintet, 1967, Sikorsky Verlag; *String Quartet* 1970–72, EMB; *Citharoedia Strigoniensis,* for guitar-trio or guitar-ensemble, 1972, *Contrafacta Hungarica* (transcription of Partita all'Ungaresca) for wind octet, 1977; *La Cour du Roi Mathieu,* octet, 1977.

PIANO PIECES: *Sonata,* 1930, MS; *Quaderno Romano,* 1931, EMB; *Canephorae,* 1931, MS, transcribed for organ: EMB, BH; *Small Piano Pieces* on Hungarian Folk Songs, 1935, MK; *Three Burlesques,* 1941, Cs, EMB; *Three Lute Fantasies* by Bálint Bakfark, piano arrangement, 1943, Cs, EMB; *Old Hungarian Dances from the 17th Century,* 1943, Püski, EMB; *Toccata,* 1945, Sidem; *Two Aquarelles,* 1955, EMB; *Five Easy Piano Pieces* on Hungarian folk songs, 1955, EMB; *Ballade,* 1955, Mills; *Régi nóta, régi tánc* (Two Small Piano Pieces), 1955, EMB; *Correspondances,* 1957, Mills; *Hybrids,* 1957, Mills; *Three Monograms,* 1962, EMB; *Nyári kirándulások* (Holydays Excursions), 1975, EMB.

FOR ALPINE HORN SOLO:
Petite Suite Alpestre, 1976.

GUITAR PIECES: *Old Hungarian Dances,* transcription for guitar by László Szendrey-Karper, EMB; *Six Pièces Brèves,* for guitar solo, 1971, Berben, Milano.

SONGS: *Pastorali,* with chamber orchestra or piano accompaniment (Italian and Hungarian texts), 1931, EMB; *Eszterlánc* (Garland), 4 songs with piano accompaniment, 1936, MK; *Gyümölcskosár* (Fruit Basket), 12 songs with piano or with chamber ensemble accompaniment (Hungarian and German texts), 1946, Püski, EMB; *Énekeljünk Cypriának* (Let Us Sing for Cypria), 7 songs with piano accompaniment, EMB; *Zöld a kökény* (Green is the Sloe), 20 Hungarian folk songs with piano accompaniment, EMB; *Selected Songs* (18 songs with piano accompaniment, Hungarian and German texts), 1932–52, EMB; *A vándor dalai* (The Wanderer's Songs), three songs with piano or chamber ensemble (Hungarian and German texts), 1956, EMB; *Naptár* (Calendar), 12 miniatures for soprano, tenor and piano, or chamber ensemble (Hungarian and German texts), 1956, UE; *Drei Lieder* with piano accompaniment (Germar and Hungarian texts), 1958, EMB; *Trois Chansons* with piano accompaniment (French and Hungarian texts), 1960, EMB; *Tibicinium* (Two Songs) with flute accompaniment (Hungarian and German texts), 1960, EMB; *Hommage à Alpbach,* four songs with piano (German and Hungarian texts), 1968, EMB; *Autumnalia,* six songs with piano (Hungarian and German texts), 1969, EMB; *Zúgj hullám* (Deep River, Negro Spirituals, Hungarian and English texts), 1965, EMB; *Karácsonyi Album* (Christmas Songs), 1970, EMB; *Cinque canzoni dei trovatori* (Old French text, with guitar accompaniment), 1971, Berben; *Török dal Júliához* (Canzone turca) with guitar accompaniment, Berben; *Rosarium* 5 songs (Latin text).

A CAPPELLA CHORAL WORKS:

MIXED VOICES: *Baranyai lakodalmas* (Wedding in Baranya), 1940, MK, EMB; *Alkony* (Sunset), 1942, MK, EMB; *Rózsamadrigál* (Rose Madrigal, Hungarian and German texts), MK, EMB; *Honszeretet* (The Love of the Country), 1948, MK, revised: 1969, NPI; *4 Canons,* 1947, MK; *2 Noëls,* 1948, MK; *Áldott éj* (It comes upon, Hungarian and English texts), MK, EMB; *Csónakos-dal* (Boatman's Song), 1958, EMB; *Földrengés* (Earthquake), 1957, EMB; *Epigramma* (Latin text), 1960, EMB; *Psalm CXXX,* 1962; *Emléksorok* (Memento), 1962, EMB; *Merre száll?* (Where is Flying?), 1962, EMB; *Az öröm illan* (The Joy is Passing), 1962, EMB; *Tavasz–Nyár–Ősz–Tél* (Spring–Summer–Autumn–Winter), 1962, EMB; *Milliók szájával* (With the Voices of Millions), 1963, NPI; *Májusi dalocska* (May-Song), 1965, NPI; *Göcseji Madrigál* (Madrigal from Göcsej), 1969, NPI, EMB; *Népek karéneke* (Choir of the Peoples), 1969, NPI, EMB; *Felhők* (Clouds), 1972, NPI, EMB; *Pataki diákdalok,* I., II. (Student Songs from Patak), 1974, NPI; *Hajdútánc* (Soldiers' Dance) 1975, NPI; *A reggel* (Morning), 1974, NPI; *Deutsches Liederbuch* (8 songs, German text) 1976; *Két vegyeskar* (Two mixed choruses) 1975, EMB; *Esztergom megvételéről* 1976, EMB; *Futás a Gond elől* (Flight from Anxiety) 1977, EMB.

MALE VOICES: *Folk Songs* in the volume "Búzavirág" (Cornflower), EMB; *Selected Folk Songs* (two volumes), NPI; *To Bacchus,* 1933; *Bacchylides békedala* (Peace-Song by Bacchylides), 1933; *Fel!* (Up!), 1938, MK; *Temetőben* (In the Churchyard), 1963, EMB/ *Hommage à Ramuz* (3 songs, French text) 1975; *Szivárvány* (Rainbow) 1974, EMB.

CHILDREN CHORUSES: *2 Petőfi Poems,* 1934, MK; *Cigánynóta* (Gipsy Song), 1935, MK, EMB; *Gyöngyöri Gyöngy* (Pearls), 1935, MK, EMB; *Párosító* (6 Folk Songs), 1935, MK, EMB; *A béke mosolya* (Le gout de la paix, French and Hungarian texts), 1964, EMB; *Keresztöltés* (Cross-stitch), 1967, EMB; *Tillió-lió,* 1969, EMB; *Öt kis gyermekkar* (Five Little Pieces) 1975, EMB; *Állatok világa* (The World of Animals, 6 easy pieces) 1976, EMB; *Ákom-bákom hadsereg* (7 little pieces), 1977, EMB.

FEMALE CHORUS: *Bakonyi pártabúcsúztató* (Maiden's Farewell) 1975, EMB.

INCIDENTAL MUSIC: to Madách's *"Tragedy of Man",* Shakespeare's *Timon of Athens, As You Like It, The Taming of the Shrew, Macbeth, Romeo and Juliet, Twelfth Night;* to radio-plays and to more than 70 feature and short films.

DISCOGRAPHY:
Prelude and Fugue
Symphony Orchestra of the Hungarian Radio and Television,

conductor: György Lehel
LPX 1273

Waiting for the Spring (Cantata) – *Piccola musica di concerto – Planctus et consolationes – Trittico concertato*
György Melis (soloist), Vera Dénes (violoncello)
Ferenc Liszt Chamber Ensemble; Hungarian State Concert Orchestra; Choir, Children's Choir and Symphony Orchestra of the Hungarian Radio and Television, conductors: Frigyes Sándor, János Ferencsik
LPX 11391

Six Pièces Brèves for guitar solo
László Szendrey-Karper (guitar)
LPX 11629 (in preparation)

St. John's Well (Cantata lirica) – *Cantus Pannonicus*
Margit László (soloist)
Budapest Choir; Hungarian State Concert Orchestra; Symphony Orchestra of the Hungarian Radio and Television, conductor: Miklós Forrai
HLX 90029

Citharoedia Strigoniensis
Karola Ágay, conductor: László Szendrey-Karper
SEP 21697

Danses Hongroises du XVII. siècle
György Sebők (piano)
ERATO EFM 42072

Hungarian Dances of the 17th Century
János Sebestyén (harpsichord)
CANDIDE CE 31032

Alte ungarische Tänze; Lavottiana
Bieler Bläserquintett
SONORDISC SO 30016

Lavottiana
Budapest Wind Quintet
NIPPON COLUMBIA OS 10117–N

Sonatina für Flöte und Cembalo
Erdmuthe Boehr, Hanns-Christoph Schuster
DARNOK DF 2024

Concertino all'antica
Miklós Perényi,
Orchestra of the Hungarian Radio and Television
conductor: György Lehel
SLPX 11749

Passacaglia and Postludium
Gábor Lehotka (organ)
SLPX 11808

ISTVÁN FEKETE GYŐR

(b. Kisgyőr, 28 March 1936). He studied in Szeged with Géza Szatmári, subsequently at the Budapest Academy of Music under Endre Szervánszky, graduating in 1966. Till 1972 he was professor at the Conservatory of Music in Győr, at present he teaches at the Béla Bartók Conservatory in Budapest.

ORCHESTRAL MUSIC: *Three Movements for Orchestra,* 1970.

CHAMBER MUSIC: *Three Duos* for flute and piano, 1969, EMB; *Sonata* for violin and piano, 1973–1977.

SONGS WITH PIANO ACCOMPANIMENT: *Bagatellek* (Bagatelles), cycle to poems by S. Weöres, 1967; *Four Songs* (Poems by L. Nagy), 1968; *Kék hegyek hidege* (Coldness of the Blue Mountains), cycle to poems by L. Nagy, 1970–71.

JENŐ GAÁL

(b. Zólyom, 16 June 1900). He completed his studies at the Academy of Music, Budapest as a pupil of Zoltán Kodály in 1931. In 1956 he was awarded the Erkel Prize.

WORKS FOR CHORUS AND ORCHESTRA: *Three Orchestral Songs,* 1956; *Fekete földrész éneke* (Song of the Black Continent, oratorio), 1962.

SYMPHONIC WORKS: *Vágyak* (Desires), 1938; *Two Notturnos,* 1939; *Rhapsody,* 1940; *Az ember és a halál* (Man and Death), 1941; *Scherzo,* 1942; *Introduzione e Allegro,* 1943; *Scherzo,* 1952; *Symphonic Adagio,* 1952; *Suite,* 1954; *First Symphony,* 1955; *Fantasy,* 1959; *Second Symphony,* 1960; *Concertino* for orchestra, 1966; *Concerto* for orchestra, 1973; *Exclamatio* for orchestra, 1976.

CONCERTOS: *Concerto for Piano,* 1951; *Concertino for Piano,* 1945–1959, EMB.

CHAMBER MUSIC: *Three String Quartets* No. 1: 1941, No. 2: 1952, No. 3: 1959–60, EMB; *Trio* for wind instruments, 1957; *Quintet* for wind instruments, 1958; *Sonata* for oboe and piano, 1956, EMB; *Harp Trio,* 1963; *Sonatina* for violin and harp, 1963; *Sextet* for string trio, flute, xylophone and celesta, 1964, EMB; *Wind quintet* No. 2, 1967; *String Quartet* No. 4, 1968; *Music for Piano and Chamber Ensemble,* 1969; *Sextet* No. 2, for string quartet, piano and clarinet, 1972.

PIANO PIECES: *Five Piano Pieces,* 1945; *Fantasy,* 1948; *First Sonata,* 1948; *Second Sonata,* 1954, EMB; *Twelve Bagatelles,* 1964; *Six Piano Pieces,* EMB; *Piano Music,* 1975; *Ten Pieces for Piano,* 1977.
Songs and choral works.

ZOLTÁN GÁRDONYI

(b. Budapest, 25. Apr. 1906). He studied composition at the Academy of Music, Budapest under Zoltán Kodály and musicology at the University of Berlin, also as a pupil of Hindemith. He obtained his doctor's degree in musicology at the Berlin University. From 1931 to 1941 he was professor at the Teachers' Training College in Sopron and conductor of the Musical Society there. From 1941 up to his retirement in 1967 he was professor at the Academy of Music, Budapest. He was awarded the music prize of Budapest in 1931, and the Gold Medal of the Order of Labour in 1966. Since 1972 he is living in the German Federal Republic.

WORKS FOR CHORUS AND ORCHESTRA: *A tékozló fiú* (The Prodigal Son), oratorio, 1971; *Memento,* cantata in the memory of the Hungarian galley-slaves, 1975.

SYMPHONIC WORKS: *Suite,* 1930; *Sinfonietta,* 1932; *Hungarian Suite* for youth orchestra, 1935, MK; *Folk Song Variations* for youth orchestra, 1935, MK; *Divertimento,* 1949; *Two Serenades* for string orchestra, 1957, (II.: EMB); *Suite, No. 2* for youth orchestra, 1963; *Symphony,* 1964.

CONCERTOS: *Concerto for Clarinet,* 1942; *Concerto for Violin* (Variazioni concertanti), 1943; *Concertino for Violin,* 1959.

CHAMBER MUSIC: *String Quartet No. 1,* 1933; *String Quartet No. 3,* 1936; *Piano Quintet,* 1941; *String Quartet No. 3,* 1954, EMB; *Quintet* for wind instruments, 1958; *Duet Sonatas.*

INSTRUMENTAL PIECES: *Prelude and Fugue* for organ, 1932, MK; *Prelude* for organ, 1933, MK; *Prelude and Passacaglia* for organ, 1941, MK; *Two Sonatas for Organ,* No. 1: 1944, MK; No. 2: 1947; *Two Preludes for Organ,* 1961, EMB; *Partita* for organ, 1962, EMB; *Toccata* for organ, 1963; *Suite for Piano,* 1937, publ. by the composer; *Sonata* for two pianos, 1938; *Sonatina for Piano,* 1952, EMB; *Two Small Rhapsodies* for violoncello and piano, 1954, EMB; *Easy Duets* for two violins, 1958, EMB; *Fantasy* for oboe and piano, 1956; *Sonatina* for clarinet and piano, 1959, EMB; *Sonata* for flute and piano, 1960; *Zsoltárrapszódia* (Psalm Rhapsody), for organ, 1971; *Meditatio* in memoriam Zoltán Kodály, for organ, 1972; *Zsoltárfantázia* (Psalm Fantasy) for organ, 1976; *Triptychon* for three pianos, 1977.

EDITIONS: Trio transcriptions from Haydn's pieces for the barytone, 1959, EMB; Transcription for Strings of Haydn's *"Zwölf kleine Divertimenti",* 1962, EMB, Schott. Between 1970 and 1972 he was one of the editors of the Neue Liszt Ausgabe (new Liszt Edition) volumes 1–4, EMB + Bärenreiter; Liszt: *Grand Duo Concertant* for violin and piano, 1971, Bärenreiter; Liszt: *Epithalam,* for violin and piano, 1971, Bärenreiter.

WRITINGS: *Die ungarischen Stileigentümlichkeiten in den musikalischen Werken Franz Liszts* (Preculiarities of Hungarian Style in the Compositions of Ferenc Liszt), 1931, De Gruyter, Berlin; *Liszt Ferenc magyar stílusa* (The Hungarian Style of Ferenc Liszt), 1936, National Széchényi Library, Budapest; *A zenei formák világa* (The World of Musical Forms), 1949, MK; *Elemző formatan* (Analytic Morphology), 1964, EMB; *The Contrapuntal Art of J. S. Bach,* 1967, EMB; Articles on Hungarian music history in "Die Musik in Geschichte und Gegenwart", since 1958, Bärenreiter; *J. S. Bach* and *Works of Liszt* in Hungarian Music Encyclopaedia; 1965, EMB; An article on Liszt in "Dictionnaire de la Musique", 1970, Bordas, Paris; *J. S. Bach kánon- és fúgaszerkesztő művészete* (J. S. Bach's Art in Fugue and Canon Composition), 1972, EMB.

MIKLÓS GRABÓCZ

(b. Budapest, 8 March 1927; d. Budapest, 1977). He studied music at the Academy of Music, Budapest where Rezső Kókai was his professor for composition and Tibor Wehner for pianoforte. Since 1951 until his death he worked at the Music Department of the Hungarian Radio, first as folk music editor, later in charge of the light music programmes. In 1955 he was prize winner at the World Youth Festival.

STAGE WORK: *Utolsó padban* (In the Last Schooldesk), (Text by Halasi— Tarbay), 1968.

WORKS FOR CHORUS AND ORCHESTRA: *Szüreti kantáta* (Vintage Cantata), 1954; *Two Orchestral Songs,* 1957; *Világok mozgatója* (Driving Force of Worlds), cantata, 1960.

SYMPHONIC WORKS: *Overture,* 1951; *Light-Music for Symphonic Orchestra,* 1958.

CHAMBER MUSIC: *Régi magyar táncok* (Old Hungarian Dances), for wind quintet and harpsichord, 1962, Bärenreiter; *Hat szépkenyerűszentmártoni népdal* (Six Folk Songs from Szépkenyerűszentmárton) for female voice and flute, 1970.

SONGS, CHORAL WORKS: *Fiatal erdők éneke* (Song of Young Forests), 1954, EMB; *Táborban* (In the Camp), 1956, EMB; folk song arrangements, mass songs.

LÁSZLÓ GULYÁS

(b. Debrecen, 3 Nov. 1928). After learning to play the piano in his native town, he entered the Academy of Music, Budapest, where he studied composition under Sándor Veress and Ferenc Farkas, conducting under János Ferencsik and András Kórodi. From 1950 to 1960 he was artistic director of the orchestra of the Hungarian State Folk Ensemble. In 1958 he was awarded the Erkel Prize. Since 1971 he has been editor at the Music Department of the Hungarian Television.

STAGE WORKS: *Kisbojtár* (The Shepherd Boy), ballet, 1955; *Pókháló* (Cobweb), ballet, 1962; *Szeplőcske* (Small Freckle), children's opera, 1965; *Three Jokes,* ballet, 1969; *Játékkatona* (Toy Soldier), ballet, 1972; *Jeles napok* (Excellent Days), ballet in four scenes, 1966; *A manók ajándéka* (The Goblins' Gift), fairy tale, 1973; *Minden egér szereti a sajtot* (Every Mouse Likes the Cheese), radio-play, 1975; *Két kicsi pingvin* (Two Little Penguins), radio-play, 1976; *A titokzatos jóbarát* (The Mysterious Friend), fairy tale, 1977; *Tündér Ilona* (Helen, the Fairy), radio-play, 1978.

WORK FOR MIXED CHOIR: *Engesztelő ének* (Propitiative Song), 1969.

ORCHESTRAL AND INSTRUMENTAL WORKS: *Rhapsody* for violoncello and orchestra, 1949; *Concerto for Trumpet,* 1959; *Chamber Suite,* 1961; *Nem én kiáltok* (It is Not Me Whom You hear), choir fantasy for baritone solo, mixed choir and symphonic orchestra, to poems by A. József, 1964.

Folk song arrangements for choir (a cappella, or with accompaniment), for popular orchestra, etc. amongst these: *Széki muzsika* (Music from Szék), arrangement of melodies collected by L. Lajtha, 1950, EMB.
Choral works, songs, incidental music to plays.

DISCOGRAPHY:
Turka – Rumanian popular Christmas customs
Choir and Orchestra of the Hungarian State Folk Ensemble
LPX 1281

LÓRÁNT HAJDÚ

(b. Bucharest, 12 Aug. 1937). He studied composition (István Szelényi), horn (Zoltán Lubik) and piano (Clara Chitz) at the Béla Bartók Conservatory of Music. He graduated from the Academy of Music in 1965 as a pupil Endre Szervánszky. His piano teacher there was Béla Ambrózy.

He was awarded the "Reihe Marie Jose" prize in 1966 at an international composer competition in Geneva. The piano concert was performed in 1967, with the composer at the piano, accompanied by the Suisse Romande orchestra.

At present he is professor at the Budapest State Music School. He performs his own piano works.

CONCERTOS: *Concerto per pianoforte e orchestra,* 1966; *Concerto per violino e orchestra,* 1967; *Concertino per pianoforte e orchestra,* 1972.

ORCHESTRAL MUSIC: *Symphony No. 1,* 1968.

CHAMBER MUSIC: *Elegy for horn and piano, 1958; Sonata* for violoncello and piano, 1958; *Horn Quartet,* 1960; *Suite* for two horns and piano, 1962; *Quintet* for wind instruments, No. 1, 1965; *Ten Miniatures* (Trio for Wind Instruments), 1970; *Sonata* for trumpet and piano, 1971; *Oscillazione* for clarinet and piano, 1972; *Quintet* for wind instruments, No. 2, 1973; *Phantasy, Scherzo and March* for percussion, 1974;

Circulatio for bass tuba and tape, 1975; *Piano Pieces* for four hands, 1975; *Stigmen* for wind instruments, percussion and piano, 1975; *Funny Waltz* for percussion, 1976.

INSTRUMENTAL MUSIC: *Two Movements* for viola, 1974; *Performance Pieces* for harp, 1978; *Concert Etudes* for horn, 1978.

PIANO PIECES: *Bagatelles,* 1955; *Sonatina* on Hungarian folk songs, 1958; *Sonatina,* 1959; *Sonata* on Hungarian folk songs, 1962; *Three Etudes,* 1963; *Three Rondos,* 1963; *Toccata,* 1972; *Scherzo-capriccio,* 1972; *Consequences,* 1976.

EDUCATIONAL MUSIC: *Small Pieces* for violin and piano, 1967; *Pieces for Violin and Piano, Violin Duets,* 1969, EMB; *Kaleidoszkóp* (Caleidoscope), 1971; *Ten Easy Piano Pieces,* 1972, EMB; *Fanfar* for horn and piano, 1972, EMB; *Duos* for oboe and recorders, 1973.

SONGS: *Songs* (Poems by E. Ady), 1965; *Children's Song* (Á. Tordon), 1966. Incidental music to radio-plays and films.

MIHÁLY HAJDU

(b. Orosháza, 30 Jan. 1909). He studied piano, later composition at the Academy of Music, Budapest. His professors were István Thomán and Zoltán Kodály, resp. He taught at several private music schools, subsequently at the Budapest Municipal Music School Organization, the Béla Bartók Conservatory, and since 1961 he has been professor of the Academy of Music. In 1957 he was awarded the Erkel Prize.

His cycle of songs won the first prize at the competition organized on the occasion of the 25th aniversary of Budapest's Liberation, in 1970. His "Capriccio all'ongarese" was awarded the Hungarian Radio's Prize of the Public.

STAGE WORK: *Kádár Kata,* opera, 1957.

CHORAL WORKS: *Fonóházi dal* (Spin Song), for female voices, 1961, EMB; *Tavaszi motetták* (Spring Motets), suite for mixed voices, 1969, EMB; *Two Mixed Choruses* to poems by S. Petőfi, 1973; *Budapest* for mixed voices, 1974, EMB; *Őszi lombok* (Autumn Leaves), three pieces for mixed voices, 1977.

ORCHESTRAL WORKS: *Suite,* 1941; *Felhők* (Clouds), cycle of orchestral songs, 1946; A munka dícsérete (In Praise of Work), symphonic poem, 1958; *Concertino* for piano and orchestra; *Capriccio all'ongarese* for clarinet and orchestra, EMB; *Eight Etudes* for string orchestra, 1970, EMB; *Herendi porcelánok* (Herend Porcelains), suite, 1976; *Divertimento* (Intrada, Serenata, Fugato) for chamber orchestra, 1978.

CHAMBER MUSIC: *String Quartet,* 1936; *Clarinet Duets,* 1951, EMB; *Hungarian Shepherd's Dances* for flute and piano, 1953, EMB; *Sonata* for violin and piano No. 1, 1953, EMB; *Variations and Rondo* for violoncello and piano, 1955, EMB; *Pieces* for clarinet, 1956, *Piano Trio,* 1957; *Trio* for wind instruments, 1958, EMB; *Sonatina* for violoncello and piano, 1969, EMB; *Énekek Budapestről* (Songs on Budapest), cycle for baritone solo and piano, 1969, EMB; *String Quartet No. 2,* 1970; *Three Pieces for Two Pianos,* 1971, EMB; *Thirty Small Pieces* for violoncello and piano or two violoncellos, 1973, EMB; *Sonata* for violin and piano No. 2, 1977, EMB.

PIANO PIECES: *Three Scherzi,* 1931; *Elegy,* 1932; *Sonata* 1940; *Sonatina,* 1952, EMB; *Five Piano Pieces,* 1955, EMB.

Songs, song-cycles, choral works for equal voices and for mixed choir, folk song arrangements and numerous educational works on music, for solo instruments and youth orchestra.

ARTUR HARMAT

(b. Nyitrabajna, 27 June 1885; d. Budapest, 20 Apr. 1962). His professors were Ferenc Kersch and, later, at the Academy of Music, Budapest, Viktor Herzfeld. He lived in Budapest from 1912, first as singing teacher, then from 1920 to 1946 he was school-inspector of singing. He taught composition at the Municipal High School for Music. From 1924 to 1959 he was professor at the Academy of Music, Budapest (theory, liturgy, church music). He organized the church music faculty at the Academy. Choirmaster of the Budapest Central Parish-Church from 1922 to 1938, and of the Saint Stephen Cathedral from 1938 to 1956. From 1921 to 1927 he was also the leader of the Palestrina Choir. Co-president, later honorary president of the Hungarian Cecilia Society. Winner of the Erkel Prize (1956) and holder of the Knight's Cross of the Papal Order Saint Gregory (1942).

SACRED WORKS:

WORKS FOR CHORUS AND ORCHESTRA: Three Masses; *Te Deum; Tu es Petrus,* 1929; *Christmas Cantata.*

CHORAL WORK WITH INSTRUMENTAL ACCOMPANIMENT: *150th Psalm,* 1929, MK.

WORKS FOR MIXED CHOIR WITH ORGAN: Two Masses; *Stabat Mater; Te Deum,* 1912–1929, Coppenrath, Regensburg; Motets.

WORKS FOR MIXED CHOIR WITHOUT ACCOMPANIMENT: Three Masses; *De Profundis,* 1932; several Offertories, Motes, Hymns, etc.

CHORAL WORKS WITHOUT ACCOMPANIMENT: Motets, Hymns, Various choral arrangements of folk hymns.

WORKS FOR ORGAN: *Three Preludes; Hungarian Ordinary,* 1954; *Sonata for Organ,* 1956; etc.

PUBLICATIONS: *Lyra coelestis,* 1923, R; *Szent vagy, Uram!* (Holy Are Thou, My Lord!), 1930, MK; new editions of works by Lassus, Palestrina, Lotti, Victoria; *Hungarian Pontifical,* 1958.

SECULAR WORKS:

WORKS FOR CHORUS AND ORCHESTRA: *Szép Ilonka* (Fair Helen), 1954; *Csikóbőrös kulacsocskám* (My Dear Little Leather Bottle), 1953.

CHORAL WORKS A CAPPELLA:

Mixed choirs: *Petőfi Songs; two Madrigals* to poems by J. Arany; K. Mikes, EMB; *A hazáról* (About the Fatherland), 1956; *Szakcsi nótázás* (Singing at Szakcs), 1957; *Song of Daniel.*

Works for male choir, for equal voices, for youth and children's choir, amongst them: *Mátyás anyja* (Matthias's Mother), 1955, EMB; *Margit asszony* (Margaret), *Honfidal* (Patriotic song), 1955, EMB. Songs to poems by Catullus, 1957.

WRITINGS: Counterpoint, Vol. I., 1947, MK; 1958, EMB; Vol. II., 1956, EMB.

FRIGYES HIDAS

(b. Budapest, 25 May 1928). He studied composition at the Budapest Academy of Music under János Viski. Between 1952–66 he was conductor and musical director of the National Theatre in Budapest. In 1959 he was awarded the Erkel Prize. Since 1974 he has been musical director of the Operetta Theatre of Budapest.

STAGE WORKS: *Színek* (Colours), one-act ballet, 1966; *Riviera,* operetta in two acts, 1963; *Asszony és az igazság* (The Woman and the Truth), one-act opera, 1965; *Tökéletes alattvaló* (The Perfect Subject), one-act opera, 1973; *Cédrus* (Cedar), ballet in two acts, 1975; *Bösendorfer,* one-act opera, 1977.

VOCAL MUSIC: Cantate de minoribus, 1959; *Hajnaltól estig* (From Dawn to Dusk), children's cantata, 1967, EMB; *Gyászzene* a Donnál elpusztult II. magyar hadsereg emlékére (Funeral Music in memory of the 2nd Hungarian army that perished at the Don), oratorio, 1973.

CONCERTOS: *Concerto for Oboe,* 1951, EMB; *Concertino for Violin,* 1957, EMB; *Concerto for Viola,* 1959; *Concerto for Flute,* 1967; *Concerto for Horn,* 1968, EMB; *Concerto for Piano,* 1972; *Concerto for Clarinet* (Concerto semplice), 1977.

SYMPHONIC WORKS: *Symphony,* 1960; *Concertino* for strings, 1960; *Concertino* for wind instruments and strings, 1969; *Adagio* (Two Dances from the ballet "Cedar"), 1977.

CHAMBER MUSIC: *String Quartet No. 1*, 1954; *Sonata* for oboe and piano, 1954; *Sonata* for organ, 1956; *Quintett* for wind instruments No. 1, 1961; *String Quartet No. 2*, 1963; *Phantasy* for clarinet and piano, 1965, EMB; *Phantasy* for organ, 1969; *Quintet* for wind instruments No. 2, 1969, GMP; *Sextet* for brass instruments, 1972, EMB; *Quintet* for brass instruments, 1973; *Quartet* for brass instruments, 1973; *Quartet* for horn, 1974; *Four Concert Etudes* for 1, 2, 3 or 4 trombones, 1977.

MUSICAL PLAYS COMMISSIONED BY THE RADIO: *Johnny Bumm*, 1965; *Veronai haragosok* (Enemy in Verona), 1967; *Guillotine térzenével* (Guillotine with Promenade Music), 1968.

Songs, incidental music, film music.

DISCOGRAPHY:

Toccata
Sebestyén Pécsi (organ)
LPX 1222

Concertino
Dénes Kovács (violin)
Symphony Orchestra of the Hungarian Radio and Television,
conductor: György Lehel
LPX 1273

Wind Quintet No.2
Hungarian Wind Quintet
LPX 11630

ZOLTÁN HORUSITZKY

(b. Pápa, 18 July 1903). He studied composition at the Academy of Music Budapest, as a pupil of Zoltán Kodály and simultaneously he obtained his doctor's degree in law. From 1927 to 1949 he was professor, then director of the Municipal High School for Music and superintendent of the music courses in Budapest. From 1938 to 1944 he was responsible editor for the periodical "A zene" (Music). In 1954 he was awarded the Erkel Prize. Between 1946 and 1968 he was professor of pianoforte teaching at the Academy of Music, Budapest, until his retirement in 1968. In 1973 he was awarded the Golden Medal of the Order of Labour. During the summers of 1975, 1976 and 1977 he conducted 3 and 4-week piano courses in Tampere, Finland, at the invitation of the summer university there. In these years he also gave a piano concert each year. In 1976 his *Piano Sonata* was among the compulsory pieces in the programme of the International Cziffra Competition in Versailles.

STAGE WORKS: *Zsigmond Báthory,* opera, 1955; transcribed: 1960; – given by the Hungarian Radio in 1955 in the form of selected pieces; first stage performance 1957 in Greiz, GDR (conductor: Dr Gerhard Friedrich); performed at the Hungarian State Opera House in 1960 (conductor: Miklós Lukács); *Kecskebőr* (Goatskin), ballet, 1962; *Fekete város* (The Black Town), ballad, 1969; *Csipkerózsika* (The Sleeping Beauty), text by J. Romhányi, musical comedy, 1971; *Egyetlen éjszakán* (In a Single Night), musical play for radio, text by József Romhányi, 1974.

WORKS FOR CHORUS AND ORCHESTRA: *Fekete hold éjszakáján* (The Black Moon's Night), cantata, 1930; *Te Deum,* 1937; *Felkelt a nap* (The Sun Has Risen), cantata, 1955; *Ünnepi kantáta* Dunaújváros alapításának 20. évfordulójára (Festive Cantata on the occasion of the 20th anniversary of the foundation of Dunaújváros), text by J. Romhányi, 1970.

CHORAL WORKS: *Missa Pannonica,* 1942, MK; *Kosztolányi Choruses,* 1962; *Petőfi Madrigals,* 1963; *Dömösön* (At Dömös), three madrigals for female choir, 1969; *Three Mixed Choruses* to poems by Á. Tóth, 1972; *Hívás* (Calling), cantata for tenor voice, mixed choir and piano, 1976; *Luonnon Kuvia,* for female choirs to poems by Saina Harmaja in Finnish; its Hungarian translation: *Finn tájképek* (Finnish Landscapes); *Őszi vázlat* (Autumn Sketch) (poem by J. Pilinszky), for female choir.

SYMPHONIC WORKS: *Symphony,* 1933, transcribed: 1941; *Báthory Suite,* 1953; *Suite* on Mari folk songs, 1955; *Four Ballet Scenes,* 1964; Two *Concertos for Piano,* 1938, 1959, EMB; *Violin Concerto,* 1954.

CHAMBER MUSIC: *Five String Quartets,* 1932 (transcribed: 1939), 1953, 1956, 1957, 1962, EMB; *Quartet* for brass instruments, 1958; *Cassazione* for three brass instruments, 1954, EMB; *Sonata* for viola and piano, 1971, EMB; *String Quartet No. 6,* 1976, first performed October 7, 1977; *Organ Sonata,* 1974–76.

INSTRUMENTAL PIECES: *Five Piano Pieces,* 1925; *Piano Pieces for Children,* 1935, R; *Three Piano Pieces,* 1940; *Children's World,* 1959; *Poétikus gyakorlatok* (Poetical Exercises), eight piano pieces, 1965, EMB; *Sonata for Piano,* 1968, EMB; *Sonata* for two pianos, 1970; *Magányos sétáló álmodozásai* (Reveries of a Solitary Stroller), 10 piano pieces, first performance by Hungarian Radio, December 1977.

SONGS: *Ady Songs,* 1929–1940; *Songs to Chinese Poems,* 1941, EMB; *Three Shakespeare Sonnets,* 1953, EMB; *Two Chamber Songs* to poems by Gy. Illyés, for soprano solo, flute, violoncello and piano, 1963; *Two Songs* to poems by M. Magyar, 1964; *Three Chamber Duets* to poems by E. Ady, 1946; *Three Songs* (Kosztolányi, Ady), EMB; *Two vocalizations,* 1967.

SONGS WITH PIANO ACCOMPANIMENT: *Őszi tücsökhöz* (To an Autumn Cricket) (Poem by M. Babits), 1975; *Szelíd esti imádság* (Gentle Evening Prayer) (Poem by E. Ady), 1975; *Találkozás* (Encounter) (Poem by F. Vaád), 1975.

SONGS TO FRENCH POEMS: *Chanson d'Automne* (Verlaine), 1977; *La vie* (Helène Faure), 1975; *Trois mèlodies* (Charles Cros), 1. Le but; 2. Paroles d'un miroir à une belle dame; 3. Romance, 1974.

LAJOS HUSZÁR

(b. Szeged, 26 Sept. 1948.) Between 1963 and 1967 he studied at the Conservatory in Szeged under István Vántus; then, until 1973 at the Academy of Music, with Endre Szervánszky and Zsolt Durkó. In 1975 he won a scholarship to the Santa Cecilia Academy in Rome where his studies were with Goffredo Petrassi; now active in Szeged.

VOCAL MUSIC: *Five Monologues to Poems by J. Parancs,* for mezzo-soprano and orchestra, 1972; *69th Psalm* for tenor and piano, 1976; *Ady Songs* for bass and piano, 1977.

CHORAL WORKS: *Hold-lepte úton* (On a Moon-Lit Road), children's cantata to poems by Sándor Weöres, for children's or female choir and small orchestra, 1969–73; *Caligaverunt,* a cappella for female voices, 1976.

CHAMBER MUSIC: *Csomorkány,* music for ten performers, 1974; *Musica concertante,* for chamber ensemble, 1975.

INSTRUMENTAL MUSIC: *Cogitatio No. 1,* 1968, *No. 2,* 1971, *No. 3,* 1972, for piano; *Five Piano Pieces,* 1977; *2 + 2* for a percussion player, 1977.

ELEK HUZELLA

(b. Budapest, 24 Aug. 1915; d. Budapest, 15 Dec. 1971.) After having entered the Academy of Music, Budapest he studied composition under Albert Siklós. Simultaneously he also took his doctor's degree in philosophy; the theme of his dissertation was Debussy. From 1943 to 1945 he worked at the Music Department of the Hungarian Radio, from 1947 to 1949 he was teaching theory at the Municipal High School for Music, from 1949 he was professor at the Béla Bartók Conservatory. At the composers' competition at Vercelli in 1957, he was one of the prize-winners.

WORKS FOR CHORUS AND ORCHESTRA: *Ten Choral Songs,* 1951; *Patak vára* (The Castle of Patak), oratorio, 1954; *Emlények* (Memorial Songs), cycle of orchestral songs, 1959.

CHORAL WORKS: *Mass,* 1941; *Offertory,* 1942; *Motet,* 1948; *Ambrosian Hymns,* 1947–59; *Folk Song arrangements,* 1952; *Water Magic,* 1962.

ORCHESTRAL MUSIC: *Nocturne,* 1943; *Meditation,* 1955; *Suite,* 1957; *Rhapsody* for piano, timpani and string orchestra, 1959; *Dance and Song,* 1960; *Concertino lirico,* for flute and string orchestra, 1963, EMB.

CHAMBER MUSIC: *String Sextet,* 1940; *Miser Catulle* (Catulli Carmina, VIII.), for soprano and tenor solo with accompaniment of 10 brass-instruments, 1967, EMB; *Kim and Kiö* (Ancient Oriental Legend) for solo voices and orchestra, 1969.

INSTRUMENTAL WORKS: *Epilogue* for organ, 1957; *Three Dances* for guitar, 1959; *Three Archaic Dances* for piano, 1960; *Cambiate* for piano, EMB.

SONGS: *Felhők* (Clouds), 1952, Ricordi; *Aranyhálóban* (In the Golden Net), 1954, Ricordi; *A hídon* (On the Bridge); *Bölcsődal* (Cradle Song), 1958, EMB; *Őszi alkonyat* (Autumn Dusk), 1960; *Shakespeare's Sonnet LXXIII.*, 1960; *Idegen népdalok* (Foreign Folk Songs), 1964.

Incidental music to radio plays.

DISCOGRAPHY:
Three Dances for Guitar (in memory of Scarlatti)
László Szendrey-Karper (guitar)
LPX 11629

PÁL JÁRDÁNYI

(b. Budapest, 30 Jan. 1920; d. 27 July 1966.) He studied violin and piano as a child (György Kósa was his piano teacher). He entered the Academy of Music, Budapest, as a pupil of Ede Zathureczky (violin). Simultaneously he took private lessons in composition from Lajos Bárdos. In 1938 he became Zoltán Kodály's pupil at the Academy of Music. He undertook his first folk song collecting tour during his student years. Having obtained his diploma, he first wrote music critiques, then he was appointed professor at the Academy of Music, Budapest (1946–1959). He worked at the Hungarian Academy of Sciences from 1948, first as research fellow of the Folklore Group, then from 1960 to his death as head of department. In 1948 he was among the prize winners of the composers' competition of the Bartók Festival. He was awarded the Erkel Prize in 1952 and in 1953, the Kossuth Prize in 1954.

CHORAL WORKS: folk song arrangements for various choirs.

SYMPHONIC MUSIC: *Sinfonietta* for string orchestra, 1940, MK; *Divertimento concertante,* 1942–49, EMB; *Dance Music,* 1950, EMB; *Tisza mentén* (Along the Tisza), 1951; *Vörösmarty Symphony,* 1953, EMB; *Borsodi rapszódia* (Rhapsody from Borsod), 1953; *Symphonic March,* 1953; *Concerto for Harp,* 1959, EMB; *Vivente e moriente,* 1963, EMB.

CHAMBER MUSIC: *Violin Duets,* 1934–37; *Sonata* for violin and piano, 1944, MK; *String Quartet No. 1,* 1947, EMB; *String Quartet No. 2,* 1953–54, EMB; *Sonata* for flute and piano, 1952, EMB; *Fantasy and Variations on a Hungarian Folk Song,* for a quintet of wind instruments, 1955, EMB; *String Trio,* 1959.

INSTRUMENTAL MUSIC: *Dances for Piano,* 1937; *Rondo for Piano,* 1939, EMB; *Sonata for Piano,* 1940; *Sonata* for two pianos, four hands, 1942, Művészeti Tanács, EMB; *Bulgarian Rhythm* for piano duet, 1946, EMB.

SONGS: *Three Songs,* 1936–37; *Love Songs,* 1957–58.

EDUCATIONAL WORKS (Solo pieces, chamber music, works for youth orchestra).

WRITINGS: *A kidei magyarság világi zenéje* (Secular Music of the Hungarian Population at Kide, Transylvania), 1943, Kolozsvár; *Magyar népdaltípusok* (Types of Hungarian Folk Songs), 1961, Budapest; numerous articles and essays on musical folklore research, the systematical arrangement of melodies in Vol. I and IV of Corpus Musicae Popularis Hungaricae.

DISCOGRAPHY:

Sonata for Flute and Harpsichord
Erdmuthe Boehrs, Hanns-Christoph Schuster
DARNOK DF 2024

SÁNDOR JEMNITZ

(b. Budapest, 9 Aug. 1890; d. Balatonföldvár, 8 Aug. 1963.) Studied at the Academy of Music, Budapest, where he was a pupil of János Koessler; in Leipzig he studied with Reger, Straube and Sitt. From 1917 to 1921 he was engaged by German opera companies, from 1921 to 1924 he studied at Schönberg's Master School in Berlin. He returned to Budapest in 1924 and was henceforward for several decades one of the most respected Hungarian music critics. (His contributions appeared in Népszava, the daily of the Social Democratic Party.) For several years he was member of the comittee of the Association of Workers' Choirs. His compositions were performed at the ISCM Festivals and have been published also in foreign countries. After 1945 for a while he was also professor at the Béla Bartók Conservatory of Music, Budapest.

STAGE WORK: *Divertimento,* ballet, 1921.

ORCHESTRAL MUSIC: *Concerto* for chamber orchestra, 1931; *Prelude and Fugue,* 1933; *Seven Miniatures,* 1948, Művészeti Tanács; *Overture,* 1951, Schott; *Concerto* for string orchestra, 1954.

CHAMBER MUSIC: *Organ Quartet,* 1918; *Flute Trio,* 1924, Zimmermann, Leipzig; Two *String Trios,* I: 1925, Kistner and Siegel, Leipzig, II: 1929, UE; *Partita* for two violins, 1932, Schott; *Guitar Trio,* 1932; *Duet Sonata* for saxophone and banjo, 1934;

Trumpet Quartet, 1925, transcribed: 1941; *Two Trios for Wind Instruments,* 1925; *Duet Sonata,* for viola and violoncello, 1927, Schott; *String Quartet,* 1950; *Trio* for wood-wind instruments, 1958.

SONATAS WITH PIANO ACCOMPANIMENT: three *Sonatas* for violin and piano, 1921, 1923, 1925, all of them: Kistner and Siegel, Leipzig; *Sonata* for violoncello and piano, 1922, Wunderhorn, München; *Sonata* for flute and piano, 1931, published by the composer; two *Suites* for violin and piano, 1952, 1953, EMB.

SOLO SONATAS: three *Sonatas* for violin solo, 1922, Wunderhorn, München, 1932, R., and New Music Edition, New York, 1938, R.; *Violoncello Solo Sonata,* 1933, R; *Harp Solo Sonata,* 1933; *Sonata for Double-Bass,* 1935; *Sonata for Trumpet,* 1938, R; *Organ Pedal Sonata,* 1941; *Sonata for Flute Solo,* 1941, published by the composer; *Sonata for Viola Solo,* 1941, R.

PIANO MUSIC: *Three Piano Pieces,* 1915, Hofmeister, Leipzig; *Two Sonatinas,* 1919, R; *Seventeen Bagatelles,* 1919, Wunderhorn, München; four *Sonatas,* 1914, Wunderhorn, München, 1927, UE, 1929, UE, 1933, R; *Recueil,* 1938–45, R; *Eight Pieces,* 1951; *Fifth Sonata,* 1954, EMB.

ORGAN MUSIC: *Introduction, Passacaglia and Fugue,* 1914, Wunderhorn, München; Two *Sonatas for Organ,* I: 1959, EMB, II: 1959.

Songs in eight series, published by Wunderhorn, München, and Kistner and Siegel, Leipzig. – Choral works.

WRITINGS: *Bachtól Bartókig,* I (From Bach to Bartók, I), Budapest, 1937; *Szenvedélyek színpadán* (On the Stage of Passions), Budapest, 1943; *Schumann élete leveleiben* (Schumann's Life in his Letters), 1958, EMB; *Mendelssohn,*Gondolat, Budapest, 1958; *Beethoven élete leveleiben* (Beethoven's Life in his Letters), 1960, EMB; *Chopin,* Gondolat, Budapest, 1960; *Mozart,* Gondolat, Budapest, 1961.

ZOLTÁN JENEY

(b. Szolnok, 4 March 1943.) He studied composition under Zoltán Pongrácz (Zoltán Kodály Conservatory, Debrecen, 1957–61), Ferenc Farkas (Academy of Music, Budapest, 1961–66) and Goffredo Petrassi (Accademia Nazionale di Santa Cecilia, Rome, Corso di Perfezionamento di Composizione, 1967–68). In 1970 he was one of the founders of the New Music Studio of the Young Communist League's Central Art Ensemble, in which he has been active as a composer and performer ever since.

VOCAL MUSIC: *Three Songs to Poems by Apollinaire,* for female voice and piano, 1962; *Five Songs to Poems by Attila József,* for soprano, clarinet, cello and harp, 1963; *Az áramlás szobra* (The Statue of Streaming), quintet for voices to a poem by S. Weöres, 1965; *Omaggio* for soprano and orchestra to a poem by L. Szabó, 1966; *Solitude,* for female choir, to Henry D. Thoreau's text, 1973–74; *Monody,* (poem by H. Melville) for mixed choir, 1974, or soprano and piano, 1977, (EMB); *said he, said she,* for soprano and piano, to a poem by E.E. Cummings, 1975.

ORCHESTRAL MUSIC: *Alef-Hommage à Schönberg* for orchestra, 1976–77; *Quemadmodum* for string orchestra, 1975, EMB; *Something round* for string orchestra, 1975; *Laude* for orchestra, 1976–77; *Sostenuto* for orchestra, 1977–78.

CHAMBER MUSIC: *Aritmie-Ritmiche,* trio for flute, viola and cello, 1967; *Wei wu*

83

wei for chamber ensemble, 1968; *Round* for piano, harp and harpsichord, or two prepared pianos, 1972, EMB; *Mandala* for three electric organs, 1972; *Yantra,* for any number of instruments and performers, 1972;*Four Pitches* for 4-11 performers, 1972, EMB; *A szem mozgásai II* (Movements of the Eye II) for two pianos, 1973; *A szem mozgásai III* (Movements of the Eye III) for three pianos, 1973; *Coincidences* (Movements of the Eye IV) for one or three chamber ensembles, 1973; *Four Quartets* for one or more string quartets, 1973; *Orfeusz kertje* (Garden of Orpheus) for eight instruments, 1974; *Desert Plants* for two prepared or unprepared pianos, 1975, EMB; *a leaf falls – brackets to e.e. cummings,* for violin or viola with contact-microphone and prepared piano, 1975, EMB; *Tropi* for two trumpets, 1975, EMB; *Százéves átlag* (Hundred Years' Average) for string quintet and two sine generators, 1977; *Caput-tropics* for flute and tuba or piano, and for Gregorian chorus and cello, 1977; *Two Mushrooms: Amanita caesarea — Amanita muscaria* for chamber ensemble, 1977; *Solitaire* for fifteen percussion instruments, 1978; *pontpoint* for six percussion instruments, 1978; *impho 102/6* for six metal percussion instruments tuned to different pitches, 1978.

INSTRUMENTAL MUSIC: *Five Piano Pieces,* 1962, EMB; *Soliloquium No. 11* for solo flute, 1967, EMB, BH; *Movements of the Eye I* for piano, 1973, EMB; *End Game* for piano, 1973, EMB; *something lost* for prepared piano, 1975, EMB; *Transcription automatique* for piano, 1975; *Arthur Rimbaud in the Desert* for optional keyboard instrument, 1976, EMB; *Supplements* for cimbalom, 1976, EMB; *Soliloquium No. 2* for solo violin, 1977–78.

JOINT COMPOSITIONS: *Undisturbed* for chamber ensemble and tape, 1974 (with L. Sáry and L. Vidovszky); *Hommage à Kurtág* for chamber ensembles and tapes, 1975 (with P. Eötvös, Z. Kocsis, L. Sáry and L. Vidovszky); *Gaga* trio for clarinet, cello and piano, 1976 (with L. Sáry and L. Vidovszky); *Hommage à Dohnányi* for 12 instruments, 1977 (with B. Dukay, Z. Kocsis, L. Sáry and L. Vidovszky).

FILM: *Round,* a pictorial transformation of the musical material of the trio of the same title; Béla Balázs Studio, 1973–75.

WRITING: *Labrador — Description of a Dream Concert* (the night from the 2nd to 3rd of April 1976); *Les Adieux,* 1977.

FRIGYES JUHÁSZ

(b. Budapest, 18 May 1925.) From 1942 on he studied composition at the National Music School with Gábor Lisznyai, and Endre Szervánszky, organ under János Schmidthauer and János Hammerschlag. He attended the Brussels Conservatoire from 1947 as a pupil of Henry Sarly, in 1954 studied composition with Rezső Sugár.

Encouraged by Zoltán Kodály and Zoltán Vásárhelyi he started composing choral works, and became a choirmaster.

He worked in the Bartók Society in 1949–50, then in the Institute of Popular Art, later in the Institute of Popular Culture from 1951 to 1966, after that he was the music editor of the Information Bureau of Public Education. Since 1971 Juhász has been editor at KÓTA's Monthly.

WORKS FOR CHORUS AND ORCHESTRA: *Tüzek* (Fires), (poem by B. Kapuvári), cantata for baritone solo, male choir and full orchestra, 1960; *Ifjak éneke* (Song of Young People), (poem by J. Kövesdy), cantata for sopran and tenor solo, male choir and full orchestra, 1965; *Munkáld a jelent!* (Work on the Present), (Poems by Gy. Hárs and J. Csanády) cantatino for male choir and full orchestra, 1963; *Az idő parancsa* (The Command of Time), (Poem by Gy. Szilágyi), cantata for bass solo, male choir and full orchestra, 1967; *Új világok felé* (Toward New Worlds), (Poem by

F. Róna), cantata for mixed choir and full orchestra, 1963; *Ikarosz* (Icarus), (Poem by J. Csanády), oratorio for soprano, tenor and bass solo, male choir and full orchestra, 1970.

CHORAL WORKS: *Galgahévíz közepébe'* (In the Middle of Galgahévíz), folk songs for mixed choir, 1954, EMB; *A gárda panasza* (Complaint of Guards), (Poem from the Si King, translated by D. Kosztolányi), for mixed choir, 1956, NI; *Őszi chanson* (Autumn Chanson), (Poem by P. Verlaine, translated by Á. Tóth), for mixed choir, 1959, NI; *Akarni kell csak!* (Where There is a Will...) (Poems by Aristophanes, Kastner, translated by I. Békés), for mixed choir, 1961, EMB; *Búcsúztató* (Farewell) (Poem by J. Kövesdy), for equal voices, 1961, NI, EMB; *Helikoni dal* (Helikon Song), (Poem by J. Csanády), for young mixed choir, 1962, KISZ; *Ébred a falu* (The Village Awakes), (Poems by I. Pákolitz and Z. Soós), for equal voices, 19162, EMB; *Ballada a vörös katonáról* (Ballad on the Red Soldier), (Poem by B. Kapuvári), for mixed choir (German text, too), 1963, EMB; *Némuljatok meg kishitűek!* (You Half-Hearted People), (Poem by M. Tompa), for male choir, 1963, NI; *Bizakodás* (Confidence), (Poem by L. Papp), for mixed choir, 1965, EMB; *Hallgatag folyó* (Silent River), (Poem by J. Yewtushenko, translated by Zs. Rab), for equal voices, 1966, NPI; *Dadogós dana* (Stammering Dana), (Poem by B. Kapuvári), for children's choir, 1966, NPI; *Esküvés* (Oath), (Poem by D. Roshdestwensky, translated by Zs. Rab), for mixed choir, 1967, NPI; *Egy kidőlt fenyőszálra* (Onto a Fallen Pine), (Poem by Z. Jékely), canon in memory of Béla Bartók, 1968, NPI; *Históriás ének* (Vers-chronicle), (Poem by L. Hollós Korvin), for mixed choir, 1970, EMB; *A másik Amerika* (The Other America), (American folk songs, translated by J. Kövesdy), cycle for mixed choir, 1968, EMB; *Ha majd a bőség kosarából...* (When We Can Share Everything Equally), (Poem by S. Petőfi), canon for choir, ad lib., 1972, EMB; *Ébred a reggel* (The Morning Awakes), cantatino for soprano and baritone solo, a cappella mixed choir, 1971; *Ünnepi kánon* (Festive Canon), (Poem by I. Raics), for mixed choir, 1972, NPI; *Proletár sors* (Fate of the Proletariat), két munkásdal-feldolgozás férfikarra, 1971, Fővárosi Tanács; *Ne feledd!* (Don't Forget!), (Poem by G. Roshdestwensky, translated by Zs. Rab), for mixed choir, 1972; *Regösének* (Vers-chronicle), (Poem by J. Kövesdy), for male choir, 1972; *Balaton* (Lake Balaton), (Poem by E. Madarász), for mixed choir, 1972; *Három férfikar* (Three Male Choruses), (Poem by F. Frideczky–Z. Jékely), 1972; *Párosének* (Pair Song), two folk song arrangements, for mixed choir, 1973, KÓTA; *Áprilisi ének* (April Song), Poem by E. Rossa, for female or mixed voices, 1973, NPI; *Párosének* (Pair Song), folk song arrangements for mixed voices, 1973, NPI; *Summásdalok* I–II (folk song arrangements), for mixed voices, 1973–1974, NPI; *Két leányének* (Two Girls' Songs), folk song arrangements, for female voices, 1977, NPI.

CHORAL WORKS WITH PIANO ACCOMPANIMENT: *Szabad tavaszi ének* (Free Spring Song), (Poem by R. Boros), 1950, Alliance Bartók; *Dombi Zsuzsa* (Zsuzsa Dombi), (Poem by G. Hajnal), for baritone solo and choir, ad lib., 1955, SZOT; *Szól a kürt* (Voice of the Horn), 1958, NI, EMB; *Munkásőr induló* (Militiamen's March), (Poem by E. Rossa), 1958, EMB; *Dal a pártház védőiről* (Song on Defenders of the

Party House), (Poem by B. Kapuvári), 1959, EMB; *Dal egy kisfiúról* (Song on a Little Boy), (Poem by B. Kapuvári), for childrens's choir, 1959; *Hansági dal* (Song from the Hanság), (Poem by B. Kapuvári), 1960, EMB; *KISZ-hívogató* (Calling to the KISZ), (Poem by E. Rossa), 1961, EMB; *Dal a párt ősz harcosáról* (Song on the Gray-Haired Fighter of the Party), 1960, KISZ; *Kommunista ifjúság* (Communist Youth), (Poem by B. Kapuvári), 1961, KISZ, EMB; *Útra föl!* (Up on the Road!), (Poem by E. Rossa), 1962, EMB; *Disznótor* (Feast at Pig-Killing), (Poem by J. Romhányi), 1962, NI; *Tavaszi ünnep* (Spring Feast), (Poem by J. Kövesdy), 1965, NI; *Szabad a sorsod!* (You Are Free), (Poem by Zs. Gál), for ad lib. choir, 1966, NPI; *Májusi dal* (May Song), (Poem by E. Bornemissza), 1967, NPI; *Soha többé!* (Nevermore!), (Poem by J. Kövesdy), 1967, EMB; *Él a Tanácsköztársaság!* (The Soviet Republic is Alive), (Poem by Á. Horváth), 1968, NPI; *Aki szegény, az a legszegényebb* (Pour Man is the Poorest), (Poem by A. József), 1970, NPI; *Hajnalnóta* (Dawn Song), (Poem by E. Gyárfás), 1970, NPI; *Kavarog a forradalom* (Whirling Revolution), (Poem by J. Kövesdy), 1971, EMB; *Nyílj ki a földön, gyönyörű béke!* (Come to the Earth, Beautiful Peace!), (Poem by I. Raics), for ad lib. choir, 1972, EMB; *Két amerikai munkásdal* (Two American Workers' Songs), (unknown translator), for equal or mixed voices, 1978, NPI; *Tábortűznél* (At Camp Fire), (Poem by J. Kövesdy), for children's voices, 1976, NPI.

Collections: Selected Chorus Works I–II, 1976, EMB.

Chansons, songs.

PÁL KADOSA

(b. Léva, 6 Sept. 1903.) From 1921 to 1927 he studied composition under Zoltán Kodály and piano with Arnold Székely at the Academy of Music, Budapest. From 1927 to 1943 he was teaching piano at the Fodor Music School, from 1943 to 1944 at the Goldmark Music School. Since 1945 he has been professor of piano at the Academy of Music, Budapest, dean of the piano faculty. He is an outstanding pianist. From 1945 to 1949 he was deputy president of the Hungarian Arts Council. He received the Kossuth Prize (1950), winner of the Erkel Prize (1955 and 1962). "Merited Artist of the Hungarian People's Republic" (1953), "Eminent Artist of the Hungarian People's Republic" (1963), Hon. member of the Royal Academy of Music, London (1967). He has been corresponding member of the Deutsche Akademie der Künste since 1970.

He was awarded the Kossuth Prize again in 1975. Since 1977 honorary doctor of the Academy of Music, Budapest.

STAGE WORKS: *Irren ist staatlich* – called also Lehrstück – (Even the Law Can be Wrong), 1931; *A huszti kaland* (The Adventure of Huszt), opera, 1949–50.

WORKS FOR CHORUS AND ORCHESTRA: *De amore fatali,* cantata, 1939–40, EMB; *Terjed a fény* (Light is Spreading), cantata, 1949; *Bartók Association; Sztálin esküje* (Stalin's Oath), cantata, 1949, EMB; *A béke katonái* (The Soldiers of Peace), cantata, 1950; *Március fia* (Son of March), cantata, 1952, EMB.

CHORAL WORKS: *Hat kórusdal* (Six Songs for Choir), to poems by J. Arany, 1969, EMB; Diverse smaller pieces.

SYMPHONIC MUSIC: *Chamber Symphony,* 1926, Schott; *Divertimento No. 1,* 1933, EMB; *Divertimento No. 2,* 1933–34, transcribed: 1960, EMB; *Symphony No. 1,* 1941–42, EMB; *partita,* 1943–44, EMB; *Gyászóda* (Mourning Ode), 1945; *March,* overture, 1948; *Symphony No. 2,* 1948, EMB; *Mezei csokor* (A Bunch of Field Flowers), 1950, EMB; *Becsület és dicsőség* (Honour and Glory), suite, 1951; *Suite,* 1954, EMB; *Symphony No. 3,* 1953–55, EMB; *Symphony No. 4,* 1958–59, EMB; *Symphony No. 5,* 1960–61, EMB; *Pian e forte,* 1963, EMB; *Suite for Small Orchestra,* 1962, EMB; *Symphony No. 6,* 1966, EMB; *Symphony No. 7,* 1967, EMB; *Symphony No. 8,* 1968, EMB + BH; *Sinfonietta,* EMB.

CONCERTOS: *Concerto for Piano* No. 1, 1931; *Concerto for Violin* No. 1, 1932, transcribed 1969–70, EMB; *String Quartet Concerto,* 1936, EMB; *Concertino for Viola,* 1937, Artisjus, EMB + BH; *Concerto for Piano,* No. 2 (Concertino), 1938, EMB; *Concerto for Violin* No. 2, 1940–41, transcribed: 1956, EMB; *Concerto for Piano* No. 3, 1953, transcribed: 1955, EMB; *Concerto for Piano* No. 4, 1966, EMB.

CHAMBER MUSIC: *String Trio No. 1,* 1929–30, Schott, EMB; *Four Duets* for two violins; *Five Studies of Rhythm* for two violins; *Small Suite* for two violins, 1931, Schott; *String Quartet No. 1,* 1934–35, EMB; *String Quartet No. 2,* 1936, EMB; *Folk Song Cantata* for voice, clarinet, violin and violoncello, 1939, EMB; *Quintet for Wind Instruments,* 1954, EMB; *String Trio No. 2,* 1955; *Piano Trio,* 1956, EMB; *String Quartet No. 3,* 1957, EMB; *Serenade* for 10 instruments, 1967, EMB + Schott.

DUET SONATAS, INSTRUMENTAL PIECES: *Sonatina for Solo Violin,* 1923, transcribed: 1960, Harmos, Budapest, EMB; *Sonatina for Solo Violoncello,* 1924, transcribed: 1961, EMB; *Sonatina for Violin and Violoncello,* 1923; *First Sonata* for violin and piano, 1925, transcribed 1969–70, EMB + BH; *Suite* for violin and piano, 1926, transcribed 1970, EMB + BH; *Partita* for violin and piano, 1931, Schott, EMB; *Suite for Solo Violin,* 1931; *Hungarian Folk Songs,* for violin and piano, 1931, Schott, EMB; *Nádi hegedű* (Peasant Fiddle), for violin and piano, 1931, Schott, EMB; *Improvisation* for violoncello and piano, 1957, EMB; *Sonatina* for violin and piano, 1962, EMB; *Sonatina* for flute and piano, 1961, EMB; *Second Sonata for Violin and Piano,* 1963, EMB.

PIANO MUSIC: Three *Suites* for piano, No. 1: 1921, Harmos, Budapest, transcribed 1969–70, EMB + BH; No. 2: 1921–23, Schott, EMB; No. 3: 1923, transcribed 1970, EMB + BH; *Seven Bagatelles,* 1923, Schott, EMB; *Three Studies,* 1923; *Epigrams,* 1923–24, Schott, EMB; *Piano Sonata,* No. 1: 1926, transcribed 1970, EMB; No. 2: 1926–27, Schott, EMB; *Al fresco,* 1926–29, Schott, EMB; *Sonatina,* 1927, Schott, EMB; *Sonata No. 3,* 1930, Schott, EMB; *Three Easy Sonatinas,* 1931, Schott, EMB; *Sketches,* 1931, Bárd, Hansen, EMB; *Folk Song Suite, 1933, Cs, EMB; Four Pieces for Children, Ten Small Piano Pieces, Six Folk Songs, Folk Song Sonatina,*

Small Suite, Five Etudes, Toccatina, Capriccio, 1935, MK, CS, EMB; *Rhapsody,* 1937, UE; *Six Small Preludes,* 1944, UE; *Small Pieces for Small People,* 1945, Cs, EMB; *Sonata for Two Pianos,* 1947, EMB; *Epistulae ex Ponto (Presto adirato), Tristia, Tollrajzok (Sketches), 1948, EMB; Mezei csokor* (A Bunch of Field Flowers), *Piano Duet,* 1950; *Suite for Piano Duet,* 1955, EMB; *Ten Bagatelles,* 1956–57, EMB; *Sonata* No. 4, 1959–60, BH, EMB; *Four Caprichos,* 1961, EMB; *Kaleidoscope,* EMB + BH; *Pillanatképek* (Snapshots), 1971, EMB + BH; pedagogical works, smaller pieces.

SONGS: *Four songs,* 1924, EMB; *Song* with orchestral accompaniment, 1926; *Songs,* 1936; *Folk Songs,* 1936; *Seven Petőfi Songs,* 1952, EMB; *Three Petőfi Songs,* 1952; *Songs,* 1952, partly EMB; *Three Radnóti Songs,* 1961, EMB; *Seven Attila József Songs,* 1964, EMB; *Four Songs* in memoriam Nelly Sachs, 1970, EMB.

DISCOGRAPHY:
Four Pieces for Organ
Sebestyén Pécsi (organ)
LPX 1222

String Quartet No. 3 – Three Radnóti Songs – Two Attila József Songs
Erika Sziklay (soprano), Loránt Szűcs (piano)
Tátrai String Quartet
LPX 1235

Pian e forte (Sonata per orchestra)
Symphony Orchestra of the Hungarian Radio and Television,
conductor: György Lehel
LPX 1273

Symphony No. 6, Op. 62 – Symphony No. 7, Op. 64 – Concerto for Piano No. 4, Op. 63
Gyula Kiss (piano)
Symphony Orchestra of the Hungarian Radio and Television, Hungarian State
Concert Orchestra, conductor: Miklós Erdélyi
LPX 11456

Sonata for Piano No. 1, Op. 7 – Four Caprichos, Op. 57 – Rhapsody, Op. 28/a – Sonata for Violin and Piano No. 2, Op. 58–Serenade for Chamber Orchestra, Op.65
Zoltán Kocsis, Dezső Ránki, Csilla Szabó (piano), Albert Kocsis (violin)
Budapest Chamber Ensemble, conductor: András Mihály
LPX 11532

LÁSZLÓ KALMÁR

(b. Budapest, 19 Oct. 1931.) He studied composition at the Béla Bartók Conservatory under Ervin Major, and subsequently took private lessons from Ferenc Farkas. Since 1957 editor in chief at EMB. Was winner of the London Kodály Foundation Prize in 1967, and of the Wolfsburg Volkswagen Prize in 1969. His Trio was performed at the 1969 Hamburg ISCM Festival.

CHORAL WORKS: *"Senecae Sententiae"* for mixed voices, 1959–65, BH; *"Soldiers Weep at Night"*, cantata (Poem by S. Quasimodo), 1962; *"Kantate für gemischten Chor"*, 1968; *Memoriale* for chorus, percussion and string orchestra (Poems by Seneca–Villon–Rilke), 1969–71; *Rubáiyát* (Poem by Omar Khájjám, translated by L. Szabó), for female voices, 1960–1972, EMB; *Négy madrigál* (Four Madrigals), (Poems by J. Pilinszky), for female voices, 1965–1974, EMB; *Motetták* (Motets), for female voices, 1966–1977.

ORCHESTRAL MUSIC: *Symmetriae* for string orchestra, 1966; *Toccata concertante* for piano and string orchestra, 1968–70; *Cicli* for string orchestra, 1971, EMB; *Notturno 1.* for chamber orchestra, 1973, EMB.

CHAMBER MUSIC: *Trio* for flute, marimba (vibraphone) and guitar, 1968, EMB + BH; *"Cantus"* for two contraltos, clarinet, violoncello and harp (Poem by Á.

Fodor), 1969–72; *Sonata* for flute and piano, 1970–71, EMB + BH; *Triangoli* for clarinet, horn, harp, violin and violoncello, 1970–71, EMB; *Distichon* for piano, harp and percusion, 1970–71, EMB; *Quartet* for English horn, viola, vibraphone and harpsichord, 1972, EMB; *Two Duets* for two trumpets, 1972, EMB; *String Trio,* 1972, EMB; *Combo* for guitar, conga drum and double bass, 1971–1973, EMB; *Sotto voce* for harmonium, vibraphone and harp, 1973, EMB; *Sereno* per violoncello e arpa, 1975; *Énekek* (Songs), (Poems by S. Weöres, J. Pilinszky, Á. Fodor, D. Tandori) for solo voice, 1975; *La stanza quarta* per tre corni, 1976; *Terzina* per violino, viola e arpa, 1976, EMB; *Anera* per vibrafono e tamburi, 1977; *Morfeo* per quartetto d'archi, 1977.

INSTRUMENTAL MUSIC: *Four Canons* for piano, 1966, EMB; *Two Fugues* for organ, 1966, EMB + BH; *Monologo* per chitarra sola, 1968, EMB + BH; *Invenzioni* per pianoforte, 1973, EMB; *Monologo 2.* per violino solo, 1973, EMB; *Monologo 3.* per flauto solo, 1974, EMB; *Monologo 4.* per violoncello solo, 1975; *Clausulae* for organ, 1975; *Monologo 5.* per clarinetto solo, 1977.

Children's choruses, educational pieces.

JÓZSEF KARAI

(b. Budapest, 8 Nov. 1927.) At the Academy of Music, Budapest he was a pupil of János Viski and later of Ferenc Farkas. He was awarded the Erkel Prize in 1972.

WORKS FOR CHORUS AND ORCHESTRA: *Estéli nótázás* (Singing in the Evening) for mixed voices and gipsy band, 1958; *Concertino* for children's voices, piano and chamber orchestra, 1967; *Tavaszi kantáta* (Spring Cantata) for children's voices and chamber orchestra, 1970; *Borsodi népdalszvit* (Borsod Folksong Suite) for children's voices and chamber orchestra; *Tündérsíp* (Fairy Flute), for children's voices with chamber orchestra accompaniment, 1976.

FOR CHILDREN'S AND FEMALE CHOIR (to poems by E. Ady, A. József, S. Weöres, I. Csanádi etc.): *Két nőikar* (Two Female Choruses), 1955–1956, EMB; *Estéli nótázás* (Singing in the Evening) with piano accompaniment, 1956, EMB; *Téli táj* (Winter Landscape), 1956, EMB; *Vadrózsa* (Wild Rose), 1956, EMB, Tonos; *Két gyermekkar* (Two Children's Choruses), 1956–1957, EMB; *Kis népdalszvit* (Small Folksong Suite), 1958, EMB, Tonos; *Tavaszi emlékezés* (Spring Remembering), 1960, EMB; *Dal az édesanyához* (Song to Mother), 1962, EMB; *A remény dalai* (Songs of Hope), 1963, EMB; *Barangolók* (Ramblers), 1963, EMB; *Táj szeretőkkel* (Landscape with Lovers), with piano accompaniment, 1964; *1848,* 1967; *Mozdonyok* (Locomotives), 1969;

A Day in a Child's Life, GMP; *Áldalak búval, vigalommal* (I Bless You with Sorrow and Gaiety), 1969, EMB; *Kodály szavai* (Kodály's Words), 1970, EMB; *Kórus Kodály emlékére* (Chorus in Memory Kodály's), 1971, EMB; *Sixteen Choruses* for children's and female voices, 1970, EMB; *Litánia* (Litany), with organ accompaniment, 1976; *Éjszaka* (Night), 1976; *Thirteen Easy Children's Choruses,* 1978, EMB.

WORKS FOR MIXED CHOIR: to poems by E. Ady, A. József, M. Babits, M. Radnóti, G. Garai): *A fonóban tánc jár* (In Spinning Room), 1951, EMB; *A grófi szérűn* (In the Threshing-Yard of Count), 1958; *Új várak épültek* (New Castles have been Built), 1959, EMB; *Vidám nóta* (Merry Song), 1961, EMB; *Májusi óda* (Ode to May), 1963; *Csodálkozás* (Amazement), 1965, EMB; *Three English Folk Songs,* 1970; *Love* (Poem by R. Browning), 1970; *Himnusz a békéről* (Hymn on Peace), 1971; *Dózsa,* 1971; *A tűz csiholói* (Tenders of the Fire) in two volumes, seven-seven mixed choruses to poems by Hungarian poets of 20th century, 1968–1969, NPI; *The Black-bird* (Welsh Folk song), 1974; *To Music,* Poem by P. B. Shelley, 1974; *Symbolum,* Poem by J. W. Goethe, 1974; *Seven Mixed Choruses,* 1976, EMB; *Twelve Spirituals,* 1978, EMB.

CHAMBER MUSIC: *Sonatina* for saxophone and piano, 1964; *Variations* on a Hungarian folk song theme, for flute and piano, 1966; *Dance Grotesque,* for flute and piano, 1967, EMB; *String Quartet,* 1972–1973.

INSTRUMENTAL PIECES: *Two Dirges, Jazz Sketches, Prelude and Fugue, Blues, Variations, Allegro* for piano, 1964–1965; *Il laboratorio* ten experiments for piano, 1969; *Ten Trumpet Pieces,* 1971, 1972, partly EMB; *Partita* for organ, 1973; *Horn Pieces,* 1972, partly EMB; *Duos* for clarinets, 1977–1978.

ORCHESTRAL MUSIC: *Táncszvit* (Dance Suite), for chamber orchestra, 1968; *Kis szvit* (Small Suite), for children's orchestra, 1978; *Zene vonósokra* (Music for Strings), 1978.

ISTVÁN KARDOS

(b. Debrecen, 6. June 1891; d. 28 Febr. 1975.) He studied composition at the Academy of Music, Budapest as a pupil of Viktor Herzfeld. Studied law at the University of Sciences, Budapest. From 1917 to 1946 he was conductor of theatres in Hungary, Switzerland and Germany. He had a European reputation as a piano accompanist. From 1948 to 1959 he was professor at the Academy of Music, Budapest, from 1952 at the Academy of Dramatic Art, too. Several of his works won prizes, e.g. first and second prize at th Jubilee competition for choral works, in 1948, at the Ministry of Education competition for choral works in 1969.

He was awarded Ferenc József Prize in 1923, and in 1971 the Gold Medal of the Order of Labour.

STAGE WORKS: Accompaniment music to *The Tragedy of Man* (Poem by Imre Madách), 1937; and to *1002nd Night* (Poem by J. Heltai), 1939; *Mátyás diák* (Matthias, the Scribe), opera, 1953.

WORKS FOR CHORUS AND ORCHESTRA: *Áprilisi hajnal* (Dawn in April), cantata, 1950; *Exegi monumentum* (Poem by Horatius), *Thermopylai* (Poem by Simonides), 1969.

SYMPHONIC MUSIC: *Dance*, 1918; *Symphony No. 1*, 1919; *Flower Suite*, 1923;

Hungarian Scherzo, 1936; *Double Fugue on Themes by Beethoven,* 1938; *Festive Prelude,* 1920; *Festivity,* 1920; *Gay Hungarian Overture,* 1923; *Janus,* 1950; *Heroic Overture,* 1957; *Symphony No. 2,* 1958; *Symphony No. 3,* 1967; *Intrada,* 1968; *Symphony No. 4,* 1968; *Visitation,* 1969.

CONCERTOS: *Concertino* for violin and orchestra, 1947; *Piano Concerto No. 1,* 1956; *Concertino,* for double bass and orchestra, 1959; *Double Concerto* for viola and double bass, 1964; *Piano Concerto No. 2,* 1963; *Alliage,* for violin and chamber orchestra, 1966.

CHAMBER MUSIC: *Six String Quartets,* I: 1917; II: 1925; III: 1951; IV: 1960; EMB; V: 1967; VI: 1971; *Sonata* for viola and piano, 1942; *Makkabeus Suite* for violin and piano, 1947; two *Sonatas* for flute and piano, 1957, 1962; *Sonata* for double bass and piano, 1949, EMB; *Sonata* for flute and piano, 1957. The Composer; *Andalgó* (Dreamy Dance), for violin and piano, 1958, EMB; *Four Small Pieces* for double bass and piano, 1958, EMB; *Quintet* for wind instruments, 1959; *Solo Capriccio* for violoncello, 1959, EMB; *Poem and Humoresque,* trio for violin, viola and harp, 1959, GMP; *Divertimento* for violin and piano, 1959, EMB; *String Trio,* 1960; *Tüzes nyíl* (The Arrow and the Fire), 1961; *Bipartitum,* for bassoon and piano, 1963, GMP; *Canto tenero,* 1964, EMB; *Canto giacoso,* 1964; *Solo Sonata* for clarinet, 1965, GMP; *Poem* for clarinet and piano, 1965, GMP; *Two Trios* for cimbalom, flute and violoncello, 1969; *Poem and Burlesque* for double bass and piano, 1969, EMB; *Duo* for clarinet and violoncello, 1970, GMP; *Noa-Noa* for violino, viola and violoncello, 1970, GMP; *Ode* for flute, bassoon and piano, 1971; *Two Sextets* for clarinet, string quartet and piano, 1971, GMP; *Grotesque* for octave flute, violoncello and double bass, 1971, GMP; *Notturno* for French horn, flute, violin and harp, 1971, GMP; *Two Duos* for bugle and piano, 1971; *Three Cimbalom Solos,* 1970.

PIANO PIECES: *Sonata,* 1916; *Suite,* 1928; *Improvisation and Fugue,* 1949; *Dickens Suite,* 1957; *Twelve Preludes,* 1956; *Three Preludes,* 1956, EMB; *Toccata,* 1960; *Variations and Fugue,* 1969; *Korszakok* (Eras), three piano pieces, 1917, 1956, 1972, EMB.

SONGS: *Petőfi Songs,* 1917, R; *Csokonai Songs,* 1917, R; *Five Songs,* 1923–43, EMB; *Literary Chansons,* 1941–64, EMB; *Fourteen Songs,* 1940–66, EMB; *Ciclus Antiquus,* 1968–69; *Six Songs* (Poems by Horatius, Simonides, Meleagros, Sappho and Catullus), 1968–69, GMP; *Songs* to poems by E. Ady, D. Kosztolányi, M. Radnóti, A. József, Á. Tóth, Gy. Illyés, Á. Fodor, M. Babits, S. Petőfi, J. Arany, I. Pákolicz, S. Weöres, M. Csokonai, S. Kisfaludy, S. Lányi, F. Móra, L. Gereblyés, Szmirnyenszki, van der Woestijne, J. W. Goethe, W. Verper, Béranger, P. Geraldy, V. Majakovszkij, J. Yewtushenko etc.

EDUCATIONAL MUSIC: *Accordion School* I–II., 1952, EMB; Choruses.

Opera and song translations. Musical writings in Nyugat, Esztendő, Zenelap, Zenei Szemle, Magyar Zene etc.

PÁL KÁROLYI

(b. Budapest, 9 June 1934.) Studied at the Béla Bartók Conservatory, first piano then composition under István Szelényi 1953–56. Then he resumed his studies at the Academy of Music in 1956, where his professor for composition was János Viski, and after Viski's death, Ferenc Farkas. He graduated in 1962; he has been teaching composition, theory and chamber music at the Municipal State Music School. He took part, with success, in several competitions; in 1965 his "Introduzione e Allegro" was awarded the third prize at the competition of composers organized in honour of the 200th anniversary of the "Harmonien" Orchestra, Bergen. His works were recorded by Radio Wien, Radio Burgenland, Kölnischer Rundfunk, Bayerischer Rundfunk Nürnberg and CBC (Canada).

CHORAL WORKS: *Chamber Musik* for mixed voices (Poem by J. Joyce), 1962; *Fragments* for mixed voices (Poem by Á. Tóth), 1963; *Six Children's Choruses, Five Children's Choruses* (Poems by S. Weöres), 1965, NI, GMP; *"Seasons"* for children's voices (Poems by S. Weöres), 1965, EMB, GMP; *"Ilona"* for mixed voices (Poem by D. Kosztolányi), 1966, EMB; *"Ad Lydiam"* for mixed voices (Poem by Horatius), 1967; *Missa brevis* for two female choruses, placed in space, 1969; *Énekkari etüdök No. 1* ("The Grape"), Poem by J. Pannonius, for mixed voices, 1971, NPI; *Énekkari*

97

etüdök No. 2 ("Synaesthesia"), for female voice, 1977; *Incanto* for double mixed choruses, 1974, EMB; *Notturno* for four female choruses, placed in space, 1974.

WORKS FOR CHORUS AND ORCHESTRA: *Aucasin et Nicolete,* oratorio, 1961–64; *Lover's Dialogue,* chamber cantata, 1969–72; *Epilógus* (Epilogue), 1974.

ORCHESTRAL MUSIC: *Concerto of "Miskolc",* 1963; *Introduzione e Allegro,* 1964; *Pantomime,* 1965; *Symphonic Fragment,* 1966; *Reminiscenze,* 1967; *Aucasin et Nicolete,* suite, 1968; *Interludium,* 1972; *Consolatio,* 1974.

CHAMBER MUSIC: *Piano Quintet,* 1960–61, revised 1968; *Three Songs* for tenor, three horns and harp (Poems by G. Lorca), 1963; *String Quartet,* No. 1, 1965; *Campane* for twelve performers, 1967–69, GMP; *Meditazione* per clarinetto e pianoforte, 1967, EMB + BH; *Serenata notturna,* for violin, viola and harp, 1970, EMB; *String Quartet,* No. 2, 1970; *Contorni* per fagotto e pianoforte, 1970, EMB; *Contemplatio* for tenor, flute, two guitars and violoncello, 1973; *Rondo* for two cimbaloms, 1975; *Két akvarell* (Two Aquarelles), for two cimbaloms, 1975; *Notturno* for two cimbaloms, 1976; *Triphtongus 3a Conclusio,* 1975, EMB; *Triphtongus 3b Constellatio,* 1975, EMB; *Epitaxia* for twelve accordions, 1977.

PIANO MUSIC: *Five Piano Pieces,* 1963, EMB + BH; *Twenty-four Piano Pieces for Children,* 1964, EMB + BH; Broekmans and van Poppel; *Toccata for the Left Hand,* 1966; *Toccata furiosa,* 1966, EMB + BH; *Accenti,* 1969, EMB; *Four Etudes,* 1972, EMB; *Hat bagatell* (Six Bagatelles), 1972–73; *Aperto,* 1977; *Equazione* for prepared piano, 1976.

ORGAN MUSIC: *Elegy and Capriccio,* 1965; *Triphtongus 1,* 1968, EMB + BH; *Triphtongus 2,* 1970, EMB.

INSTRUMENTAL MUSIC: *Four Pieces for Dulcimer,* 1966, EMB; *Aquarelles* for harp, 1970; *Aspetto* for accordion, 1973, VEB Deutscher Verlag für Musik, Leipzig; *Motivo 1* for viola, 1973, EMB; *Motivo 2* for violin, 1975, EMB; *Változások* (Changes) for cimbalom, 1975, EMB; *Formations* for vibraphone and percussion, 1976, EMB.

WORKS FOR YOUTH: *Little Suite* for string orchestra, 1964, EMB; *Children's Symphony,* 1964; *Little Trio* for two violins and piano, 1964; *Three Bagatelles* for three violins and piano duet, 1968; besides works for two violins, for violin and piano, EMB (in educational musics, for clarinet and piano, EMB, Broekmans, Belwin), (in "Clarinet Music for Beginners"); *Színek* (Colours) for orchestra, 1973; *Kamarazene* (Chamber Music) for two violins and piano, 1973; *Pásztorjáték* (Pastoral), suite, (Poem by B. Balassi), 1976.

TREATMENTS: *Early Hungarian Dance Tunes,* for violin, viola and harp, 1969; *Divertimento,* for violin, violoncello and piano, 1969; *Dances from Hungary from the 18th Century,* for violin, viola and harp, 1970; etc.

INCIDENTAL MUSIC: *A villámszóró kard* (The Lightning Sword) (written by G. Albert from Irish folk tales), radio-play, 1971; *Argirus királyfi* (Prince Argirus), musical play for radio, 1972; *Szép magyar komédia,* radio-play, (Poem by B. Balassi), 1975.

ARRANGEMENTS: *Concerto in F major* by A. Vivaldi (PV 278), EMB; *Concerto in Si♭ major by A. Vivaldi (PV 44), EMB; Five Triosonatas* by D. Scarlatti, EMB.

Cadenzas to Clarinet Concerto in C major by Vanhal, EMB.

TIBOR KAZACSAY

(b. Budapest, 12 March 1892; d. Budapest, 5 Oct. 1977.) Studied composition at the Academy of Music, Budapest, with Viktor Herzfeld, Albert Siklós and Zoltán Kodály. He had been teaching since 1920; first at the Scharwenka Conservatory, Berlin, then at the National Conservatory, Budapest. Since 1933 he was inspector of all music schools in Hungary and played an important role in establishing an overall network of music schools in the country.

Between 1926–1936 he held the post of piano accompanist at the Hungarian Radio. His composition "Ének a Margitszigetről" (Song on Margaret Island) won the prize of the Capital.

STAGE WORK: *Tilalom és szabadság* (Prohibition and Liberty), (Poem by G. Hegedüs), one act ballet, 1969; *Bacchus ünnep* (Bacchus Feast), dance-play in one act, (Poem by G. Hegedüs), 1977, MS.

WORKS FOR CHORUS AND ORCHESTRA: *A szeretet dala* (Song of Affection), cantata for mixed choir, solo voices and orchestra, to a poem by E. Ady, 1942; *Ének a Margitszigetről* (Song on Margaret Island), 1956–57, EMB; *Balatoni szimfónia* (Balaton Symphony), 1958–59; *Egy eltávozotthoz* (To One Who Departed), 1962.

SYMPHONIC MUSIC: *Max und Moritz,* 1919–22, to Design by Wilhelm Busch; *Egy humorista vázlatkönyvéből* (From the Sketchbook of a Humorist), 1928; *Rag Caprice,* 1930; *Álomország* (Dream Land), 1931; *Keleti jelenet* (Oriental Scene), 1932, Harmónia; *Circus,* satiric suite; *Satiric Symphony,* 1934; *Variations for Orchestra,* 1948; *Pantomime Suite* for wind orchestra, 1951; *Madách emlékére* (In Memory of Madách) symphonic poem for full orchestra, 1952; *Symphonic Elegy* for full orchestra, 1952; *Orientália,* three pieces for full orchestra, 1964; *Four Episodes,* for wind orchestra, 1964; *Three Hungarian Dances in Old Style,* for wind orchestra, 1971; *Szimbolikus táncminiatürök* (Symbolical Dance Miniatures), for full orchestra, 1972; *Két szentimentális keringő* (Two Sentimental Waltzes), 1974; Wind Transcription of a Schubert March, 1974; *Röntgenfelvételek* (X-ray Photographs), mosaic suite in eight movements, 1976; *Két tanulmány* (Two Studies) for full orchestra, 1976; *Four Pieces* for wind orchestra, 1977.

CONCERTOS: *Concerto for Violin,* 1933; *Concerto for Bassoon,* 1955–56, EMB, transcription for bassoon and piano, 1974, EMB; *Concerto for Trumpet,* 1965, EMB, transcription for trumpet and piano, 1972, EMB; *Concert Rhapsody* for oboe, piano and orchestra, 1957.

CHAMBER MUSIC: *Böcklin Suite,* for clarinet and piano, 1926; *Two Impressions,* for violin and piano, 1929, Zimmermann, Berlin; *Sonata for Flute and Piano,* 1938; *Falusi képek* (Village Images), six easy pieces for violin and piano, 1942, R; *Sonata* for violin and piano, 1946; *Divertimento* for contrabass, with piano accompaniment, 1946, EMB; *Small Suite* for violin and piano, 1955, EMB; *Two Concert Duets* for oboe and English horn, 1955–56, EMB; *Rhapsody* for violoncello, with piano accompaniment, 1965; *Rhapsody* for trumpet, with wind orchestra accompaniment, 1968; *Életemből — Gyász és újjászületés* (My Life — Mourning and Revival) for violin and piano or chamber orchestra, 1968; *Elegy Fantasy,* for clarinet and piano, 1971; *Chamber Music for Ten Instruments,* 1973.

PIANO PIECES: *Portrék* (Portraits), five pieces, 1920, Leuckart; *Egy humorista vázlatkönyvéből* (From the Sketchbook of a Humorist), 1924–28, Bárd; *Meseképek* (Fairy-tale Sketches), piano duet, 1930; *Two Burlesques,* 1931; *Two Concert Pieces,* 1931; *És most hallgassatok ide* (And Now Listen To Me), 1933, R; *Látomások* (Visions), five concert pieces for piano, 1935; *Hungarian Pastorale and Rondo,* 1946; *Úton, útfélen* (Here and Everywhere), 1953–54; *Three Small Pieces,* 1954, EMB; *Two Concert Pieces,* 1961, EMB; *Miniatürök* (Miniatures), for the left hand, 1968; *Sonata dramatica,* 1969; *Bucolic,* three pictures on painting by Boucher, 1971; *Pro Memoria II,* 1974, EMB; *Furcsaságok* (Grotesques), six virtuoso programme pieces, 1977, EMB.

SONGS: *Children's Songs,* 1915, Bárd, Budapest; *Chinese Songs,* 1930, Bárd, Budapest; *Small Songs About Animals,* 1936, Dante, Budapest; *Két drámai dal* (Two Dramatic songs) with orchestra or piano acc., 1937; *Verlaine Songs,* 1939, Bárd, Budapest; *Two Duets,* 1941, R; *Móra songs* for soprano and tenor voices, with piano acc., 1940,

Bárd; *Four Ady Songs,* 1941; *Two Sonnets,* Poem by G. Baffo, 1942; *Monológ a halálról* (Monologue on Death), for baritone solo and piano, 1950; *Petőfi Songs* for mezzosoprano or baritone solo and piano, 1960; *Pro Memoria* cycle for baritone solo with orchestra, 1960, EMB; *Lorca Songs,* 1962, EMB.

WRITING: *Az új zene összhangzattana* (Harmony Book of New Music), 1945, University Press.

HUGÓ KELEN

(b. Budapest, 7 March 1888; d. 1956.) He studied in Berlin and in Vienna under Joseph Marx, and Franz Schreker resp.

For a while he was répétiteur at the Opernschule in Berlin, then singing teacher in Budapest. From 1943 on he was professor of the Goldmark Music School (singing). After 1945 he took part in the work of the Association of Hungarian Musicians.

STAGE WORKS: *Leánynéző* (Wooing), comic opera, 1932; incidental music to the play "A csodarabbi" (The Rabbi of Miraculous Powers), 1935.

WORKS FOR CHORUS AND ORCHESTRA: *Sirató* (Dirge), 1930; *Chor der Toten* (Chorus of the dead), 1932; *Johannisfeuer,* 1932; *Job,* 1940; *Zsoltár a mindenség szeretetéről* (Psalm of Loving the Universe), 1944; *A szocializmus útja* (The Way of Socialism), 1949; *Kommunisták* (Communists), 1950; *Pillantás előre* (A Glance into the Future), 1950; *Üzenet* (Message), 1953.

CHORAL WORKS WITHOUT ACCOMPANIMENT: *Psalm No. 9,* 1932; *Napittas földön* (On Sunny Soil), 1942.

ORCHESTRAL MUSIC: *Two Pieces for Orchestra,* 1930; *Concerto Grosso,* 1943; *Concerto for Oboe,* 1954.

CHAMBER MUSIC AND INSTRUMENTAL PIECES: *Four Piano Pieces,* 1920; *Piano Quartet,* 1925; *Small Suite* for violoncello and piano, 1925; *Jewish Suite,* for violoncello and piano, 1932; *Variations on a Theme* for violoncello and piano, 1951; *Ifjúság* (Youth), string trio, 1952; *Three Pieces for Violin and Piano,* 1952; *Three Pieces for Violoncello,* 1953; *Two Pieces for Oboe and Piano,* 1954.

SONGS to poems by E. Ady, B. Balázs, J. Arany, S. Petőfi, Rosenfeld, Bierbaum, Tchipatchof and others, among them: *Four Songs,* 1952, EMB; several songs and song-cycles with orchestral accompaniment, choral works with piano accompaniment.

The works composed by Hugó Kelen previous to 1944 perished during the siege of Budapest.

JENŐ KENESSEY

(b. Budapest, 23 Sept. 1905; d. Budapest, 19 Aug. 1976.) Studied music at the National Conservatory with László Lajtha, and later at the Academy of Music, Budapest under Albert siklós. After having obtained scholarship he made study-tours to Italy and to Austria, among others he attended also Franz Schalk's course for conductors in Salzburg. From 1929 on he was a member of the Budapest Opera House, where he became conductor in 1932. In 1953 he was awarded the "Merited Artist of the Hungarian People's Republic" title and the Kossuth Prize. He was conductor of the symphony orchestra at Ganz-MÁVAG and held the post of conductor of the Symphony Orchestra of Vasas Central Art Ensemble for several decades. He was awarded the Gold Medal of the Order of Labour in 1955 and the SZOT Prize in 1966.

STAGE WORKS: *Montmarte,* ballet, 1930; *Csizmás Jankó* (Johnny in Boots), ballet, 1935; *Enyém a vőlegény* (Mine is the Bridegroom), ballet, 1938; *Az arany meg az asszony* (The Gold and the Woman), opera, 1942, EMB; *Majális* (May Festival), ballet, 1948; *A keszkenő (The Kerchief), ballet, 1951; Bihari nótája* (Bihari's Song), ballet, 1954; *The Ballerina* (text by Gy. Krudy), unfinished.

WORKS FOR CHORUS AND ORCHESTRA: *Cantata from Goethe's "Pandora",* 1960; *Fényküllők* (Beams of Light), cantata, 1960; *Dawn at Balaton,* in memoriam

Gábor Devecseri, symphonic poem to a poem by G. Devecseri, for narrator and female voices, 1972.

CHORAL WORKS: *Four Old Hungarian Songs,* 1940; *Bocsásd meg Úristen* (Forgive Me God), 1946, MK; *Kuruc istenes ének* (Pious Kuruc Song), 1946, MK; *Kuruc bordalok* (Kuruc Drinking Songs), 1946; Association of Workers' Choirs.

ORCHESTRAL MUSIC: *Small Suite,* 1930; *Two Dances,* 1933; *Dance Impressions,* 1933; *Falusi képek* (Village Scenes), 1934; *Divertimento,* 1945; *Dances from Sárköz,* 1953.

CHAMBER MUSIC: *Piano Quartet,* 1928–29; *Sonata for Harp and Flute,* 1940; *Sonata for Harp, Flute and Viola,* 1940; *Divertimento,* for viola and harp, 1963; *Canzonetta* for flute and chamber orchestra, 1970; *Harp Trio* No. 2, for violin, viola and harp, 1972.

INSTRUMENTAL MUSIC: *Three Piano Pieces,* 1927, Bárd, Budapest; *Three Fugues for Piano,* 1928; *Sonata for Organ,* 1928; *Toccata for Organ,* 1941; *Fantasy for Organ,* 1949; *Two Recruiting Songs* for piano, 1949; *Variations on Children's Songs* for piano, 1970; *Pastorale per organo,* 1972; *Elegy and Scherzo* for piano, 1973.

SONGS: six series, among them: *Attila József cycle,* 1960, EMB.

MIKLÓS KOCSÁR

(b. Debrecen, 21 Dec. 1933.) He studied composition at the Academy of Music, Budapest under Ferenc Farkas. He was musical director and conductor of the Madách Theatre. Since 1972 he has been professor at the Béla Bartók Conservatory, Budapest, teaching composition and theory of music. In 1973 he was awarded the Erkel Prize. Since 1974 he has been working at the Music Department of the Hungarian Radio.

CHORAL WORKS: *Three Children Choruses* (Poems by S. Weöres), 1956, EMB; *Magyar nyár* (Hungarian Summer), (Poem by Gy. Juhász), 1958, NI; *Szikla* (Rock), (Poem by Gy. Sárközi), 1959, NI; *Two Mixed Choruses* to poems by Gy. Juhász, 1960, NI; *Új Kőmíves Kelemen* (New "Kelemen, the Mason"), (Poem by Gy. Juhász), for male choir, 1960, NI; *Süssél nap!* (Shine Sun, Shine!), (Poem by L. Drégely), Three Children Choruses, 1962, NI, EMB; *Évszakok zenéje* (Music of the Seasons), Eight Choruses for female choir to poems by L. Áprily, 1967, EMB; *Tűz, te gyönyörű* (Fire, You Wonderful), (Poem by L. Nagy), for mixed choir, 1970, EMB; *Liliomdal* (Lily Song), (Poem by L. Nagy), for mixed choir, 1971, NI; Three Female Choirs to poems by L. Nagy: *Szerelem emléke* (Memory of Love), 1971, EMB; *Ábránd* (Fancy), 1971; *Ó, havas erdők némasága* (Oh, Stillness of Snowy Forests), 1972, EMB; *Tűzciterák*

(Fire Zithers), (Poem by L. Nagy), for female voices, 1973, EMB; *Gyermekkarok* (Children's Choruses) I, II, III, Poems by I. Csanády, 1974, EMB; *Csili-csali nóták* (Seven Children's Choruses), (Poems by S. Weöres), 1977, EMB.

WORKS FOR CHORUS AND ORCHESTRA: *Hegyi legények* (Mountain Lads), cantata for male choir, brass instruments and percussion, based on new Greek popular poetry, 1957; *Suhanj, szerelem* (Glide Away, Love), cantata for mixed choir, with piano accompaniment to poems by J. Joyce, 1961, NI.

ORCHESTRAL MUSIC: *Horn Concerto,* 1957; Capriccio, 1961; *Serenate per archi,* 1959, 1971; *Five Movements* for clarinet and strings (ad lib. zimbalo ungherese o clavicembalo), 1976; *Változatok zenekarra* (Varianti per orchestra), 1977.

CHAMBER MUSIC: *Duo Serenade* for violin and viola, 1955; *Divertimento* for woodwind trio, 1956, EMB; *Rongyszőnyeg* (Ragcarpet), Six Short Songs for soprano solo and chamber ensemble to poems by S. Weöres, 1956; *Wind Quintet,* 1956, 1959, EMB; *Three Duets* for oboe and clarinet, 1956; *Brass Trio* for two trombones and trumpets, 1958, EMB; *Ungaresca per due fiati di legno,* 1968, EMB + BH; Broekmans and van Poppel; *Variazioni per Quintetto a Fiati,* 1968, EMB + BH; *Magányos ének* cycle for soprano solo and chamber ensemble to fragments by A. József, 1969; *Repliche* per flauto, e zimbalo ungherese (o clavicembalo), 1971, EMB + BH; *Sestetto d'ottoni,* 1972, EMB; *Kassák-dalok* (Kassák songs) for mezzosoprano solo, flute and cimbalom, 1976; *Repliche No. 2* per corno in Fa e zimbalo ungherese, 1976.

INSTRUMENTAL PIECES: *Capriccio* for flute, 1956; *Sonatina* for piano, 1956; *Sonata* for violin and piano, 1957; *Movimento* for violin, 1961–62; *Dialoghi* for bassoon and piano, 1964–65, EMB + BH; *Improvvisazioni per pianoforte,* 1972, EMB; *Furulyamuzsika* (Musica pastorale), 1975, EMB; *Tizenöt kis zongoradarab* (Fifteen Small Piano Pieces), 1975, EMB.

SONGS WITH PIANO ACCOMPANIMENT: *Three Attila József Songs,* 1955; *Fájva szeretni* (To Love with Sorrow) to a cycle by Á. Tóth, 1958; *Kései szelek* (Belated Winds) to a cycle by L. Kassák, 1958; *A kísértet dala* (Song of the Phantom), to a poem by S. Weöres, 1958; *Falusi sirató* (Dirge in the Village), to a poem by G. Szabó, 1959; *Lamenti,* cycle to poems by F. García Lorca, 1966–67, BH + EMB; *Három Petőfi-dal* (Three Petőfi Songs), 1973, EMB.

DISCOGRAPHY:

Kiszejárás (Hungarian folk Custom) – *Wedding in Nagyréde*
Choir and Orchestra of the Hungarian State Folk Ensemble,
conductors: Rezső Lantos, Miklós Pászti
LPX 1281

Days of Celebration (Midsummer Night Fire – Devil's Wedding – Harvest Celebration)
Choir and Orchestra of the Hungarian State Folk Ensemble, conducted by Rezső Lantos and Miklós Pászti
LPX 18010

Improvvisazioni
Ádám Fellegi (piano)
SLPX 11692

Repliche per flauto e zimbalo ungherese; Variazioni per quintetto a fiati; Lovely Song to Poems by A. József
István Matuz (flute), Márta Fábián (cimbalom)
Hungarian Wind Quintet
Erika Sziklay (soprano), Budapest Chamber Ensemble,
conductor: András Mihály
SLPX 11635

Brass Sextet
Hungarian Brass Ensemble
SLPX 11811

Évszakok zenéje (Music of the Seasons)
Girl's Chorus of Győr, conductor: Miklós Szabó
SLPX 11764

ZOLTÁN KODÁLY

(b. Kecskemét, 16 Dec. 1882; d. Budapest, 6 March 1967.) In his early years he studied music at Nagyszombat (Trnava). In 1900 he came to Budapest, where he was a pupil of János Koessler at the Academy of Music. Simultaneously with his musical studies he took his degree of Doctor of Philosophy. (His thesis was "A magyar népdal strófaszerkezete". Strophic Structure of the Hungarian Folk Song, 1906.) He began his folk song collecting tours in 1905; from 1906 on, he was accompanied by Béla Bartók. In 1906 and in 1907 he visited Berlin and Paris, respectively. From 1907 until his retirement he was professor of the Academy of Music, Budapest. From 1946 to 1949 he was appointed president of the Hungarian Academy of Sciences, from 1945 to 1949 president of the Hungarian Arts Council, honorary president of the Association of Hungarian Musicians, from 1963 to his death president of the International Society for Musical Education (ISME). He was awarded the Kossuth Prize in 1948, 1952 and 1957, the "Outstanding Artist of the Hungarian People's Republic" title in 1952.

STAGE WORKS: *A Notre-Dame-i toronyőr* (The Hunchback of the Notre Dame), 1902, lost; *Cid,* 1903, lost; *A nagybácsi* (The Uncle), 1904; *Pacsirtaszó* (Song of the Lark), incidental music to a play by Zs. Móricz, 1917; *Háry János,* 1925–27, UE; *Székely fonó* (Spinning Room), 1924–32, UE; *Kuruc mese* (Kuruc Tale), ballet, choreography on the music of Dances of Marosszék and Dances of Galánta, 1935; *Kádár Kata,* music to a film, 1943, UE; *Czinka Panna,* 1946–48.

WORKS FOR CHORUS AND ORCHESTRA: *Ave Maria,* prior to 1897, lost; *Assumpta est,* 1902; *Psalmus Hungaricus,* 1923, UE, EMB; *Te Deum of Budavár,* 1936, UE, EMB; *Missa brevis,* 1944, BH, EMB; *Vértanúk sírjánál* (At the Graves of the Martyrs), 1945; *Kállai kettős* (Double Dance of Kálló), 1950, EMB, BH; *An Ode* (O'Shaughnessy), 1964.

CHORAL WORKS WITH ACCOMPANIMENT OF ORGAN, PIANO OR OTHER INSTRUMENTS: parts from a Mass, Mixed Choir and Organ, prior to 1897, lost; *Ave Maria,* mixed choir and organ, prior to 1900; *Five Tantum Ergos,* children's choir and organ, 1928, UE, MK; *Pange lingua,* mixed choir and organ, or children's choir and organ, 1929, UE; *Katonadal* (Soldiers' Song), male choir, trumpet and drum, 1934, MK, EMB; *Karácsonyi pásztortánc* (Shepherds' Dance at Christmas), children's choir and recorder, 1935, MK, UE, EMB; *Ének Szent István királyhoz* (Hymn to King Stephen), for equal voices and organ, 1938, MK, EMB; *Első áldozás* (The First Holy Communion), chorus and organ, 1942, published by the composer; *Molnár Anna,* chorus and small orchestra, 1942, transcribed: 1959; *Song at Advent,* mixed choir and organ, 1943, MK; *Vejnemöjnen muzsikál* (Veinemoinen's Music), for equal voices and piano, 1944, MK; *Missa brevis* mixed choir and organ, 1942–44, BH, EMB; *Jézus és a gyermekek* (Jesus and the Children), children's choir and organ, 1947, MK; *A 114., 121. genfi zsoltár* (The Geneva Psalms No. 114 and No. 121), mixed choir and organ, 1952, BH, EMB; *Intermezzo from "Háry János",* with text, mixed choir and piano, 1956, EMB; *Laudes Organi,* for mixed choir and organ, 1966, BH, EMB.

WORKS FOR SOLO VOICE WITH ORCHESTRAL OR INSTRUMENTAL ACCOMPANIMENT: *Two Songs,* 1913–16, UE, BH, EMB; *Fáj a szívem* (My Heart is Aching), voice and gipsy orchestra from the play "Pacsirtaszó", 1917; *Three Songs,* 1924–29; *Molnár Anna,* 1942; *Kádár Kata,* 1943, UE.

ORCHESTRAL MUSIC: *Overture,* 1897, lost; *Nyári este* (Summer Evening), 1906, transcribed: 1929–30, UE; *Magyar rondó* (Hungarian Rondo), violoncello and orchestra, under the title "Régi magyar katonadalok" ("Old Hungarian Soldiers' Songs"), 1917; *Ballet music,* originally intended to "Háry János", 1925, UE; *Háry Suite,* 1927, UE, EMB; *Marosszéki táncok* (Dances of Marosszék), 1930, UE, EMB; *Galántai táncok* (Dances of Galánta), 1933, UE, EMB; *Fölszállott a páva* (The Peacock), 1938–39, published by the composer, BH, EMB; *Concerto,* 1939–40, published by the composer, BH, EMB; *Minuetto serio,* 1953, EMB; *Symphony,* 1961, BH, EMB.

CHAMBER MUSIC: *Trio* for two violins and viola, previous to 1900; *Intermezzo* for string trio, 1905, Publishing House of the Hungarian Academy of Sciences; *String Quartet* No. 1, 1908–09, R, EMB; *Sonata* for violoncello and piano, 1909, UE; *Duet* for violin and violoncello, 1914, UE; *String Quartet* No. 2, 1916–18, UE; *Serenade* for two violins and viola, 1919–20, UE.

INSTRUMENTAL SOLO PIECES: *Adagio* for violin and piano, 1905, R, EMB, transcriptions for viola, violoncello, orchestral accompaniment and small orchestra;

Valsette for piano, 1905, R, EMB, transcription for violin and piano, R, EMB; *Méditation* sur un motif de Claude Debussy, for piano, 1907, UE, EMB; *Piano Music* (later: Nine Piano Pieces), 1909, R, UE, EMB; *Sonata* for violoncello solo, 1915, UE; *Capriccio* for violoncello, 1915, EMB; *Hungarian Rondo* for violoncello and piano, 1917; *Seven Piano Pieces,* 1910–18, UE, EMB; *Hívogató tábortűzhöz* (Invitation to the Campfire), for clarinet, 1930, UE, EMB; *Organ Prelude* (to Pange lingua), 1931, UE; *Exercise* for the Vásárhelyi-Gábriel violin tutor, 1942, MK; *Organ Mass,* 1942, MK; *Twenty-four Small Canons on the Black Keys* for piano, 1945, R, EMB; *Children's Dances* for piano, 1945, BH, EMB; *Epigrams* for voice or instruments with piano, 1954, EMB.

INSTRUMENTAL TRANSCRIPTIONS: J. S. Bach: *Three Choral Preludes* for violoncello and piano, 1924, R, UE; J. S. Bach: *Chromatic Fantasy* for viola solo, 1950, BH; J. S. Bach: *Prelude and Fugue* in E flat minor for violoncello and piano, 1951; J. S. Bach: *Lute Prelude* for violin and piano, 1959, EMB; Haydn: *Rondo from the Sonata No. 5* (Hoboken XVI:43 bis) for youth orchestra, 1965.

SONGS AND FOLK SONGS ARRANGEMENTS FOR VOICE AND PIANO AC-COMPANIMENT: *Ave Maria,* prior to 1897, lost; *Vadon erdő a világ* (A Wilderness is the World), prior to 1900; *Szeretném itthagyni a fényes világot* (I Should Like to Leave This Bright World), 1905; *Hungarian Folk Songs,* in collaboration with Béla Bartók, 1906, Rozsnyai, EMB; *Four Songs,* 1907, UE, BH, EMB; *Énekszó* (16 Songs), 1907–09, R, EMB; *Himfy-Song,* 1915; *Megkésett melódiák* (Late Melodies), 1912–16, UE, EMB; *Two Songs,* 1913–16, UE, BH, EMB; *Fáj a szívem* (My Heart is Aching), 1917; *Five songs,* 1915–18, UE, BH, EMB; *Three Songs,* 1924–29, UE, BH, EMB; *Hungarian Folk Music,* ten volumes, 1924-32, UE, EMB; *Eight Small Duets,* following Bicinia Hungarica, 1953, EMB, BH; *Epigrams* for voice or instrument, without words, 1954, EMB; *Öt hegyi-mari népdal* (Five Folk Songs of the Mari People), 1960, EMB; *Hungarian Folk Music XI.,* 1964, UE, EMB; *Epitaphium Joannis Hunyadi,* 1965, EMB.

A CAPPELLA CHORAL WORKS:

MIXED VOICES: *Este* (Evening), 1904, UE, MK, EMB; *Nagyszalontai köszöntő* (A Birthday Greeting), 1931, MK, UE, OUP, EMB; *Mátrai képek* (Mátra Pictures), 1931, MK, UE, EMB; *Öregek* (The Aged), 1933, MK, UE, EMB; *Székely keserves, Jézus és a kufárok* (Székely Lament, Jesus and the Traders), 1934, MK, UE, EMB; *Akik mindig elkésnek* (Too Late), 1934, MK, UE, EMB; *Horatii Carmen* II. 10., Students' mixed choir, 1934, MK, EMB; *Liszt Ferenchez, Molnár Anna* (To Ferenc Liszt, Molnár Anna), 1936, MK, UE, EMB; *A magyarokhoz* (To the Magyars), canon, 1936, MK, EMB; *Fölszállott a páva* (The Peacock), transcription for mixed choir, 1937, EMB; *Ének Szent István királyhoz* (Hymn to King Stephen), three different arrangements for mixed choir, 1938, MK, BH, EMB; *Esti dal* (Evening Song), 1938, MK, EMB; *János köszöntő* (Greeting John), boys' mixed choir, 1939, published by the composer, EMB; *Norvég lányok* (Norwegian Girls), 1940, MK, BH, EMB; *Balassi Bálint elfelejtett éneke* (The Forgotten Song of Bálint Balassi), 1942, MK, EMB; *Első áldozás* (First Communion), 1942, MK, EMB; *Szép könyörgés, A székelyekhez, Cohors generosa,*

Gömöri dal (Invocation, To the Székelys, Cohors generosa, Song from Gömör), 1943, MK, EMB; *Adventi ének* (Advent Song), 1943, MK, EMB; *Csatadal* (Battle Song), 1943, MK, EMB, BH; *Sirató ének* (Lament), 1947, MK, EMB; *A magyar nemzet* (The Hungarian Nation), 1947, MK, EMB; *A szabadság himnusza* (The Hymn of Liberty "La Marseillaise"), 1948, MK, EMB; *Adoration,* 1948, Cs, EMB; *Jelige* (Motto), 1948, MK, EMB; *Az 50. genfi zsoltár* (The Geneva Psalm No. 50), 1948, MK, EMB; *Békesség-óhajtás – 1801. esztendő* (Wish for Peace – The Year 1801), 1953, EMB; *Zrínyi szózata* (Zrinyi's Appeal), 1954, EMB; *Magyarország címere* (The Arms of Hungary), 1956, EMB; *I Will Go Look for Death,* 1959, BH, EMB; *Sík Sándor's Te Deum,* 1961, EMB; *Media vita in morte sumus,* 1961, BH, EMB; *Mohács,* 1965, EMB.

MALE VOICES: *Stabat Mater,* previous to 1900, EMB; *Two Choruses* for male choir, 1913–17, UE, MK, EMB; *Jelenti magát Jézus* (Jesus Appears), 1927, MK, EMB; *Canticum nuptiale,* 1928, EMB; *Karádi nóták* (Songs of Karád), 1934, MK, BH, EMB; *Kit kéne elvenni* (Whom to Marry), 1934, MK, BH, EMB; Horatius: *Justum et tenacem,* 1935, published by the composer, EMB; *Huszt,* 1936, MK, UE, EMB; *Fölszállott a páva* (The Peacock), 1937, MK, EMB, BH; *Ének Szent István királyhoz* (Hymn to King Stephen), 1938, MK, EMB; *Esti dal* (Evening Song), 1938, MK, EMB; *Semmit ne bánkódjál* (Don't Despair), 1939, MK, EMB; *Rabhazának fia, Isten csodája* (The Son of an Enslaved Country – Still, by a Miracle, Our Country Stands), 1944, MK, EMB; *Élet vagy halál – Hej, Büngözsdi Bandi* (To Live or Die – Hey, Bandi Büngözsdi), 1947, MK, EMB; *A szabadság himnusza* (The Hymn of Liberty), two arrangements of the "Marseillaise", 1948, MK, EMB; *Jelige* (Motto), 1948, MK, EMB; *Nemzeti dal* (National Ode), 1955, EMB; *Emléksorok Fáy Andrásnak – A nándori toronyőr* (Dedication to András Fáy – The Guard at the Tower of Nándor), 1956, EMB.

FEMALE VOICES: *Két zoborvidéki népdal* (Two Folk Songs from Zobor), 1908, UE, EMB; *Hegyi éjszakák* I. (Nights in the Mountains I), 1923, II–IV: 1955–56, V: 1962, EMB, BH; *Four Italian Madrigals,* 1932, MK, EMB; *Ave Maria,* 1935, MK, UE, EMB; *Harmatozzatok* (Rorate), 1935, MK, EMB; *Ének Szent István királyhoz* (Hymn to King Stephen), 1938, MK, EMB; *Semmit ne bánkódjál* (Don't Despair), 1939, MK, EMB, BH; *Árva vagyok* (I am Lonely), 1953, EMB; *Ürgeöntés* (Children's Song), 1954, EMB; *Meghalok, meghalok* (Woe is Me), 1957, EMB.

CHILDREN'S CHORUSES, CHOIRS FOR EQUAL VOICES: *Villő – Túrót eszik a cigány* (Villő – The Gipsy is Munching Curd), 1925, UE, MK, OUP, EMB; *Gergelyjárás* (St. Gregory's Day), 1925, MK, OUP, EMB; *Lengyel László* (Children's Song), 1927, MK, OUP, EMB; *Jelenti magát Jézus* (Jesus Appears), 1927, MK, OUP, EMB; *Juhásznóta* (Shepherd's Song), 1928, MK, EMB; *A süket sógor – Cigánysirató – Isten kovácsa* (The Deaf Boatman – Gipsy Lament – God's Blacksmith), 1928, MK, OUP, EMB; *Gólyanóta – Pünkösdölő – Táncnóta – Új esztendőt köszöntő* (Children's Song – Whitsuntide – Dancing Song – New Year's Greeting), 1929, MK, OUP, EMB; *Nagyszalontai köszöntő* (A Birthday Greeting), 1931, MK, OUP, EMB; *Vízkereszt* (Epiphany), 1933, MK, UE, OUP, EMB; *Nyulacska* (Bunnykin), 1934, MK, UE, EMB; *Harmatozzatok* (Rorate), 1935, MK, EMB; *Angyalok és pásztorok* (The Angels and the Shepherds), 1935, MK, UE, EMB; *Seven Easy Children's Choirs and Six Canons,* 1936, MK, EMB; *A magyarokhoz* (To the Magyars), canon, 1936, MK, EMB; *A 150. genfi zsoltár* (The Geneva Psalm No. 150), 1936, MK, EMB; *Harangszó* (Bells), 1937, MK, EMB; *Angyalkert* (Angels' Garden), 1937, MK, EMB; *Hajnövesztő* (Children's Song) – *Katalinka* – *Három gömöri népdal* (Three Folk Songs from Gömör), 1937, MK, EMB; *A csikó* (The Filly), 1937, MK, EMB; *Egyedem-begyedem* (Children's Song), – *Cú, föl lovam* (Gee-up, my Horse) – *Csalfa sugár* (Treacherous Gleam), 1938, MK, EMB; *Esti dal* (Evening Song), 1938, MK, OUP, EMB; *Szolmizáló kánon* (Solmization canon), 1942, Singing youth, EMB; *Magyar magyart rontja* (Hungarian against Hungarian), 1944, Singing youth, EMB; *Szent Ágnes ünnepére* (St. Agnes' Day), 1945, EMB; *A szabadság himnusza* (Hymn of Liberty), two arrangements of the "Marseillaise", 1948, MK, EMB; *Jelige* (Motto), 1948, MK, EMB; *Békedal* (Peace Song), 1952, EMB; *Ürgeöntés* (Children's Song), 1954, EMB; *Arany szabadság* (Wonderful Liberty), canon, 1957, EMB; *Házasodik a vakond* (Children's Song), 1958, EMB; *Méz, méz, méz* (Honey, Honey, Honey), 1958, EMB; *Tell Me Where is Fancy Bred...,* 1959, EMB; *Harasztosi legények* (Lads of Harasztos), 1961, EMB; *Az éneklő ifjúsághoz* (To the Singing Youth), 1962.

EDUCATIONAL MUSIC, SINGING EXERCISES: *Fifteen two-part exercises,* 1941, published by the composer, MK, BH, EMB; *Énekeljünk tisztán!* (Let Us Sing Correctly!), 1941, published by the composer, MK, BH, EMB; *Bicinia Hungarica* I–IV, 1937–42, published by the composer, MK, EMB, BH; *333 olvasógyakorlat* (333 Elementary Exercises), 1943, MK, EMB, BH; *Ötfokú zene* I–IV (Pentatonic Music I–IV), 1945–48, published by the composer, MK, EMB, BH; *Thirty-three two-part exercises,* 1954, EMB, BH; *Forty-four two-part exercises,* 1954, EMB, BH; *Fifty-five two-part exercises,* 1954, EMB, BH; *Tricinia,* 1954, EMB, BH; *Tricinium* No. 29, 1954, EMB; *Kis emberek dalai* (Fifty Nursery Songs), 1961, EMB; *Sixty-six two-part exercises,* 1962, EMB, BH; *Twenty-two two-part exercises,* 1964, EMB, BH; *Seventy-seven two-part exercises,* 1966, EMB, BH.

MISCELLANEOUS: *Festive Military March* for wind orchestra, 1948, EMB.

WRITINGS: *Erdélyi Magyarság, Népdalok* (The Hungarians of Transylvania, Folk Songs), in collaboration with Béla Bartók, 1921, Budapest, R; *A magyar népzene* (Hungarian Folk Music), 1937, 1943, 1951, 1960, 1969, in German: 1956, in English: 1960; *Iskolai énekgyűjtemény* I–II (Songs for Schools I–II), Budapest, 1943; *Szó-mi* I–VIII (Sol-Fa I–VIII), in collaboration with Jenő Ádám, Budapest, 1944–45; *Énekeskönyv az általános iskolák I–VIII. osztálya számára* (Song Book for Forms I–VIII in Primary Schools), in collaboration with Jenő Ádám, Budapest, 1948; *Arany János népdalgyűjteménye* (The Folk Song Collection of János Arany), in collaboration with Ágost Gyulai, Budapest, 1953; *Visszatekintés* I–II (Retrospection I–II), a collected edition of Kodály's Essays and Writings, Budapest, 1964, EMB.

DISCOGRAPHY:

Háry János (suite) – *Dances of Galánta* – *Dances of Marosszék*
Budapest Philharmonic Society Orchestra, conductor: János Ferencsik
LPX 1194

Nights in the Mountains 1-4. – *Two Folk Songs from Zobor* – *Treacherous Gleam* –
Veinemoinen's Music – *Evening* – *Lament* – *Greeting John* – *Too Late* – *Beseeching* –
Székely Lament – *Wish for Peace*
Debrecen Kodály Choir, conductor: György Gulyás
LPX 1211

Duo for Violin and Violoncello, Op. 7 – *Sonata for Violoncello and Piano, Op. 4* –
Adagio for Violoncello and Piano
Vilmos Tátrai (violin), Ede Banda, Vera Dénes (violoncello), Endre Petri (piano)
LPX 1149

Two Songs, Op. 5 (Winter is coming – To cry) – *Three Songs, Op. 14* (Sorrow for Me –
Open – Wait for Me, my Bird) – *Molnár Anna* – *Kádár Kata*
György Melis, József Simándy, Márta Szirmay (soloists)
Symphony Orchestra of the Hungarian Radio and Television,
conductor: György Lehel
LPX 11450

Trio Serenade, Op. 12 – *Intermezzo for String Trio* – *Sonatina for Violoncello and Piano* – *Adagio for Violoncello and Piano* – *Capriccio for Violoncello solo* – *Prelude and Fugue* (transcription of J. S. Bach's Wohltemperiertes Klavier I. 8.)
Vilmos Tátrai, István Várkonyi (violin), György Konrád (viola), Ede Banda, László
Mező (violoncello), Loránt Szűcs (piano)
LPX 11449

ARCHIVE RECORDING

Zoltán Kodály conducts his own works
Missa brevis – *Te Deum of Budavár* – *Psalmus Hungaricus* – *Concerto* – *Summer
Evening*
Mária Gyurkovics, Edit Gáncs, Timea Cser, Magda Tiszay, Irén Szecsődy, Endre
Rösler, Tibor Udvardy, András Faragó, György Littasy (soloists)
Budapest Choir, Hungarian State Concert Orchestra, Budapest Philharmonic Society
Orchestra
HLX 90053/55

KODÁLY ZOLTÁN'S WORKS ON HUNGAROTON

VOCAL MUSIC
Psalmus Hungaricus Op. 13
The Peacock, Variations on a Hungarian Folk Song
József Simándy, Budapest Choir

Children's Choir of the Hungarian Radio and Television
Hungarian State Orchestra
conductor: Antal Doráti
SLPX 11392

Te Deum of Buda Castle – Missa Brevis
Éva Andor, Alice Ekkert, Klára Makkay, Éva Mohácsi (soprano), Márta Szirmay
(contralto), József Réti (tenor), József Gregor (bass)
Choir and Orchestra of the Hungarian Radio and Television
conductor: János Ferencsik
SLPX 11397

Háry János – complete recording
(A Play with Music)
Imre Palló, Magda Tiszay, Oszkár Maleczky, Andor Lendvay, Anna Báthy, Judit
Sándor, Endre Rösler, György Melis
Chorus of the Hungarian State Opera
Budapest Philharmonic Orchestra
conductor: János Ferencsik
LPX 1023–25
(only mono)

Spinning Room – complete recording
(A Lyrical Play on Folk Texts)
Erzsébet Komlóssy, György Melis, Zsuzsa Barlay, József Simándy, Éva Andor,
Sándor Palcsó
Choir of the Hungarian Radio and Television
Budapest Philharmonic Orchestra
conductor: János Ferencsik
SLPX 11504–5

ORCHESTRAL SONGS:
Two Songs, Op. 5 – Three Songs Op. 14 – Mónár Anna – Kádár Kata
György Melis (baritone), József Simándy (tenor), Márta Szirmay (contralto)
Orchestra of the Hungarian Radio and Television
conductor: György Lehel
SLPX 11450

*Songs for Voice and Piano – Énekszó – 16 Songs, Op. 1 – 4 Songs, (Without Opus
Number) – 7 Songs, Op. 6 – 5 Songs, Op. 9 – Himfy Song – Epitaphium Joannis
Hunyadi*
Éva Andor, Attila Fülöp, István Gáti, József Gregor, Boldizsár Keönch, Kolos Kováts,
György Melis, Sylvia Sass, Sándor Sólyom-Nagy, Ilona Tokody (voice)

Loránt Szűcs (piano)
SLPX 11766–7

CHORAL WORKS I.
Horatii Carmen – Cohors generosa – Advent Song – Media vita in morte sumus –
Pangue lingua – Four Italian Madrigals – Psalm No.150 – Ave Maria – Fancy – I am
Dying – Nights in the Mountain No. 4
"Zoltán Kodály" Children's Choir
Choir of the Hungarian Radio and Television
conductor: Ilona Andor, Zoltán Vásárhelyi
SLPX 1259

CHORAL WORKS II.
Whitsuntide – Straw Guy – New Years Greeting – St.Gregory's Day – László Lengyel –
Angels and Shepherds – Peace Song – Evening Song – Birthday Greeting –Hey Ho – I
am an Orphan – Honey, Honey – Lands of harasztos – Gopher
Hunting – The Mole is to Marry – Four Pieces from the Bicinia Hungarica – Three Pie-
ces from the Tricinia – Singing Youth
"Zoltán Kodály" Children's Choir
conductor: Ilona Andor
LPX 11315

CHORAL WORKS III.
Mátra Pictures – Molnár Anna – Songs from Gömör – See, the Gipsy Munching
Cheese – Kálló Double Dance – The Ruins – The Miracle of God – The Peacock –
Songs from Karád – Hejh Büngözsdi Bandi – Drinking Song – Merrymaking –
Password
Choir of the Hungarian Radio and Television
Male Choir of the Hungarian People's Army
Hungarian State Orchestra
conductor: Zoltán Vásárhelyi
SLPX 11339

CHORAL WORKS IV.
Nights in the Mountains Nos. 1-5. – God's Blacksmith – Gee-Up, My Horse
–Children's Song – The Deaf Boatman – The Bells – The Hawk – Little Rabbit – Kata-
linka – Children's Song – In the Green Forest – The Foal – See, the Gipsy Munching
Cheese – Dancing Song – Jesus Appears – Xmas Shepherd's Dance – Veinemoinen's
Music
"Zoltán Kodály" Chorus of the Klára Leöwey Secondary School, Budapest
conductor: Ilona Andor
SLPX 11409

CHORAL WORKS V.
Two-Part Singing Exercises
"Zoltán Kodály" Girls' Chorus
conductor: Ilona Andor
SLPX 11469

CHORAL WORKS VI.
Jesus and the Traders – Norwegian Girls – I will go look for Death – Too Late –Old People – Lament – The Forgotten Song of Bálint Balassi – The Hungarian Nation – To the Transylvanians – Mohács – To Ferenc Liszt
Choir of the Hungarian Radio and Television
conductor: Zoltán Vásárhelyi
SLPX 11522

CHORAL WORKS VII.
Adoration – First Holy Communion – Twelfth Night – Geneva Psalm CXXI – Do not Despair – Geneva Psalm CXIV – Geneva Psalm L – Laudes Organi
Chorus of the Hungarian Radio and Television
Budapest "Zoltán Kodály" Girls' Chorus,
Gábor Lehotka (organ)
conductor: János Ferencsik
LPX 11612

CHORAL WORKS VIII.
Evening Song – Székely Lament – A Birthday Greeting – Two Folk Songs from Zobor – Justum et tenacem – Advent Song – Come, Holy Ghost – Lovely Invocation – Battle Song – Too Late – Hymn to King Stephen – Wish for Peace – Evening – Sándor Sik's Te Deum
Kodály Chorus of Debrecen
conductor: György Gulyás
SLPX 11606

ORCHESTRAL AND CHAMBER MUSIC
Symphony
Ballet Music
Budapest Philharmonic Orchestra
conductor: János Ferencsik
SLPX 1245

Háry János – Suite for Orchestra
Dances of Galánta
Dances of Marosszék

Budapest Philharmonic Orchestra
conductor: János Ferencsik
SLPX 11914

String Quartets No. 1 and 2
Tátrai Quartet
SLPX 11322

CHAMBER MUSIC I.
Adagio for Cello and Piano
Capriccio for Cello Unaccompanied
Intermezzo for String Trio
Prelude and Fugue
Serenade for two Violins and Viola Op.12
Sonatina for Cello and Piano
László Mező, Loránt Szűcs, Vilmos Tátrai, György Konrád, Ede Banda, István Várkonyi
SLPX 11449

CHAMBER MUSIC II.
Duo for Violin and Cello Op.7
Epigrams for Voice or Instrument with Piano Accompaniment
J. S. Bach – Zoltán Kodály: Three Choral Preludes for Cello and Piano
Péter Komlós, Ede Banda, Béla Kovács, Kornél Zempléni, Ádám Fellegi
SLPX 11559

CHAMBER MUSIC III.
Sonata for Cello and Piano Op.4
Sonata for Cello Unaccompanied Op.8
Miklós Perényi, Jenő Jandó
SLPX 11864

PIANO MUSIC
Dances of Marosszék
Children's Dances
Seven Piano Pieces, Op.11
Valsette
Méditation
Kornél Zempléni (piano)
SLPX 1260

REZSŐ KÓKAI

(b. Budapest, 15 Jan. 1906; d. 6 March 1962.) He studied composition at the Academy of Music, Budapest under Prof. János Koessler, and piano with Emanuel Hegyi. He took his D. Mus. degree at the University of Freiburg under W. Gurlitt. From 1926 to 1934 he was professor at the National Conservatory, from 1929 on at the Academy of Music. (Musical aesthetics, methods of music-education, composition.) He was awarded the Erkel Prize in 1952, 1955 and 1956.

STAGE WORKS: *István király* (King Stephen), scenic oratorio, 1942; *A rossz feleség* (The Bad Wife), dance ballad, 1946; adaptation of Erkel's opera "Brankovics", 1961.

ORCHESTRAL MUSIC: *Two Rondos for Small Orchestra,* 1947; *Recruiting Suite,* 1950, EMB; *Short Recruiting Music,* for youth orchestra, 1954, EMB; *Széki táncok* (Dances from Szék), 1952, EMB; *Concerto all'Ungherese,* 1957, Mills, London; *Hungarian Dance,* for youth orchestra, 1960, EMB.

CONCERTOS: *Concerto for Violin,* 1952, EMB; *Rhapsody for Clarinet and Popular Orchestra,* 1952.

CHAMBER MUSIC: *Serenade for String Trio,* 1949–50, EMB; *Small Quartet* for clarinet and string trio, 1952.

INSTRUMENTAL PIECES: *Toccata* for piano, 1927, R; *Four Improvisations* for piano, 1949–50, Arts Council; *Sonata* for two pianos, 1949, EMB; *Two Dances* for violoncello and piano, 1950, EMB; *Four Hungarian Dances* for clarinet and piano, 1951, EMB; *Recruiting Rhapsody* for violin and piano, 1952, EMB; *Capriccio,* for violin and piano, 1952, EMB; *Two Pieces for Violin and Piano,* 1953, EMB.

Songs, music to radio plays and films.

WRITINGS: *Franz Liszt in seinen frühen Klavierwerken* (Ferenc Liszt in His Early Piano Works), Diss., Leipzig, 1933; *Rendszeres zeneesztétika* (Methodical Aesthetics of Music), Budapest, 1933; *Századunk zenéje* (The Music of our Century), in collaboration with Imre Fábián, Budapest, 1961, EMB.

GYÖRGY KÓSA

(b. Budapest, 24 Apr. 1897.) At seven he became Bartók's pupil for piano playing. At the beginning of the 1910s he was already admitted to the Academy of Music where he studied composition with Zoltán Kodály and Viktor Herzfeld. He obtained his artist's diploma in piano playing under Ernő Dohnányi. In 1917 he was coach at the Budapest Opera House, and afterwards made several concert tours as piano accompanist. In 1920–21 he was employed as conductor at the Theatre Tripolis. In 1921 he returned to Budapest, and in 1927 he became professor of pianoforte playing at the Academy of Music. In 1955 he was awarded the Erkel Prize, in 1963 the "Merited Artist of the Hungarian People's Republic" title, and in 1967 the Gold Medal of the Order of Labour. In 1972 he was awarded the "Outstanding Artist of the Hungarian People's Republic" title.

STAGE WORKS: seven *Operas,* amongst them: *Az két lovagok* (Those Two Knights), 1934; *Tartuffe,* 1951; *Eleven Ballets* and *Pantomimes,* amongst them: *Phaedra,* 1918; *Laterna Magica,* 1922; *Árva Józsi három csodája* (The Three Miracles of Józsi Árva), 1932, UE; *Ének az örök bánatról* (Song about the Everlasting Sorrow), 1955; *Pázmány lovag* (Knight Pázmány), opera, 1962–63; *Kocsonya Mihály házassága* (Marriage of Mihály Kocsonya), opera comedy, 1971.

ORATORIOS AND CANTATAS: seven *Biblical Oratorios,* four *Secular Oratorios,* amongst them: *Laodameia,* 1924; *De profundis* for soprano solo with two violins accompaniment, 1947; transcribed with organ accompaniment 1970; three *Biblical Cantatas, three Secular Cantatas,* three *Masses,* 1946, 1949, 1951; *Requiem,* 1949; *Te Deum,* 1949; *Stabat Mater,* 1949; twelve *Offertories,* 1949; *Villon,* 1960–61; *Requiem No. 2,* 1966; five other Sacred Works: *Hajnóczy,* 1954; *Manole,* 1965; *A bárányka* (The Lambkin), Rumanian ballad for soprano and bass, flute, cello, harp and kettle drum, 1965; *Orpheus* (Poem by Rilke), 1967; *Cantata Humana* (Poem by J. Pannonius), 1967; *Susanna,* chamber cantata, 1971; *Az üresek* (The Empty Ones), cantata to a poem by T. S. Eliot, vocal quartet, flute, bassoon, four percussion instruments, four strings; *Simeon's Song,* to a poem by T. S. Eliot, for bass solo, three female voices, harp; *Karinthy Cantata* for tenor and string trio, 1973; *Bikasirató* (Bull Dirge), cantata to a poem by G. Devecseri, for tenor solo, mixed choir and orchestra, 1974–75 (won the "Critics' Prize" of the Hungarian Radio in 1977); *Kakasszó* (Cock Crow), cantata to a poem by I. Vas, for baritone solo, female choir, wind quintet and vibraphone, 1975; *Todesfuge,* cantata to a poem by P. Celan, for soprano solo, wind quintet, string quartet, harp, percussion, 1976.

CHORAL WORKS: *Csendes dal* (Quiet Song), 1925, MK; *Iciri-piciri* (Zs. Móricz text), for children's choir, 1932; *Istenes ének* (Religious Song), (Poem by B. Balassi), for mixed choir, 1938; *Suite to Poems by Po-Tshu-Ye,* with harp 1955; *Csokonai Suite,* 1958, EMB; *Erdélyi havas balladák* (Transylvanian Snowy Ballads), for mixed choir, 1964, EMB; *Phaedrus mesék* (Phaedrus Fables), for children's choir, 1970; *Látomások* (Visions), (Poems by J. Pilinszky), for mixed choir, 1972; *XX. századi freskó* (Twentieth Century Fresco), a cappella chorus (Poem by S. Weöres), 1976; *Psalm,* a cappella chorus to a poem by S. Weöres, 1976; *Damján és Rémanyó* (Damyan and Aunt Spook), fantastic Rumanian folk ballad for girls' choir, 1977.

ORCHESTRAL MUSIC: nine *Symphonies,* 1921, 1927, 1933, 1934, 1937, 1946, 1957, 1959, 1969, EMB; *Six Pieces,* 1919, UE; *Suite,* 1924, UE; *Fairy-tale Suite,* 1931; *Fantasy on Three Folk Songs,* 1948; *Dance Suite,* 1951, EMB; *Small Suite,* 1955; *Jutka Ballad,* 1946; *Suite* for string orchestra, 1958; *Ballad and Rondo* for violin and wind orchestra, 1961; three orchestral song-cycles, etc.

CHAMBER MUSIC: eight *String Quartets,* 1920, Hansen, Copenhague, 1929, EMB, 1933, 1937, 1956, 1959–60, 1963, 1965; *Duet* for violin and double bass, 1928; *Music for Seventeen Instruments,* 1928; *Six Portraits,* 1933; *Quintet* for harp and wind instruments, 1938; *Trio* for flute, viola and violoncello, 1941, Arts Council; *Trio* for two violins and viola, 1946, EMB; *Trio* for voice, violin and clarinet, 1947; *Kis cipő* (Small Shoes), *Quintet* for wind instruments, 1955; *Quintet* for wind instruments, 1960; *Piano Trio,* 1962; *Duet* for violin and violoncello, 1964; *Miniatürök* (Miniatures), twelve pieces for voice without words, with piano accompaniment or other instrumental ensemble; *Johannes,* cantata to poems by Chr. Morgenstern (German text), for bass solo and string quartet, 1972; *Szálkák* (Splinters), cantata to poems by J. Pilinszky, for alto solo, viola and violoncello, 1972; *Dialogue* for tuba and marimbaphone, 1974; *Three Fantastic Rumanian Folk Ballads* for soprano solo, cimbalom, viola and cello, 1976; *A vak szonettje* (The Blind Man's Sonnet), song based on Milton's poem for soprano solo and string trio, 1976; *Este az édenben* (Evening in Eden), song based on Milton's poem for soprano solo, harp and vibraphone, 1976; *Megemlékezés* (Commemoration), for viola sola, 1977; *Homályban* (In Dusk), for cello solo with orchestra, 1977.

PIANO PIECES: three *Sonatas,* 1941, 1947, 1956; *Fantasy,* 1971; *Thirteen Bagatelles,* 1918, UE; *Three Sad and Three Gay Bagatelles,* 1924, UE; *Jutka,* 1928, UE; *Variations,* 1933; *Jutka Ballad,* 1946, EMB; *To the Memory of Béla Bartók,* 1947; *Kis cipő* (Small Shoes), 1954, EMB; *Mesemadár* (The Fabulous Bird), 1957, EMB; *Divertimento,* 1960, EMB; etc.

INSTRUMENTAL PIECES WITH OR WITHOUT PIANO ACCOMPANIMENT:
VIOLIN: *Duet,* 1919; *Fairy-Tale Suite,* 1931; *Sonata,* 1937; *Four Pieces,* 1942, EMB; *Four Pieces,* 1954; *Gaby Sonata,* 1958, EMB; *Concerto Patetico,* 1960; *Elegy* for violin solo, 1964.

VIOLONCELLO: *Solo Sonatina,* 1928, UE; *Andante and Vivace,* 1948, EMB; *Violoncello Cantata* with organ, piano and percussion, 1963; *Sonata* for violoncello and piano, 1965.

MISCELLANEOUS: *Divertimento* for cimbalom (dulcimer), 1938; *Notturno* for flute, 1966, EMB; *Four Easy Pieces* for bassoon, 1967, EMB, BH.

SONGS WITH PIANO ACCOMPANIMENT: 27 series, amongst them: *Szegény kisgyermek panaszai* (Complaints of a Poor Little Child), 1938; *Seven Árpád Tóth Songs,* 1940, EMB; *Eight Ady Songs,* 1947, EMB; *Angelus Silesius,* 1953; *Four Csokonai Songs,* 1954, EMB; *Two Series of Chinese Songs,* 1954–56, EMB; *Twelve Gyula Juhász Songs,* 1958, EMB; *Four Aragon Songs,* 1962; *Seven Pilinszky songs,* 1964; *Cycle to Poems by G. Devecseri,* six songs for alto solo, with piano accompaniment, 1972; *Csúfolkodó dalok* (Mocking Songs), to poems by S. Weöres for voice with piano accompaniment, 1974; *Three Songs* to poems by S. Petőfi, 1974; *Ősz elején. A csavargó. Ilyen óriás.* (In Early Autumn. The Tramp. Such a Giant), songs with piano accompaniment; *Búcsúzás Kemenesaljától* (Farewell to Kemenesalja), song for bass with piano accompaniment, 1974; *Homályban* (In Twilight), ten songs to poems by A. Hajnal, with piano accompaniment, 1977.

WITH OTHER ACCOMPANIMENT: *Istenes énekek* (Religious Songs), viola accompaniment, 1936; *Ének a teremtésről* (Song about Creation), violoncello, 1939; *Krisztus szemű asszony* (The Women with Christ's Eyes), string quartet, 1946; *Five L. Szabó Songs,* piano quartet, 1942; *Two Songs,* harp, 1949; *Furcsa, rímes játék* (Strange Play with Rhymes), trio of wind instruments and harp, 1957; *Three Petrarca Sonnets,* vocal quartet with guitar, 1957; *Three French Recitatives,* string quartet, 1961; *Eclogue,* string sextet, 1964, etc.

DISCOGRAPHY:
Symphony No. 8
Hungarian State Concert Orchestra, conductor: Endre Kemény
LPX 1297

Sonata for Violoncello – *Twelve Miniatures* for Harp Trio – *Orpheus, Eurydice, Hermes* (Chamber Cantata)
Ede Banda (violoncello), György Kósa (piano), Anna Sz. Molnár, Mária Vermes, Gusztáv Szeredi (harp), Katalin Szőkefalvy-Nagy, Klára Takács, Gabriella Zsigmond, Attila Fülöp, Gábor Németh, Péter Kovács (soloists), Péter Lukács (viola), Árpád Szász (violoncello), László Som (double bass), Henrik Pröhle (alto flute), Hédi Lubik (harp), András Gärtner (percussion), conductor: Miklós Erdélyi.
LPX 11628

GYÖRGY KURTÁG

(b. Lugos, 19 Febr. 1926.) He has played the piano ever since he was five years old. At fourteen he started regular studies in piano and composition. In 1946 he came to Budapest, where he entered the Academy of Music. Pál Kadosa was his piano tutor; he attended the chamber music courses of Leo Weiner, and studied composition with Sándor Veress and Ferenc Farkas. From 1957 to 1958 he studied with Marianne Stein in Paris, and attended courses of Messiaen and Milhaud. Active as a composer, he is also professor at the Academy of Music. He was awarded the Kossuth Prize in 1973.

WORKS FWITH OPUS NUMBERS:

CHAMBER MUSIC: *String quartet* Op. 21, 1959, EMB; *Quintet* for wind instruments Op, 2, 1959, EMB; *Eight Duets* for violin and cimbalom (dulcimer), Op. 4, 1961, EMB;, UE; *Bornemisza Péter mondásai* (The Sayings of Péter Bornemisza), concerto for soprano solo and piano Op. 7, 1963–68, EMB, UE; *Egy téli alkony emlékére* (In Memory of a Winter Sunset), four fragments for soprano solo, violin and dulcimer, to poems by P. Gulyés, Op. 8, 2969, EMB, UE; *Four Capriccios* Op. 9 (Poem by I. Bálint), for soprano solo, and chamber ensemble, 1972, EMB, UE; *Négy dal Pilinszky János verseire* (four Songs to Poems by J. Pilinszky). Op. 11, for voices and chamber ensemble, 1974; *Eszká-emlékzaj* (Seven Songs), Poems by D. Tandori, Op. 12, for soprano solo and violin, 1975.

INSTRUMENTAL PIECES: *Eight Piano Pieces,* Op. 3, 1960, EMB; *Jelek* (Signs), for viola solo, Op. 5, 1961, EMB; *Cinque merrycate,* for guitar, Op. 6, 1962; *Szálkák* (Splinters) Op. 6c, for dulcimer, 1973, EMB, UE; *Játékok* (Games), Op.   for piano, 1973–76.

WORKS WITHOUT OPUS NUMBERS: *Suite for Piano Duet,* 1950, EMB; *Piano Suite,* 1951; *Cantata,* 1953; *Viola Concerto,* 1954, EMB.

Other piano pieces, incidental music to plays, mass songs, choruses.

DISCOGRAPHY:

Szálkák (Splinters), Op. 6c; *Nyolc duó* (Eight Duos), Op. 4; *Egy téli alkony emlékére* (In Memory of a Winter Sunset), Op. 8
Márta Fábián (cimbalom), Judit Hevesi (violin), Alice Németh (soprano)
SLPX 11686

Bornemisza Péter mondásai (The Sayings of Péter Bornemisza), Op. 7; *Négy dal Pilinszky János verseire* (Four Songs to Poems by J. Pilinszky), Op. 11
Erika Sziklay (soprano), István Gáti (bassbaritone), Loránt Szücs (piano), Budapest Chamber Ensemble, conductor: András Mihály
SLPX 11845

LÁSZLÓ LAJTHA

(b. Budapest, 30 June 1892; d. Budapest 16 Febr. 1963.) He studied composition at the Academy of Music, Budapest, with Viktor Herzfeld, at the same time also graduated from the University of Sciences. Having completed his studies, he spent considerable time abroad: viz., in Leipzig, Geneva and Paris. In 1913 he joined the staff and later became musical director of the Budapest Ethnographic Museum, and soon emerged as one of the leading figures of the folk music research movement initiated by Kodály and Bartók. From 1919 to 1949 he was professor at the National Conservatory (for some time the director of that institute) teaching composition and chamber music. In 1930 he was elected president of the Music Department of the Comité International des Arts Populaires. He was member of the artistic and literary committee of the League of Nations. In 1955 he became corresponding member of the French Académie des Beaux Arts. In 1929 he was awarded the Coolidge Prize and in 1951 the Kossuth Prize.

STAGE WORKS: *Lysistrata,* ballet, 1933, L.; *Le bosquet des quatre dieux,* ballet, 1943, L.; *Capriccio,* ballet, 1944, UE; *Le chapeau bleu,* comic opera, unfinished, L.

WORKS FOR CHORUS AND ORCHESTRA: *Trois nocturnes,* 1941, L.; *Missa in tono phrygio,* 1950, L.; *Ballada és verbunk* (Ballad and Recruiting Music), 1951, L.

CHORAL WORKS (WITH OR WITHOUT ACCOMPANIMENT):

CHORUSES FOR MIXED VOICES: *Esti párbeszéd, A hegylakók* (Nocturnal Dialogue, The Mountaineers), 1932, Salabert; *Chanson et Rondel,* 1936, L.; *Quatre Madrigeaux,* 1939, L.; *Hol járt a dal?* (Where Has the Song Been?), 1940, L.

CHORUSES FOR FEMALE VOICES WITH ORGAN: *Magnificat,* 1954, L.; *Trois Hymnes pour la Sainte Vierge,* 1958, L.

CHORUS FOR MIXED VOICES WITH ORGAN: *Missa,* 1952, L.

ORCHESTRAL MUSIC: *Concerto for Violin,* 1931, the manuscript perished; *Lysistrata* – overture, 1933, L.; *Lysistrata* – suite, 1933, L.; *Hortobágy Suite,* 1935, L.; *Symphony No. 1,* 1936, L.; *Divertissement No. 1,* 1936, L.; *Symphony No. 2,* 1938; *Divertissement No. 2,* 1939, L.; *Les Soli,* 1941, UE; *In memoriam,* 1941, UE; *Evasion Fuite Liberté,* 1942, the manuscript perished; *Le bosquet des quatre dieux,* suite, 1943, L.; *Capriccio,* suite, 1944, UE; *Sinfonietta No. 1,* 1946, L.; *Variations,* 1947; *Symphony No. 3,* 1948, L.; *Shapes and Forms,* for chamber orchestra, 1949, the manuscript perished; *Symphony No. 4,* (Le printemps), 1951, L, EMB; *Symphony No. 5,* 1952, L.; *Suite No. 3,* 1952, L.; *Symphony No. 6,* 1955, L.; *Sinfonietta No. 2,* 1956, L.;- *Symphony No. 7,* 1957, L.; *Symphony No. 8,* 1959, L.; *Symphony No. 9,* 1961, L.

CHAMBER MUSIC: *String Sextet,* 1921, the manuscript perished; *Dramma per musica, Piano Quintet,* 1922; *String Quartet No. 1,* 1923; *Piano Quartet,* 1925; *String Quartet No. 2,* 1926; *String Trio No. 1,* 1927; *Piano Trio,* 1928; *String Quartet No. 3,* 1929, UE; *String Quartet No. 4,* 1930, R; *String Trio No. 2,* 1932, L.; *String Quartet No. 5* (Cinque Études), 1934, L.; *Trio for Harp, Flute and Violoncello No. 1,* 1935, L.; *Marionettes,* suite for flute, violin, viola, violoncello and harp, 1937, Salabert; *String Quartet No. 6* (quatre études), 1942, L.; *String Trio No. 3* (Soirs Transylvans), 1945, UE; *Quatre hommages* for quartet of wind instruments, 1946, L.; *Second Quintet* with harp, 1948, L.; *Trio with Harp No. 2,* 1949, L.; *String Quartet No. 7,* 1950, L.; *String Quartet No. 8,* 1951, L.; *String Quartet No. 9,* 1953, L.; *String Quartet No. 10* (Suite Trnsylvaine), 1953, L.

INSTRUMENTAL MUSIC (WITH OR WITHOUT PIANO):

PIANO: *Des esquisses d'un musicien,* 1913, R.; *Contes,* 1913, Harmónia, Budapest; *Sonata,* 1914, Harmónia; *Contes II.,* 1914–18, the manuscript got lost; *Scherzo and Toccata,* 1930, L.

VIOLIN: *Sonatina,* 1930, L.; *Sonate en concert,* 1962, L.

VIOLONCELLO: *Sonata,* 1932, L.; *Concerto,* 1940, L.

FLUTE: *Sonate en concert,* 1958, L.; *2 pièces pour flûte seule,* 1958, L.

SAXOPHONE: *Intermezzo,* 1954, L.

SONGS: *Hungarian Folk Song Arrangements,* 1924, EMB; *Motet,* 1928, L.; *Vocalise étude,* 1930, L.

WRITINGS: *300 magyar népdal* (Three-hundred Hungarian Folk Songs), Budapest, 1932; *Szépkenyerű-szentmártoni gyűjtés* (Collection at Szépkenyerű-Szentmárton), 1954, EMB; *Széki gyűjtés* (Collection at Szék), 1954, EMB; *Kőrispataki gyűjtés* (Collection at Kőrispatak), 1954, EMB; *Sopron-megyei virrasztó énekek* (Wake Songs from

Sopron County), 1956; *Dunántúli táncok és dallamok I.* (Transdanubian Dances and Melodies I.), 1962; Posthumous publications: *Dunántúli táncok és dallamok II.* (Transdanubian Dances and Melodies II.), 1965; *Dunántúli népi énekek* (Transdanubian Folk Hymns).

DISCOGRAPHY:
Symphony No. 4, "The Spring", Op. 52; Symphony No. 9, Op. 67
Hungarian State Concert Orchestra, conductor: János Ferencsik
LPX 11564

ISTVÁN LÁNG

(b. Budapest, 1 March 1933.) He studied composition at the Academy of Music, Budapest with János Viski and later with Ferenc Szabó. Since 1966 he has been musical adviser of the State Puppett Theatre; since 1973 lecturer at the Academy of Music, Budapest (first score-reading, later chamber music). He won the Ludwigshafen Composer Competion in 1961, and was awarded the Erkel Prize in 1968 and 1975.

STAGE WORKS: *Pathelin mester* (Master Pathelin), opera, 1958; *Mario és a varázsló* (Mario and the Magician), dance drama, 1962, Hungarian Copyright Office; *Hiperbola,* ballet, 1963 – suite from the ballet, 1968; *Lebukott* (Nabbed), mini-ballet, 1968; *A gyáva* (The Coward), opera, 1964–68; *Csillagra-törők* (Star Besiegers), ballet-cantata, 1971; *A nagy drámaíró* (The Great Dramatist), opera, 1960, rev. 1974.

ORCHESTRAL MUSIC: *Concerto per archi,* 1960, Mannheimer Musikverlag; *Concertino* per silofono e orchestra, 1961, EMB; *Variazioni ed Allegro,* 1965, EMB; *Laudate Hominem,* cantata, 1968, EMB; *Gyász-zene* (Funeral Music), 1969, EMB + BH; *Impulsioni* per oboe e gruppo di strumenti, 1969, EMB + BH; *Három mondat a Rómeó és Júliából* vonósokra (Three sentences from Romeo and Juliet for strings), 1969–70, EMB; *Concerto bucolico* per corno solo e orchestra, 1970–71, EMB + BH; *In*

Memoriam N.N., cantata, 1971, EMB + BH; *Symphony No. 2*, 1972–74, EMB; *Ecloga* (Eclogue), 1976, MS; *Concerto for Violon*, 1976–77, EMB.

CHAMBER MUSIC: *Chamber Cantata* for soprano, clarinet, violoncello, piano and percussion, 1962, EMB; *Duo for Two Flutes*, 1963, EMB; *Quintet No. 1* for wind instruments, 1964, EMB; *Pezzi* for soprano and 5 players (flute, clarinet, viola and percussion), 1964; *Quintet No. 2* for wind instruments, 1965, EMB; *Quartet No. 2* for strings, 1966, EMB + BH; *Cassazione* per sestetto d'ottoni, 1971, EMB + BH; *Töredékek* (Fragments), for female voice, oboe, bassoon and harp, 1971–72; *Rhymes* for flute, clarinet, viola, violoncello and piano, 1972, EMB + BH; *Constellations* for oboe, violin, viola and violoncello, 1974–75, EMB; *Hullámok I* (Waves I) for soprano and vibraphone, 1975, MS; *Quintet No. 3* for wind instruments, 1975, EMB; *Hullámok II* (Waves II) for flute, guitar and cimbalom, 1976, MS; *Two Preludes for a Postlude*, for bassoon, violin, viola and violoncello, 1977, EMB.

INSTRUMENTAL WORKS: *Sonata for Violoncello Solo*, 1960, EMB + BH; *Monodia for Clarinet Solo*, 1965, EMB + BH; *Dramma breve* per flauto solo in Sol, 1970, EMB + BH; *Intermezzi* per pianoforte solo, 1972, EMB + BH; *Villanások* (Flashes) for violin solo, 1973, EMB + BH; *Improvisation* for cimbalom, 1973, EMB; *Solo* for bass-flute, 1975, EMB; *Monologue* for horn, 1974, EMB; *Láncolat* (Concatenations) for piano, 1975–76, EMB; *poco a poco dim.* per tromba, 1977, EMB; *Percussion Music* for one player, 1978, EMB.

DISCOGRAPHY:
Wind Quintet No. 1
Hungarian Wind Quintet
LPX 1246

Variations and Allegro
Symphony Orchestra of the Hungarian Radio and Television,
conductor: János Ferencsik
LPX 1298

Impulsioni per oboe solo e gruppe di strumenti
Péter Pongrácz (oboe),
Budapest Chamber Ensemble, conductor: András Mihály
LPX 11494

Laudate Hominem (Cantata)*; Chamber Cantata to Poems by Attila József; Musica funebre per orchestra; Monodia* per clarinetto solo; Quartetto d'archi No. 2
Miklós Gábor (narrator), Erika Sziklay (soprano), Tibor Dittrich, Béla Kovács (clarinet), Ádám Fellegi (piano), Gábor Lehotka (organ), Árpád Szász (violoncello), Ferenc Petz (percussion)
Bartók String Quartet

Choir and Orchestra of the Hungarian Radio and Television, conductors: János Sándor, Ervin Lukács
LPX 11523

Wind Quintet No. 2
Hungarian Wind Quintet
LPX 11630

Improvisation
Márta Fábián (cimbalom)
SLPX 11686

Intermezzi
Ádám Fellegi (piano)
SLPX 11692

In memoriam N.N. (cantata); *Three Sentences from Romeo and Juliet for strings; Concerto bucolico for horn and orchestra*
Magda Kalmár (soprano), Gábor Lehotka (organ), Chorus of the Hungarian Radio and Television (Choir master: Ferenc Sapszon), Budapest Symphony Orchestra conducted by János Sándor, – Liszt Ferenc Chamber Orchestra, conducted by Frigyes Sándor – Ferenc Tarjáni (horn), Budapest Symphony Orchestra conducted by Géza Oberfrank
SLPX 11784

Cassazione per sestetto d'ottoni
Hungarian Brass Ensemble
SLPX 11811

Symphony No. 2; Rhymes for chamber ensemble; Constellations for oboe, violin, viola and cello
Budapest Philharmony Orchestra, conducted by András Kórody – Tihamér Elek (flute), Béla Kovács (clarinet), Ádám Fellegi (piano), Mihály Barta (violin), Gábor Fias (viola), János Devich (cello), Péter Pongrácz (oboe)
SLPX 11900

Waves II for flute, guitar and cimbalom
Tihamér Elek (flute), Béla Sztankovics (guitar), Márta Fábián (cimbalom)
SLPX 12012

KAMILLÓ LENDVAY

(b. Budapest, 28 Dec. 1928.) He studied composition at the Academy of Music, Budapest with János Viski. Since 1960 he has been reader of Hungarian Radio, since 1973 professor at the Academy of Music Budapest. Winner of the Erkel Prize in 1962 and 1964.

STAGE WORKS: *A bűvös szék* (The Magic Chair), one-act opera comedy, text by Fr. Karinthy and G. Devecseri, 1972, Artisjus; *A tisztességtudó utcalány,* opera in three parts, text by K. Lendvay to drama by J.-P. Sartre, 1976–78, Artisjus.

WORKS FOR CHORUS AND ORCHESTRA: *Orogenesis* – oratorio in memory of Lenin. Text by Gy. Urbán, 1969–70, EMB; *Pro Libertate,* cantata for tenor and baritone solo, male voices and orchestra, (Text by Zs. Kőháti), 1975, EMB; *Kocsiút az éjszakában* (A Ride at Night), cycle for contralto and seven performers, to poems by E. Ady, 1970, EMB.

A CAPPELLA WORKS: *Három férfikar* (Three Male Choruses), (Poems by L. Hollós Korvin), 1959, EMB; *Téli reggel* (Winter Morning) for mixed voices, (Poem by L. Hollós Korvin), 1966, NPI; *Dózsa siratója* (Lament for Dózsa), (Poem by J. Kövesdy), for male voices (1964), mixed voices (1965), EMB; *Éjszaka No. 1* (Night), (Poem by M. Radnóti), for female voices, 1967, EMB; *Tizenegy kétszólamú gyermekkar* (Eleven

Two Voice Children's Choruses), (Poems by S. Weöres), 1971, NPI; *Éjszaka No. 2* (Night), (Poem by M. Váci), for mixed voices, 1974, EMB.

ORCHESTRAL MUSIC: *Tragikus nyitány* (Tragic Overture), 1958, EMB; *Mauthausen,* symphonic poem, 1958, EMB; *A rendíthetetlen ólomkatona* (The Unyielding Tin Soldier), suite to a tale by Andersen, 1961; *Négy zenekari invokáció* (Four Orchestral Invocations), 1966, EMB; *Kifejezések* (Expressions), for strings, 1974, EMB.

CONCERTOS: *Concertino* for piano, wind instruments, percussion and harp, 1959, EMB; *Concerto for Violin,* 1961–62, EMB; *Pezzo concertato* per violoncello ed orchestra, 1975, EMB.

CHAMBER MUSIC: *Trio Serenade* for violin, viola and violoncello, 1954; *Rhapsody* for violin and piano, 1955, EMB + BH; *String Quartet,* 1962, EMB; *Four Duos* for flute and piano, 1965, EMB + BH; *Kamarakoncert* (Chamber Concert) for thirteen performers (wind quintet + string quintet, piano, harp, percussion), 1969, EMB; *Kifejezések* (Expressions) version for eleven solo strings (six violins, two violoncellos, two violas, and contrabass), 1974, EMB.

INSTRUMENTAL PIECES: *Disposizioni* for cimbalom, 1975, EMB. Incidental music to films, plays, radio-plays, television-plays, songs to plays.

DISCOGRAPHY:
Concertino
Gloria Lanni (piano)
Symphony Orchestra of the Hungarian Radio and Television,
conductor: János Sándor
LPX 1166

Téli reggel (Winter Morning)
Choir of the Hungarian Radio and Television, conductor: Zoltán Vásárhelyi
LPX 11330

Kamarakoncert (Concerto da camera)
Budapest Chamber Ensemble, conductor: András Mihály
LPX 11494

Orogenesis
Éva Andor, Márta Szirmay, József Réti, Sándor Palcsó, József Dene (soloists), László Kozák (narrator)
Choir and Orchestra of the Hungarian Radio and Televišion,
conductor: György Lehel
LPX 11524

Négy zenekari invokáció (Four Orchestral Invocations); *Kocsiút az éjszakában* (A Ride at Night); *Pezzo concertato; Kifejezések* (Expressions)
Symphonic Orchestra of the Hungarian Radio and Television,
conductor: György Lehel
Budapest Chamber Ensemble, conductor: András Mihály
Zsuzsa Barlay (alto), Márta Fábián (cimbalom), András Kiss (violin), János Kovalcsik (bass flute), Tivadar Popa (viola)
SLPX 11860

Disposizioni per cimbalo ungherese
Márta Fábián (cimbalom)
SLPX 11899

ISTVÁN LORÁND

(b. Budapest, 14 June 1933.) Studied composition at the Academy of Music, Budapest, as a pupil of Ferenc Szabó and later of Ferenc Farkas. He was music teacher, then director of a music school, from 1956 to 1965 worked with Editio Musica, Budapest, presently he is teacher at a secondary school.

In 1976 he won the first prize at the OIRT International Composers' Competition, and in 1977 was awarded the Erkel Prize.

WORKS FOR CHORUS AND ORCHESTRA (cantatas): *Májusi óda* (May Ode), 1959; *Először gyúlt a csillag* (For the First Time Shone the Star), 1961; *American Worker's Songs,* 1966; *Children's Cantatas; Dózsa-sirató* (Dózsa Lament), small cantata, 1972; *Az örökség* (The Inheritance) (Poem by J. Arany), 1975; *Gesta Hungarorum* (based on text by Anonymus), cantata, 1977; Mass Songs, Pioneers' Songs, Folk Song Arrangements.

CHORAL WORKS: *Teérted haltak* (They Died for You), 1959, EMB; *Mindvégig* (To the Last), 1961, EMB; *Gyászkórus* férfikarra (Mourning Chorus for Male Choir), 1963, EMB; *Alkonyi madrigál* (Twilight Madrigal), 1964, EMB; *Tengeri-hántás* (Cornhusking), (Poem by J. Arany), 1965; *Két karodban* (In Your Arms), (Poem by M. Radnóti), 1967, NI; *Balatoni tábor* (Camping at Lake Balaton), suite for children's choir, 1967, NI; *Háromszor kiáltott a madár* (Three Times the Bird Cried), 1968, NI; *Piros volt az ég* (The Sky Was Red), 1968, EMB; *Selected Children's Choruses and Pioneers' Songs,* 1971, EMB; *Seven Mixed Choruses to Poems by Classical Hungarian Poets,* 1972, NPI; *A tél halála* (Death of the Winter), (Poem by S. Petőfi), 1972; *Twelve Children's Choruses to Poems by S. Weöres,* 1972; *Új vallomás* (New Confession), (Poem by Gy. Juhász), 1972; *6 Bicinia on Hungarian Folk Songs,* 1973, EMB; *Gyászkar* (Funeral Chorus), (Poem by L. Ápriliy), 1973, NPI; *Szüreti ének* (Vintage Song), (Poems by M. Csokonai Vitéz), 1974, NPI; *Fujj, szél* (Blow, Wind), (Poem by M. Váci), 1974, NPI; *Hármasének* (Ternary Song), (Poem by J. Kövesdy), suite, 1974, NPI; *Spring Madrigal,* 1976, EMB; *Csipp-csepp* (Drip-Drop), (Poem by S. Weöres), children's choir, EMB; *Legend* (Poem by M. Váci), 1976; *A kovács* (The Blacksmith), (Poem by L. Nagy), male choir, 1977; *Látjátok, feleim* (You see, My Brethren), (Poem by Gy. Juhász), 1977; *Choral Ballads* to folk texts, 1977.

ORCHESTRAL WORKS: *Symphony* for string orchestra, 1962; *Dalosünnep* (Song Feast), overture for wind orchestra, 1965; *Concertino* for piano and chamber orchestra, 1976.

CHAMBER MUSIC: *String Quartet,* 1959, EMB; *Sonata for Violin and Piano,* 1967, EMB, BH.

INSTRUMENTAL PIECES: *Rondo for Piano,* 1957, EMB; *Small Pieces* for piano, for violoncello and for violin, several of them: EMB; *Sonata per flauto solo,* 1973, EMB.

SONGS: Songs to poems by four Hungarian poets, 1962, EMB; Songs to poems by A. József, Zs. Várnai, etc., 1963.

ORCHESTRAL SONG: *Megtartó varázslat* (Retaining Magic), 3 orchestral songs to poems by Hungarian poets, 1977.

Music to radio plays.

IVÁN MADARÁSZ

(b. Budapest, 10 Febr. 1949.) He started his musical studies with the piano at the age of seven. He first studied composition at the Béla Bartók Conservatory under István Szelényi, then became a pupil of Endre Szervánszky, for composition at the Ferenc Liszt Academy of Music. He graduated in 1972. The same year he was awarded the Albert Szirmai Prize for young composers. In 1972 the Hungarian Television commissioned him to write an opera buffa. The comic opera from the one-act play by Tamás Emőd was transmitted on television several times. In 1975 two of his works won prizes at the choral competition invited by the Council of Budapest in commemoration of the country's Liberation. Under the title -1^0 Centigrade he wrote ballet music for a Television competition film which received the jury's special prize at the Montreaux Festival. At present he is assistant professor of musical theory and musical aesthetics at the Pécs Faculty of the Ferenc Liszt Academy of Music, and teaches musical theory at the Béla Bartók Conservatory in Budapest.

INCIDENTAL MUSIC: -1^0 Centigrade, ballet music, 1974; Hipermodern idők (Ultra-Modern Times), (with Máté Victor), 1975.

OPERA: A nő meg az ördög (The Woman and the Devil), a one-act comic opera, 1972.

STAGE MUSIC: *Messze még a holnap* (Tomorrow Is Still Far Away), musical comedy, 1977.

WORK FOR CHAMBER ORCHESTRA: *Tetrachtis,* 1972.

CHAMBER MUSIC: *Metamorphosis* for piano, 1974, EMB; *Ludi* for piano, 1976, EMB; *Mozaikok* (Mosaics) for violin, 1977, EMB; *Párhuzamos monológok* (Parallel Monologues) for flute, cello and harpsichord, 1977; *Erdélyi táncok* (Transylvanian Dances) for flute, cello and harpsichord, 1977; *Ütős zene két zongorára* (Percussion Music for Two Pianos), 1978.

CANTATA: *Sonnet* for percussion, piano and voice, 1976.

SONGS: *Catullus énekek* (Catullus Songs I–II), 1971–72; *Two Songs* to poems by Sándor Weöres, 1977.

CHORAL WORKS: *Szív dobban* (Heart-Beat), cycle to poems by Sándor Weöres, 1977, EMB; *Dal a reményről* (Song on Hope), 1975; *Testvériség* (Fraternity), 1977.

RUDOLF MAROS

(b. Stachy, 19 Jan. 1917.) He was a pupil of Zoltán Kodály for composition and of Temesváry for viola at the Academy of Music, Budapest, then studied in Prague under Alois Hába, and from 1958 repeatedly in Darmstadt. From 1942 to 1949 he taught at the Conservatory of Pécs, and from 1949 to 1978 he was professor at the Academy of Music in Budapest (chamber music, theory of orchestration, composition). He was awarded the Erkel Prize in 1954, 1955 and 1957, the "Merited Artist of the Hungarian People's Republic" title in 1973; Artist-in-Berlin 1971–72, ISCM-Presidium 1971–75

STAGE WORKS: *Miner's Ballad,* ballet, 1961; *Cinque Studi,* ballet, 1967, EMB; *Quadros Soltos* (Musica da ballo), ballet, 1968, EMB; *Reflexionen,* 1971, Southern, N.Y.; *Dance Pictures,* 1971, EMB; *Metropolis,* 1972, EMB, Southern, N.Y.; *The Poltroon,* 1972, EMB.

ORCHESTRAL MUSIC: *Sinfonia per Archi,* 1956, EMB, Mills, London; *Ricercare,* 1959, EMB; *Cinque Studi,* 1960, EMB; *Musica da ballo,* 1962, EMB; *Eufonia 1,* 1963, Southern, N.Y.; *Eufonia 2,* 1964, Southern, N.Y.; *Eufonia 3,* 1965, EMB – Southern, N.Y.; *Gemma,* 1968, Southern, N.Y.; *Monumentum,* 1969, Southern, N.Y.; *Notices* for strings, 1972, EMB – Southern, N.Y.; *Fragment,* 1977; *Landscapes* for strings, 1975, EMB.

CHAMBER MUSIC: *Musica Leggiera* for wind instruments, 1956, EMB; *Two Dirges* for soprano and chamber ensemble, 1963, EMB; *Musica da Camera per 11.* for chamber ensemble, 1966, Southern, N.Y., EMB; *Trio* for harp, violin and viola, 1967, EMB – Southern, N.Y.; *Lament* for soprano and chamber ensemble, 1969, Southern, N.Y., EMB; *Consort* for wind quintet, 1970, Southern, N.Y., EMB; *Albumleaves* for double-bass, 1977, Southern, N.Y., EMB; *Strophen* for soprano, harp, and percussion, 1977; *Kaleidoscope* for chamber ensemble, 1976; *Four Studies* for percussion ensemble, 1977, EMB.

WORKS FOR MIXED VOICES: *Messzeségek* (Remoteness), 1975, EMB; *Nyúlfark-kantáta* (A Tiny Cantata) for mixed voices, strings and piano, 1976, EMB; *Cheremiss Folk-songs,* 1977.

INSTRUMENTAL PIECES: *Six Bagatelles* for organ, 1961, EMB + BH; *Suite* for harp, 1966, Southern, N.Y.; EMB.

DISCOGRAPHY:
Bagatelles (Preludio, Siciliana, Scherzo, Aria, Rondo)
Sebestyén Pécsi (organ)
LPX 1222

Two Laments
Erika Sziklay (soprano), Attila Lajos (alto flute), Hédi Lubik (harp), Loránt Szűcs (piano), József Marton, Ferenc Petz (percussion), conductor: György Lehel
LPX 1273

Eufonia 1, 2, 3 – Five Studies for Orchestra
Symphony Orchestra of the Hungarian Radio and Television,
conductor: György Lehel
LPX 11362

Lament
Erika Sziklay (soprano)
Budapest Chamber Ensemble, conductor: András Mihály
LPX 11494

Gemma; Monumentum; Notices; Musica da camera; Trio
SLPX 11775

Six Bagatelles
Gábor Lehotka (organ)
SLPX 11808

Messzeségek (Remoteness)
Vándor Chorus
SLPX 15052

ANDRÁS MIHÁLY

(b. Budapest, 6 Nov. 1917.) At the Academy of Music, Budapest, he studied violoncello with Adolf Schiffer, chamber music with Leo Weiner and Imre Waldbauer. He studied composition privately with Pál Kadosa and István Strasser. From 1946 to 1950 he was member of the Budapest Opera House, first as violoncello leader, subsequently as secretary general. Since 1950 he has been teaching chamber music at the Academy of Music, and since 1962 he has been musical adviser to the Hungarian Radio. In 1955 he was awarded the Kossuth Prize, and was winner of the Erkel Prize in 1952, 1954 and 1964.

STAGE WORK: *Együtt és egyedül* (Allied and Alone), opera, 1964–65, Artisjus.

WORKS FOR CHORUS AND ORCHESTRA: *Szabadság és béke* (Liberty and Peace, 1942, MS lost, second version: 1949; *Védd a békét, ifjúság!* (Youth! Defend Peace!), 1950; *Kedves magyar hazám* (My Beloved Hungarian Fatherland), 1952; *A vörös szekér* (The Red Cart), 1957; *"1871"*, 1960.

CHORAL WORKS: *Ének Ságvári Endréről* (Song about Endre Ságvári), for mixed choir with piano accompaniment to a poem by B. Kapuvári, 1952; *Emlék és intelem* (Memory and Warning), for male choir with piano accompaniment to poem by Zs. Gál, 1959, EMB; *Szállj költemény!* (Fly, Poem!), for mixed choir to poems by A. József, 1967.

ORCHESTRAL MUSIC: *Symphony No. 1,* 1946; *Festive Overture,* 1959; *Symphony No. 2,* 1950; *Symphony No. 3,* 1962, EMB; *Monodia* per orchestra, 1971, EMB.

CONCERTOS: *Concerto* for violoncello, 1953, EMB; *Concerto* for piano, 1954; *Fantasy* for wind quintet and orchestra, 1955, EMB; *Concerto* for violin with piano obbligato and orchestra, 1959, EMB.

CHAMBER MUSIC: *Piano Trio,* 1940; *String Quartet No. 1,* 1942; *Rhapsody* for viola and piano, 1947, Hungarian Arts Council; *Serenade* for trio of wind instruments, 1956; *String Quartet No. 2,* 1960, EMB; *Three Apocrypha,* for three female voices, clarinet and percussion, 1962, EMB; *Three Movements,* for chamber orchestra, 1969, EMB; *Musica per 15,* for chamber ensemble, EMB; *String Quartet No. 3,* EMB.

INSTRUMENTAL PIECES: *Suite* for violoncello and piano, 1957; *Sonata for Piano,* 1958; *Rondo* for piano, 1958; *Four Small Piano Pieces,* 1958; *Ciaccona* two piano pieces in old style, 1961, EMB; *Movement* for violoncello and piano, 1962, EMB; *Musica per viola e piano,* EMB.

SONGS: *Chamber Music,* to poems by J. Joyce, 1958; *Attila József Songs,* 1961, EMB; *Az áhítat zsoltárai* (Psalms of Piety), for voice and piano, to poems by M. Radnóti, 1969.

Incidental music to films and plays.

DISCOGRAPHY:
Fly, Poem!
Sándor Nagy (baritone)
Choir of the Hungarian Radio and Television, Hungarian State Concert Orchestra, conductor: Ervin Lukács
LPX 11352

Symphony No. 3 – Apocrypha – Psalms of Piety
Sándor Nagy, Éva Andor (soloists), Loránt Szűcs (piano), Ferenc Petz (percussion)
Girls Choir of Győr
Budapest Chamber Ensemble, Symphony Orchestra of the Hungarian Radio and Television, conductors: György Lehel, András Mihály
LPX 11455

Three Movements for Chamber Orchestra
Budapest Chamber Orchestra, conductor: András Mihály
LPX 11494

Concerto for Violoncello and Orchestra
Miklós Perényi (violoncello)
Symphony Orchestra of the Hungarian Radio and Television
conductor: György Lehel
LPX 11556

ANTAL MOLNÁR

(b. Budapest, 7 Jan. 1890.) He studied violin and composition under Viktor Herzfeld at the Academy of Music, Budapest. From 1910 to 1913 he played the viola in the Waldbauer String Quartet, from 1917 to 1919 in the Dohnányi-Hubay Piano Quartet. From 1912 to 1918 he was professor at the Municipal Music School, from 1919 to 1959 professor at the Academy of Music (history of music, aesthetics, chamber music, theory). In the 1910s he took part in folk song collecting tours. From 1933 to 1940 he was editor of the "Népszerű zenefüzetek" (Popular Music Brochures) series. He was awarded the Francis Joseph Prize in 1914, the Baumgarten Prize in 1938 and the Kossuth Prize in 1957.

His significant musicological work includes historical, aesthetical and musical-sociological research. He also gained great distinction as a critic, in particular as the first commentator and publicist of Bartók's and Kodály's art.

SOME OF HIS MORE IMPORTANT COMPOSITIONS INCLUDE:

STAGE WORK: *Savitri* – a legend, 1912.

ORCHESTRAL MUSIC: *Tavasz* (Spring), 1914; *Grotesque March,* 1914; *Volt egyszer egy király* (Once There Was a King), 1919; *Operetta Music,* 1920; *Napkeleti monda*

(Oriental Tale), 1921; *Budapest,* overture, 1921; *Suite,* 1925; *Variations,* 1928; *Hungarian Comedy Overture,* 1928; *Bohózat-nyitány* (Overture to a Comedy), 1948.

CONCERTOS: *Concerto for Violoncello,* 1916; *Múlt és jelen* (Past and Present), for violin and orchestra, 1923; *Concerto for Harp,* 1952.

CHAMBER MUSIC: *Serenade* for violin, clarinet and harp, 1912, R.; *Flute Quartet,* 1912; two *Piano Trios,* 1912, 1917; three *String Quartets,* 1912, 1926, 1928; *Quintet for Wind Instruments,* 1926.

INSTRUMENTAL PIECES: *Two Impromptus* for piano, 1910, Weinberger, Leipzig; *Children's Pieces for Piano,* 1910, R.; *Fantasy* for flute and piano, 1910, R.; *Prelude* for violin solo, 1911, Rozsnyai; *Sonatina* for violin and piano, 1911, R.; *Hungarian Fantasy* for violin and piano, 1929, R.; *Suite* for violin and piano, 1930, R.; *Szól a hegedű* (Violin Music), 1935, Korda, EMB.

Songs, choruses, folk song arrangements, pedagogical pieces and smaller instrumental works.

SOME OF HIS MORE IMPORTANT WRITINGS INCLUDE: *A zenetörténet szelleme* (The Spirit of Music History), Budapest, 1914, Franklin; *Beethoven,* Budapest, 1917, Franklin; *Bach és Händel zenéjének lelki alapjai* (The Spiritual Basis of the Music of Bach and Händel), Budapest, 1920, Franklin; *Az európai zene története 1750-ig* (The History of European Music up to 1750), Budapest, 1920, Franklin; *A zeneművészet könyve* (The Book of Music), Budapest, 1922, Dante; *A zenetörténet szociológiája* (The Sociology of Music History), Budapest, 1923, Franklin; *Az új zene* (The New Music), Budapest, 1925, Révai; *A zeneesztétika feladata* (The Tasks of Musical Aesthetics), Budapest, 1927, Amicus; *A gyermek és a zene* (The Child and Music), Budapest, 1931, Somló; *Zoltán Kodály,* Budapest, 1936, Somló; *Zeneesztétika* (Aesthetics of Music), Budapest, 1939, author; *Népszerű zeneesztétika* (Popular Aesthetics of Music), Budapest, 1940, Széchenyi; *Az új muzsika szelleme* (The Spirit of New Music), Budapest, 1948, Dante; *Bartók művészete* (The Art of Bartók), Budapest, 1948, R.; *Brahms,* Budapest, 1959, Gondolat; *Repertórium a barokk zene történetéhez* (Repertory to the History of Baroque Music), Budapest, 1959, EMB; *Selected collection of essays: Írások a zenéről* (Papers on Music), Budapest, 1961, EMB; *A zenéről* (On Music), Budapest, 1963, EMB; *A Léner-vonósnégyes* (The Léner String Quartet), Budapest, 1968, EMB; *A zeneszerző világa* (The World of the Composer), Budapest, 1969, Gondolat; *Gyakorlati zeneesztétika* (Practical Aesthetics of Music), 1940, EMB, 1971.

IMRE MEZŐ

(b. Szeghalom, 6 Apr. 1932.) At first he studied at the Music School of Békéstarhos then transferred to the Academy of Music where his teacher was Endre Szervánszky. From 1958 to 1968 he was professor of music theory at the Municipal Music School Organization, and since 1968 he has been working as editor at Editio Musica. Most of his works are written for the youth. He was among the prize winners at the composers' competition of the World Youth Festival in 1958.

CHORAL WORK: *Piliga* for children's or female choir, 1957, EMB.

WORK FOR CHORUS AND ORCHESTRA: *Dózsa,* cantata for bass solo, mixed choir and orchestra.

ORCHESTRAL MUSIC: *Variations,* for youth string orchestra, 1963, EMB; *Variations on a Hungarian Folk Song,* for youth string orchestra, 1967.

CHAMBER MUSIC: *Suite* for flute and piano, 1956, EMB; *Elegy* for violoncello and piano, 1957, EMB; *Sonata* for violoncello and piano, 1957–59; *Trio* for three violins, 1960, EMB; *Quartettino* for youth string quartet, 1961, EMB; *Variations* for three trumpets, 1963, EMB; *Nine Small duos* for two violoncellos, 1966, EMB; *Quintetto* for two flutes, clarinet, bassoon and contrabass, 1966, EMB.

INSTRUMENTAL PIECES: *Third-playing* for piano, 1954, EMB; *Toccatina* for piano, 1954, EMB, Supraphon, Prague; *Sonatina* for piano, 1961, EMB.

Works in educational collection and instrumental methods.

LAJOS PAPP

(b. Debrecen, 18 Aug. 1935.) He obtained his musical education at the Academy of Music, Budapest as a pupil of Ferenc Szabó. He was professor at the Municipal Music School Organization from 1959 to 1968, teaching theory of music. At present he devotes himself solely to composition.

WORK FOR CHORUS AND ORCHESTRA: *Arezzói ének* (Arezzo Song), in memory of Zoltán Kodály, cantata in two movements, 1969–72.

ORCHESTRAL MUSIC: *Sketches* for string orchestra, 1964; *Suite,* 1965; *Concerto for Violoncello,* 1965; *Dialogo* for piano and orchestra, 1966, EMB; *Meditációk Füst Milán emlékére* (Meditation in Memory of Milán Füst), for soprano solo and orchestra; *Kalevipoeg második pokoljárása* (Kalevipoeg's Second Descent to Hell), symphonic poem.

CHAMBER MUSIC: *Sonata* for violoncello and piano, 1962, EMB; *Miniatűrök* (Miniatures), for harp and violoncello; *Quintet* for dulcimer and string quartet; *Impressioni* for flute, piano and gong, 1970; *Variazioni* per clavicembalo e percussioni, EMB.

INSTRUMENTAL PIECES: *Three Rondos* for piano, 1957; *Piano Variations,* 1959, EMB + BH; *Four Pieces for Violoncello Solo,* 1963; *Sonata* for violoncello and piano, 1962, EMB; *Improvvisazione* for piano, 1964; *Six Bagatelles* for piano, 1964, EMB; *Ricercare* per arpa, EMB; *Nine Bagatelles* for cimbalom, EMB; *Sketches* for violin, EMB; *Skizze* for piano, 1971.

SONGS: Trakl Songs, 1960; *Weöres Songs,* 1964.

IVÁN PATACHICH

(b. Budapest, 3 June 1922.) He studied composition at the Academy of Music, Budapest under Albert Siklós, János Viski and Ferenc Szabó. He conducted in theatres, then became musical director of the Budapest Film Studio in 1952. In 1957 he was prize winner at the World Youth Festival. In 1971 he organized an electronic music studio, the EXASTUD (Experimentum auditorii studii) in Budapest. In 1976–77 he carried out electroacoustic and computer musical experiments in Stuttgart and Utrecht. He realized his new works at Columbia University, New York (1969), in Stockholm (1974), in Bratislava (1975), in Stuttgart (1976) and in Utrecht (1977).

STAGE WORKS: *Fekete-fehér* (Black and White), ballet, 1958; *Theomachia,* opera, 1962; *Bakaruhában* (Sunday Romance), ballet, 1963; *Mngongo and Mlaba,* ballet, 1965; *Fuente Ovejuna,* opera in 3 acts, 1969; *Studio sintetico,* ballet, 1973.

WORKS FOR CHORUS AND ORCHESTRA: *Missa Simple,* 1949; *Szirtország* (Country of Cliffs), cantata, 1953; *Messe di Santa Marguereta,* 1967; *Music of the Bible* (Sir cha Sirim), cantata for tenor solo, chorus and orchestra, 1968; *Pinty és ponty,* for children's voices and percussion, 1973.

ORCHESTRAL MUSIC: *Poema sinfonico,* 1958; *Serenade for Strings,* 1960, EMB; *Sinfonietta Savariensis,* 1964, EMB; *Symphony No. 1,* 1965; *Miniature Suite,* 1965;

Symphony No. 2, 1966; *Divertimento No. 1,* 1962; *Quadri di Picasso* per orchestra, 1965; *Colori67,* 1967; *Quadri Sportivi,* 1964; *Divertimento No. 2,* 1969; *Tre Schizzi* per orchestra, 1969; Zwei ungarische Tänze, 1972, Schulz; Drei ungarische Skizzen, 1975, Schulz.

CONCERTOS: *Concerto for Harp No. 1,* 1956, EMB; *Concertino per contrabasso,* 1957; *Concerto for Flute,* 1958; *Concerto for Viola,* 1959; *Concerto for Oboe,* 1959; *Three Pieces* for clarinet and orchestra, 1961, EMB; *Concerto for Guitar,* 1961; *Concerto Breve for violoncello,* 1962; *Concerto for Piano No. 1,* 1963; *Concerto for Violin,* 1964; *Concerto per fagotto,* 1965; *Concerto per percussioni,* 1966; *Concerto per arpa,* No. 2, 1968; *Concerto per piano No. 2,* 1968; *Concerto per violino e piano,* 1969, Gerig, Köln; *Due pezzi* per trombe e orchestra di camera, 1969; *Due pezzi* per trombone e orchestra di camera, 1969; *Tre pezzi* per violino e orchestra di camera, 1969; *Concerto per organo,* 1972, EMB; *Concertino per pianoforte e orchestra di fiati,* 1972; *Presentazioni* (Concertino) per zimbalo ungherese, 1975, EMB; *Rapsodia piccola* per violino e orchestra, 1970.

CHAMBER MUSIC: *Sonata* for violin and piano No. 1, 1948; *Sextet* for harp and wind instruments, 1957; *Quintet* for harp, flute and strings, 1958; *Trio* with harp, 1958, EMB; *Duet* for violin and viola, 1959; *Quintet* for wind instruments, 1960; *Sonatina* for double-bass, 1960, Astoria-Verlag, Berlin; *Duet* for violin or flute and guitar, 1961, EMB; *String Quartet No. 1,* 1961; *Tower Music* for brass, 1961; *Quartet* for two harps, viola and double bass, 1962; *Piano Trio No. 1,* 1962; *Sonata* for viola 1962; *Sonata* for violoncello, 1963; *Sonata* for violin and piano No. 2, 1964; *Sonata* per arpa e corno, 1964; *Trio* per fiati, 1965; *Trio* per archi, 1965; *String Quartet No. 2,*1966; *Ritmi dispari* per fiati ed ottone, 1966, EMB; *Elementi* per percussioni, 1966; *Antitesti* per due pianoforti, 1964, EMB; *Piano Trio No. 2,* 1967; *Quattro studii* per percussioni, 1968; *Costruzioni* per percussioni, 1969; *Table Music* for wind instruments (flute, oboe, bassoon), 1970; Verbunkos és friss (Recruiting Dance), for brass instruments (three trumpets, two trombones and tuba), 1971; *Sonata* per oboe e arpa, 1971; *Bagatelli* per organi, flauto e corno, 1971; *Inventioni* per chitarra e contrabasso, 1971; *Proporzioni* per percussioni, 1972; *Sonata* per chitarra, 1972; *Quartettino* per sassofoni, 1972, GM; *Capriccii* per fagotto e pianoforte, 1972; *Sonata* per flauto e arpa, 1977; *Vier Stücke für drei Klarinetten,* 1974, Schulz; *Balkan,* Vier Stücke für fünf Bläser, 1975, Schulz; *Modelli* per flauto, viola e chitarra, 1975; *Terzettino* für drei Trompeten, 1976, Schulz; *Ja amidohele,* quintetto per 5 violoncelli, 1976, Astoria; *Septetto* per 3 tromba, 2 trb., tuba e arpa, 1976; *Quartettino per corni,* 1976; *Hispanica* für sechs Bläser, 1977 Schulz.

INSTRUMENTAL PIECES: *Antiche danza ungherese* per arpa, 1955; *Tre pezzi* per flauto e arpa, 1956; *Tre Abbozzi* per chitarra e clarinetto, 1961; *Sonata* for Cimbalom (dulcimer), 1962; *Petite Suite* pour deux clarinettes, 1962, Leduc, Paris; *Solo Sonata* for violin, 1964; *Two Etudes* for guitar, 1962; *Sonata for Harp,* 1964; *Five Piano Pieces,* 1964, EMB; *Sonata* per pianoforte, 1965; *Nove pezzi* per pianoforte, 1965; *Sonatine* per pianoforte, 1966; *Sedici pezzi* per chitarra, 1966; *Tre pezzi* per organo,

1966; *Episodi* per flauto e pianoforte, 1967; *Duo* per chitarra, 1968; *Due studii* per contrabasso e pianoforte, 1968; *Contorni* per arpa, 1968, EMB; *Quattro disegni* per violino e pianoforte, 1969; *Rapsodia piccola* per violino e pianoforte, 1969; *Bagatelli* per flauto e chitarra, 1969; *Balcanophonia* per arpa, 1970; *Pezzi lirico e satirico* per trombone o tuba e pianoforte, 1970; *Inventio e ritmo bulgaro* per due clarinetto, 1970, EMB; *Quattro pezzi piccoli* per pianoforte, 1971; *Quattro pezzi* per oboe e pianoforte, 1971; *Canzone moro e caccia* per corno e pianoforte, 1971, EMB; *Ritmi pari e dispari* per due corni, 1972, Schulz; *Studii* per arpa, 1972; *Pieces for Guitar* I–II., 1972; *Tre quadri* per due flauti o due oboi, 1972, Schulz; *Aquarelli* per due tromboni, 1972, EMB; *Ludi piccoli* per due trombi, 1972, Ed. Molenaar's; *Figuri* per due fagotti, 1972, EMB; *Epigramme* per due flauti, 1972; *Minuscoli pezzi* per trombe e pianoforte, 1972; *Intermezzi* per due zimbali, 1974; *Duettino* für zwei Klarinetten, 1974, Schulz; *Ritmi* per clarinetto e percussione, 1975; *Danze* per due arpi, 1975; *Charaktere* für zwei Gitarren, 1976; *Draws* for guitar and percussion, 1976; *24 Pezzi per Chitarra,* 1976; *Antiphoni* per violino e percussione, 1977; *Salmo e ballata* per violoncello e pianoforte, 1977; *Solitaire* for flute, 1977.

ELECTRONIC MUSIC: *Studio sintetico,* 1973; *Spettri,* 1974, Stockholm; *Funzione acustica,* 1975, Bratislava; *Ta foneénta,* 1976, Budapest; *Movimenti spaziale,* quadrophonic, 1976, Budapest; *Ballad – Barna Jancsi,* 1976, Budapest; *Ludus sinteticus,* 1977, Stuttgart; *Calling Sounds,* quadrophonic, 1977, Utrecht; *Hommage à l'électronique,* 1978.

LIVE ELECTRONIC MUSIC: *Experimenti,* 1974, Ed. Döring; *Metamorphosis* per marimba e nastro magnetico, quadrophonic, 1977; *Metamorphosis* per flauto e nastro magnetico, quadrophonic, 1977; *Kínai templom* (Chinese Church), (Poem by S. Weöres), quadrophonic, 1978; *Ludi spaziali* per pianoforte, quadrophonic, 1978.

WRITING: *Hang és zene a filmművészetben* (Sound and Music in Film Art), 1973, NPI.
Incidental music to plays and films.

DISCOGRAPHY:

Quartettino per sassofono
The Rascher Saxophone Quartet
Corone LPS 3030

Sonata per zimbalo ungherese
Gyöngyi Farkas
EMI Electrola C 065-30 249 1c 0233

Music of the Bible
Qualiton

Ritmi dispari
Hungarian Brass Ensemble
SLPX 77877

Funzione acustica
Qualiton

Ta foneénta
Qualiton

EMIL PETROVICS

(b. Nagybecskerek, 9 Febr. 1930.) Up to 1941 he lived in Belgrade, then he came to Budapest where he studied composition with Ferenc Farkas at the Academy of Music. From 1960 to 1964 he was musical director of the Petőfi Theatre. At present he is professor at the Academy of Dramatic Arts. He was awarded the Erkel Prize in 1960 and 1963, the Kossuth Prize in 1966. He was also prize winner at the World Youth Festival in 1955 and at the String Quartet Competition at Liege in 1959.

Since 1968 he is professor of composition at the Academy of Music, Budapest.

STAGE WORKS: *C'est la guerre* (Three Cups of Tea), one-act opera, 1961, Artisjus; *Bűn és bűnhődés* (Crime and Punishment), (Novel by Dostoievsky), three act opera, 1969, Artisjus.

WORKS FOR CHORUS AND ORCHESTRA: *Jugoslavian Songs* for voice and chamber orchestra, 1955; *Lysistrate,* comic opera for concert performance, 1962, EMB; *The Book of Jonah,* oratorio after M. Babits' poem, 1966; *2nd cantata – Ott essem el én* (Let Me Die There), (Poems by S. Petőfi, Gy. Illyés), for male choir and orchestra, 1972, EMB.

ORCHESTRAL WORKS: *Concerto for Flute,* 1957, EMB; *Symphony for Strings,* 1964, EMB.

CHAMBER MUSIC: *Cassazione* for brass instruments, 1953, EMB; *String Quartet,* 1958, EMB; *Wind Quintet,* 1964, EMB; *Egyedül az erdőn* (Alone in the Woods), solo cantata, 1956.

INSTRUMENTAL PIECES: *Four Self-Portraits in Masks* for harpsichord, 1958, EMB; *Passacaglia in Blues,* for bassoon and piano, 1964, EMB; *Magyar gyermekdalok* (Hungarian Children's Songs), for flute and piano, 1974, EMB; *Nocturne* for cimbalom, 1974; *Mouvement en Ragtime* for two dulcimers, 1977.

SONGS AND CHORAL WORKS: among them: *Játszik a szél* (The Wind is Playing), 1957, EMB; *Triangulum,* 1958, EMB; *Nagyváros* (Big City), EMB; *Évszakok zenéje* (Music of the Seasons), choral suite for female choir to poems by L. Ápriliy, 1967, EMB; *Divertimento* to poems by Gy. Czigány, for mixed choir, 1971, NPI; *Lassú táncnóta* (Slow Dance Tune), (Poem by L. Nagy), for mixed voices, 1974, EMB; *Mennyi minden* (How Much Everything), (Poems by Á. Nemes Nagy), for female or children's voices, 1976, EMB.

Folk song arrangements, incidental music to theatre plays, radio and television plays, music to twenty films.

WRITING: *Ravel,* Budapest, 1958.

DISCOGRAPHY:

C'est la guerre (Opera in one act)
György Radnai, Mária Dunszt, Róbert Ilosfalvy, József Réti, Éva Gombos, Sándor Palcsó, József Dene, András Faragó, Tivadar Bódy (soloists)
Choir and Orchestra of the Hungarian State Opera House, conductor: Tamás Blum
LPX 1208

The Book of Jonah (Oratorio)
József Réti, László Palócz, Sándor Palcsó, Endre Ütő (soloists)
Budapest Choir, Hungarian State Concert Orchestra, conductor: Miklós Erdélyi
LPX 11420

Wind Quintet
Hungarian Wind Quintet
LPX 11630

Nocturne
Márta Fábián (cimbalom)
SLPX 11686

String Quartet
New Budapest Quartet
SLPX 11847

Cassazione for Brass Quintet
Hungarian Brass Ensemble
SLPX 11811

Lysistrate (Concert Comic Opera in one act)
Veronika Kincses, Magda Kalmár, Sándor Palcsó (soloists)
Chorus of the Hungarian Radio, Budapest Symphony Orchestra,
conductor: György Lehel
SLPX 11810

ZOLTÁN PONGRÁCZ

(b. Diószeg, 5 Febr. 1912.) He studied composition at the Academy of Music, Budapest, under Zoltán Kodály and conducting with Rudolf Nilius (Vienna) and Clemens Krauss (Salzburg), then went to the Humboldt University, Berlin to do comparative musical studies at the Institut für Lautforschung. From 1938 he was répétiteur at the Budapest Opera House and subsequently joined the Music Department of the Hungarian Radio. Later, until 1964 he was professor at the Conservatory in Debrecen. He visited Darmstadt and Köln, attending the course of Professor Koenig in Utrecht and experimented with electronic music in Bilthoven. He has awarded the Francis Joseph Prize in 1939.

Since 1975 professor of electronic composition at the Academy of Music Budapest. In 1974 his work "Mariphonia" was awarded the first prize in Bourges. Since 1977 he is member of the managing committee of "Circuit International des Musiques Électroacoustiques" and member of the board of "Journées d'Études Internationales des Musiques Électroacoustiques".

STAGE WORKS: *Az ördög ajándéka* (The Devil's Present), ballet, 1936; *Odysseus and Nausikaa,* opera, 1949–50.

WORKS FOR CHORUS AND ORCHESTRA: *Christmas Cantata,* 1935; *St.*

Stephen Oratorio, 1938; *Apollo musagètes,* cantata, 1958; *Negritude* for speech-choir, chorus and percussion, 1962; *Ispirazioni* for mixed choir, orchestra and tape-recorder, 1965; *Nyírségi muzsika* (Music from the Nyírség), for voices, mixed choir and folk orchestra, 1965, County-council of Szabolcs-Szatmár; *Rapszódia* (Rhapsody) for mixed voices and gipsy band, 1976.

ORCHESTRAL MUSIC: *Pastorale,* 1941; *Gamelán zene* (Javanese Music), 1942; *Symphony,* 1943; *Ballo ongaro* for youth orchestra, 1955, EMB; *Three Orchestral Etudes,* 1963; *Hangok és zörejek* (Tones and Noises), aleatoric-graphic music for orchestra, 1966; *Színek és vonalak* (Colours and Lines), for youth orchestra, 1971.

CHAMBER MUSIC: *Music for Five Violoncellos,* 1954; *Quintet* of wind instruments, 1956; *Three Small Pieces* for Orff ensemble, 1966, EMB; *Three Improvisations* for piano, percussion, and three tape-recorders, 1971, Schott; *Three Bagatelles* for percussion, 1972.

PIANO PIECES: *Slovak Folk Dances,* 1939, Cantate, Budapest; *Six Soliloquia,* 1955; *Toccata,* 1957.

ELECTRONIC MUSIC: *Phonothèse,* 1966; realized at Studio voor Eletronische Muziek, Utrecht; *Luna 9,* 1966–67; *Az öreg hölgy látogatása* (The Visit of the Old Lady), stereophonic-electronic incidental music to Dürrenmatt's drama, 1967; *Halmazok és párok* (Sets and Pairs), electronic variations for piano and celesta, 1968; *Sárkány* (Dragon), incidental music to dramà by E. Schwarz, 1970; *Mariphonia* (Maryphonie), concrete music for female voices, realized at Electronic Studio, Bratislava, 1972; *Zoophonia,* concrete music from voices of animals, realized at Studio MAFILM, Budapest, 1973; *Rotációk* (Rotations), realized at the Electronic Studio of the Hungarian Radio, 1975; *Egy Cisz-dúr akkord története* (History of a Harmony C sharp major), realized at "Charybde" Studio, Bourges, 1975; *Közeledni és távolodni* (Approaching and Moving off) sound drama to poem by Gerhard Rühm, realized at the Electronic Studio of the Hungarian Radio, 1975; *Bariszféra* (Barisphere), realized at Exaustud of MAFILM, 1975; *Les parfumes,* multimedia for colours, parfumes and sounds, realized at the Electronic Studio of the Hungarian Radio, 1976; *Tizenkét körszalag* (Twelve Loops), realized at the "Charybde" Studio, Bourges, 1977; *144 hang* (144 Sounds), realized at the Electronic Studio of the Hungarian Radio, 1977.

WRITINGS: Zeneirodalmi ismeretek (Musical Literature), 1956; *Népzenészek könyve* (Book of Popular Musicians), 1965, EMB; *Mai zene – mai hangjegyírás* (Contemporary Music – Contemporary Notation), 1970, EMB; *Az elektronikus zene* (The Electronic Music).

DISCOGRAPHY:
Phonothèse
Deutsche Grammophon Gesellschaft, Hamburg,
Avantgarde, Stereo 137011.

Mariphonia; Egy Cisz-dúr akkord története (History of a Harmony C sharp major)
Qualiton

GYÖRGY RÁNKI

(b. Budapest, 30 Oct. 1907.) He studied composition with Zoltán Kodály. He devotes himself solely to composition. He was awarded the Erkel Prize (1952 and 1957), the Kossuth Prize (1954), *"Merited Artist of the Hungarian People's Republic"* title (1963),the Golden Medal of the Order of Labour (1967), "Pro Arte" (1970) and the "Medal for Socialist Hungary (1977).

STAGE WORKS: *Hóemberek* (Snow Men), ballet music, 1939; *A csendháborító* (The Rioter), musical comedy, 1950, transcribed 1959, Artisjus, Budapest; *Pomádé király új ruhája* (King Pomade's New Clothes), opera, 1953–69, Artisjus, Budapest; *A győztes ismeretlen* (The Winner is Unknown), children's musical comedy, 1961, Artisjus, Budapest; *Hölgyválasz* (Spoon-dance), operetta, 1961, Artisjus, Budapest; *Egy szerelem három éjszakája* (Three Nights), tragedy with music, 1961, Artisjus, Budapest; *Muzsikus Péter új kalandjai* (New Adventures of Peter Musician), children's opera, 1962, EMB; *Cirkusz* (The Circus), symphonic dance drama, 1965, Artisjus, Budapest, EMB; *The Tragedy of Man,* mystery opera, 1970, Artisjus, Budapest; *The Magic Drink,* ballet comedy, 1975, Sikorski.

WORKS FOR CHORUS AND ORCHESTRA: *Arany Ballads,* 1934, the manuscript perished; *A város peremén* (At the Outskirts of the City), cantata, 1947; *1848. évben*

(In the Year 1848), 1948; *A Szabadság Éneke* (Freedom Song), cantata, 1950; *Dal a népek egyetértéséről* (Song on the Concord of Peoples), 1952, EMB; *Ütközet békében* (Battle in Peace), cantata, 1951; *A walesi bárdok* (The Bards of Wales), 1957; *Sóhajtás békesség után* (Yearning for Peace), 1959; *Békedal* (Peace Song), 1960; *"1944"*, oratorio, 1967, EMB; *Lament* in memoriam Zoltán Kodály, 1971, EMB; *Cantus Urbis* (T. Déry), oratorio, 1972, EMB; *Phoenix – Ars Poetica,* 1974, EMB.

SYMPHONIC MUSIC: *Kardtánc* (Sword Dance), 1949, EMB; *Hungarian Dances from the Sixteenth Century,* 1950, EMB; *Hajdutánc* (Heyduck Dance), 1951; *Suite* No. 1, and No. 2, from "King Pomade's New Clothes", 1954, EMB; *Három cimbora* (The Three Chums), dance suite, 1954–55; *"1514"*, fantasy for piano and orchestra, after woodcuts by Derkovits, 1962, EMB; *Don Quijote and Dulcinea* for oboe and small orchestra, 1960, EMB; *7 Pieces for Orchestra* (Orchestration of Kodály's 7 Pieces for Piano Op. 11), 1962; *Aurora Tempestuosa,* 1967, EMB; *Raga di Notte* per violino solo e orchestra, 1974, EMB; *First Symphony,* 1977, EMB.

CHAMBER MUSIC: *Quintet* for wind instruments and piano. 1929, the manuscript perished; *Horn Quartet,* 1931, the manuscript perished; *Aristophanes,* suite for violin and piano, 1947, EMB; *Sonata* for rcorder and cimbalom (dulcimer), 1948; *Serenata all'antiqua* for violin and piano, 1956, EMB; *Kardtánc* (Sword Dance), the orchestral work transcribed for violin and piano, 1957, EMB; *Pentaerophonia* for quintet of wind instruments, 1958, EMB; *Don Quijote and Dulcinea* for oboe and piano, 1961, EMB; *Két bors ökröcske* (Two Wonder Oxen), a tale with music, narrator and thirteen instruments, Hungarian, English, German texts, EMB.

INSTRUMENTAL PIECES: *Sonata for Piano No. 1,* 1931, the manuscript perished; *Sonata for Clarinet,* 1931, the manuscript perished; *Sonata for Piano No. 2,* 1947, Arts Council, EMB; *Scherzo* for piano, 1961, EMB; *Pomádé király új ruhája* (King Pomade's New Clothes), piano arrangement for children, 1962, EMB; *"1514"*, transcription for piano duet and percussion, 1962, EMB; *Pas de Deux & Circus Gallop* for piano, 1966, EMB; *Two Wonder Oxen* (Easy Piano Duets for Children), 1969, EMB; *Raga di Notte* for violin and piano, 1974, EMB; *Two Easy Pieces* for violin and piano in Viet-Namese style, EMB; *Seven Easy Piano Pieces* on Viet-Namese folksongs, 1973, EMB.

SONGS: *Dúdoló, Medvetánc* (Humming, Bear-Dance), 1942, Cs; *Emberiség* (Mankind), 1942, EMB; *Fekete szőlő* (Black Grapes), folk song arrangements, 1964, EMB.

Incidental music to several theatre plays, music to about eighty films, radio plays, choral works (EMB, NPI).

DISCOGRAPHY:
Pentaerophonia
Hungarian Wind Quintet
LP 1607

Three Historical Tableaux (1514 [Fantasy after Derkovits' woodcuts] – 1944 [Oratorio]
– Aurora Tempestuosa [Preludio per orchestra])
Endre Ütő, Margit László, Sándor Palcsó (soloists), Endre Petri (piano)
Chamber Choir of the Academy of Music
Hungarian State Concert Orchestra, conductor: Miklós Erdélyi
LPX 11481

Don Quijote y Dulcinea
Maurice Bourgue (oboe), Colette Cling (piano)
LPX 11534

Tongue Twister Canon
Children's Choir of the Hungarian Radio and Television, conductor: Valeria Botka
LPX 5012

Cantus Urbis
Margit László, Márta Szirmay, György Korondy, Endre Ütő, Gábor Lehotka, János
Sebestyén, Hungarian State Orchestra, conductor: András Kórodi
SLPX 11699

The Tragedy of Man (Excerpts)
György Melis, Margit László, István Rozsos, Kodály Chorus of Debrecen, Orchestra
of the Hungarian State Opera House, conductor: János Ferencsik
SLPX 11714

Three Nights (Excerpts)
Sándor Angyal, Zsolt Bende, János Boros, Ottó Földi, Miklós Gábor, Tivadar
Horváth, Margit László, György Miklósy, János Pagonyi, Vera Sennyei
Orchestra of the Petőfi Theatre, conductor: Emil Petrovics
SHLX 90047

Two Wonder Oxen
Teri Horváth, The Budapest Nonet (augmented)
LP 1596

King Pomade's New Clothes (Suite No. 1)
Hungarian State Orchestra, conductor: László Somogyi
LP 133

ANTAL RIBÁRI

(b. Budapest, 8 Jan. 1924.) He studied composition at the Academy of Music, Budapest with Rezső Kókai, and later under Ferenc Szabó. He was prize winner at the World Youth Festival in 1955.

STAGE WORKS: *Lajos király válik* (The Divorce of King Louis), one-act opera, 1959; *Liliom,* opera, 1960; *Az aranypróbás legény* (Fortunio), ballet in one act (text by F. Jankovich), 1969.

WORKS FOR CHORUS AND ORCHESTRA: *A megsebzett galamb és a szökőkút* (The Wounded Pigeon and the Fountain), cantata, 1962; *A könnyek kútja* (The Well of Tears), cantata, 1964; *Hellas,* cantata, 1965; *Clown-cantata* for tenor solo, mixed choir and orchestra to a poem by H. Michaux, 1967; *Dylan Thomas,* cantata, 1971; *Requiem for the Lover,* cantata for alto and tenor solo, chamber choir and small orchestra to poems by W. Blake (The Birds), P. B. Shelley (Lines), A. C. Swinburne (A Leave-Taking), 1973; *Hat sor a Satyriconból* (Six lines from the Satyricon), for two contralto solo, mixed voices and five instruments, 1975; *The Visions of Venus,* (Poems by Auden, Drinkwater and J. Joyce), cantata for mixed voices, piano and orchestra.

CHORAL WORKS: *Himnusz a békéről* (Hymn on the Peace), chorus poem, 1972, EMB; *Nyugalom* (Rest), chorus poem (Chr. G. Rosetti – D. Kosztolányi), 1972; *Két*

Petőfi-töredék (Two Petőfi Fragments), 1972; *Tavaszi virradat* (Spring Daybreak), 1972; *Szerelem* (Love), 1973.

ORCHESTRAL MUSIC: *Sinfonietta,* 1956; *Symphony No. 1,* 1960; *Musica per archi,* 1961, EMB; *Pantomime,* 1962; *Symphony No. 2,* 1964; *Metamorphoses,* 1966; *Symphony No. 3,* 1970; *Sinfonia Festiva,* 1972; *Concerto grosso* for flute, clarinet, harp and full orchestra, 1975; *Variations* for orchestra, 1976; *Six Improvisations* for full orchestra, 1977.

CONCERTOS: *Concerto per violoncello e orchestra,* 1958, Bens, Brussels; *Violino concertino,* 1965; *Dialogues* pour alto et orchestre, 1967; *Renewal concerto* for violoncello and orchestra, 1977.

CHAMBER MUSIC: *Sonata for Violin and Piano No. 1,* 1953, EMB; *Sonata for Violin and Piano, No. 2,* Bens, Brussels; *String Quartet No. 1,* 1955; *String Quintet,* 1956; *Sonata for Viola and Piano,* 1958, EMB; *Sonata for Violoncello and Piano,* 1959, GMP; *String Quartet No. 2,* 1964; *Nine Miniatures* for string quartet, 1966; *Five Miniatures* for wind trio, 1969, EMB + BH; *Chamber Music* for five instruments, 1970, GMP; *Dialogues* for flute and piano, 1971, GMP; *Fantasia* per violino, viola e violoncello, 1971, GMP; *Sonata No. 3,* pour violon et piano, 1972; *Sonata* for cello and piano, 1973; *Quatre préludes en lumière,* pour orchestre à chord, 1976; *Doppelquartett,* für Streicher, 1977.

INSTRUMENTAL MUSIC: *All'antica,* suite per pianoforte, 1968, GMP; *Sonata* for piano, 1971, GMP.

SONGS: *Three Songs* (Poem by P. B. Shelley), 1972, GMP; *Due liriche per sonetti* (Poem by B. Michelangelo), 1972, GMP; *Five Shakespeare Sonets,* 1972; *Három önarckép* (Three Self-Portraits), 1972; *Nähe des Geliebten* (Poem by J. W. Goethe), 1973; *Five Villon Songs* for soprano and piano, 1977.

TIBOR SÁRAI

(b. Budapest, 10 May 1919.) He studied composition with Pál Kadosa. In 1948 he was secretary general of the Union of Hungarian Musicians, in 1949 head of the Music Department at the Ministry of Culture, from 1950 to 1953 he was head of the Music Department of the Hungarian Radio. From 1953 to 1959 he was teaching at the Béla Bartók Conservatory, and since then he has been professor at the Academy of Music, Budapest. Since 1959 he has been also secretary general of the Association of Hungarian Musicians. He was awarded the Erkel Prize in 1959, the Kossuth Prize in 1975. For a while he was member of the Executive Committee of the International Music Council (1971–77), vice-president of the International Music Council (1975–77), presently he is individual member of the International Music Council since 1978.

WORKS FOR CHORUS AND ORCHESTRA: *Elment a nyár* (Summer is Gone), 1957, a cappella version: EMB; *Csalogató* (Alluring), 1957, a cappella version: EMB; *Mi legyek?* (What Should I Be?), 1957–58, version with piano accompaniment, EMB; *Változatok a béke témájára* (Variations on the Theme of Peace), oratorio, 1961–64; *Jövőt faggató ének* (Future Questioning), (Poems by M. Váci), for alto and baritone solo, male choir and orchestra, 1971; *Krisztus vagy Barrabás* (Christ or Barabbas), (text by Fr. Karinthy), for tenor, baritone, bass solo, mixed voices and orchestra, 1976–77.

CHORAL WORKS: *Budapesti rapszódia* (Budapest Rhapsody), 1954; *Változások balladája* (The Ballad of Transformations), 1956; *Falraírók* (Party Workers), 1958, EMB; *Októberi magyar hangok – 1917* (Hungarian Voices in October, 1917), for male choir, 1966–67; *Debrecen dicsérete* (Praise of Debrecen), (Poem by M. Jókai), for three children's voices, 1973, EMB.

ORCHESTRAL MUSIC: *Serenade* for string orchestra, 1946, EMB; *Tavaszi Concerto* (Spring Concerto), 1955, EMB; *Six Scenes* from the dance play "János vitéz", 1956–57; *Symphony No. 1*, 1965–67, EMB; *Diagnosis '69*, for tenor solo and symphonic orchestra, to a poem by M. Váci, 1969, EMB; *Musica per 45 corde*, 1970–71, EMB; *Symphony No. 2*, 1972–73, EMB; *Sírfelirat Szabó Ferenc emlékére* (Epitaph in Memory of Ferenc Szabó), 1974, EMB.

CHAMBER MUSIC: *Humoresque* for viola and piano, 1953, EMB; *String Quartet No. 1*, 1958, EMB; *Lassú és friss* (Slow and Quick), for violin and piano, 1958, EMB; *Quartet* for flute, violin, viola and violoncello, 1961–62, EMB; *Studio per flauto e pianoforte*, 1964, EMB; *De profundis* solo cantata for tenor solo and wind quintet, to poems by A. József, 1968; *String Quartet* No. 2, 1971, EMB.

PIANO PIECES: *Rondoletto*, 1941, EMB; *Suite*, 1942; *Sonatina*, 1959, EMB; *Eight Small Piano Pieces*, 1965, EMB; *Distances* pour le piano, 1974, EMB.

SONGS: *Falusi képek* (Village Scenes), 1953.

Pedagogical pieces.

WRITING: *A cseh zene története* (The History of Czech Music), 1959, EMB.

DISCOGRAPHY:
Spring Concerto
János Szebenyi (flute), Anna Mauthner (viola), Vera Dénes (violoncello)
Hungarian State Concert Orchestra, conductor: Frigyes Sándor
LPX 1166

Symphony No. 1; Serenade for string orchestra; *String Quartet No. 2; Diagnosis '69* for tenor solo and orchestra
Sándor Palcsó (tenor)
Kodály String Quartet, Hungarian Chamber Orchestra, Symphony Orchestra of the Hungarian Radio and Television, conductors: Miklós Erdélyi, György Lehel
LPX 11636

Musica per 45 corde; String Quartet No. 1; Symphony No. 2
Katalin Szőkefalvy-Nagy (soprano)
Kodály String Quartet
Ferenc Liszt Chamber Orchestra, conductor: György Lehel
SLPX 11753

JÓZSEF SÁRI

(b. Lenti, 23 June 1935.) He began studying music at the Conservatory in Győr (organ and composition), transferred to the Academy of Music, Budapest in 1954 (chorus conducting, also composition). Graduated in 1962. School singing teacher, music master, and director of the Chemical Trade-union's Artistic Ensemble. His works—mostly folk song arrangements—won prizes several times at local competitions.

CHORAL WORKS: *Dawn Comes,* cantata for baritone solo, male voices and orchestra, 1962; *Sorrow Begone* for chorus and youth string orchestra, 1963; *Two Choruses* for mixed voices (Poem by Gy. Juhász), 1963–64; *Spring Salute* for chorus and piano accompaniment, 1965, Institute of Popular Culture; *Hold my Hand O Fellow Mine* for chorus and piano accompaniment, 1966, Institute of Popular Culture; *Rain* for chorus, 1966, Institute of Popular Culture; *Dry-grained Fiddle* for chorus and piano accompaniment, 1967, Institute of Popular Culture; *Five Children's Songs* for chorus (or solo voice) with piano accompaniment, 1967; *Ten Canons* for chorus, 1967; *Ten Sun Enflames* for chorus, 1968; *Work* for chorus, 1968; *Sing for Peace but Ever so Often* for mixed voices, 1969.

ORCHESTRAL MUSIC: *Introduction and Allegro* for oboe solo and orchestra, 1959–65; *Divertimento* "Omaggio a Bartók" for youth symphony orchestra, 1969; *Fossilien,* for string orchestra, EMB.

CHAMBER MUSIC: *Brass Quartet,* 1959; *Cinque duetti facili* per due violini, 1964, EMB + BH; *Musica da casa* for violin, violoncello and percussion, 1966; *Meditation* for bassoon and piano, 1967–68, EMB; *Contemplazione* per flauto e pianoforte, 1970, EMB + BH; *Diaphonia* musica da camera per venti strumenti, 1971, EMB; *Movimento cromatico indiretto* per flauto, pianoforte e percussioni, 1972; *Capriccio disciplinato* per violoncello e pianoforte, 1972; *Pezzo spregiudicato* per oboe, clarinetto e fagotto, 1972; *String Quartet,* EMB.

VOCAL CHAMBER MUSIC: *Two Songs* for baritone and chamber ensemble (Poems by L. Szabó), 1965; *Two Intermezzi* for tenor, clarinet and violoncello (Poems by D. Kosztolányi), 1965.

INSTRUMENTAL PIECES: *Six Piano Pieces,* 1958, EMB; *Solo sonata* for violin, 1964; *Stati* per clarinetto solo, 1968, EMB + BH; *Episodes* for piano, 1968, EMB + BH; *Acciaccature* per organo, 1971, EMB + BH.

ISTVÁN SÁRKÖZY

(b. Pesterzsébet, 26 Nov. 1920.) He studied composition at the Academy of Music, Budapest with Zoltán Kodály, Ferenc Farkas, Géza Szatmári and János Viski. Since 1959 he has taught theory at the Academy of Music.

STAGE WORKS: *Az új traktorállomás* (The New Tractor Station), ballet, 1949; *Liliomfi* (E. Szigligeti – D. Mészöly), musical play, 1950, EMB; *Szelistyei asszonyok* (The Women of Szelistye), (K. Mikszáth – A. Benedek – J. Semsey – V. E. Innocent), musical play, 1951, Henschel Verlag, Leipzig; *Pettyes* (Gy. Soós), musical comedy, 1955; *A cigány* (The Gipsy), (E. Szigligeti), musical play, 1958.

INCIDENTAL MUSIC TO THE FOLLOWING PLAYS: Gáli: *Erős János* (John, the Strong), children's play, 1951; Akszakov: *Bíborszínű virág* (Purple Flower), puppet play, 1953; K. Kisfaludy: *Pártütők* (The Conspirators), 1954; J. Eötvös: *Éljen az egyenlőség* (Long Live Equality), 1954; S. Tatay: *Ház a sziklák alatt* (House under the Rocks), music to a film, 1958; E. Vészi: *Don Quijote utolsó kalandja* (Don Quijote's Last Adventure), 1962; W. Saroyan: *Halló, ki az?* (Hello, Who is It?), for television, 1963; I. Dobozy: *Az idegen ember* (The Stranger), for television, 1964; Zs. Móricz: *Odysseus bolyongásai* (Ulysses' Adventures), musical play for radio, 1964; I. Dobozy: *Váltás* (Shift), for television, 1964; I. Dobozy: *A tizedes meg a többiek* (The Sergeant and the Others), music to a film, 1965; E. Szigligeti – G. Heller: *Liliomfi,* musical comedy for Television (new version), 1967; G. Lorca: *A csodálatos Vargáné* (The Miraculóus Wife of the Shoemaker), music play for Television, 1968.

WORKS FOR CHORUS AND ORCHESTRA: *Óda Sztálinhoz* (Ode to Stalin), (Poem by G. Képes), cantata, 1949, EMB; *Ijúság* (Youth), (Poem by E. Sárközy), suite, 1952, EMB; *Júlia énekek* (Júlia Songs), (Poems by B. Balassi), lyrical chamber cantata for tenor solo, mixed choir and four instruments, 1958, EMB; *Reng már a föld...* (The Earthquake Approaches), (Poem by I. Raics), cantata for baritone solo and mixed choir, 1958; *Aki szegény...* (Who is Poor), (Poem by A. József), Rappresentazione profana in 12 movements for sopran solo and mixed choir, 1967, EMB; *Az Ypszilon-háború* ("Y" War), (Poem by M. Vörösmarty), comedy in oratorio for ten solo voices, vocal quintet and eight instruments, 1971.

ORCHESTRAL MUSIC: *Concerto grosso,* 1943, new version (Ricordanze I.): 1969, EMB; *Small Suite,* 1951; *Bulgarian Dance* for children's orchestra, 1951, Verlag Volk und Wissen, Berlin; *Fantasy and Dance* for gipsy orchestra, 1952; *Az Ifjúsághoz* (To Youth), overture, 1953, EMB, transcription for wind band by A. Prévost: 1958, CIMI-Publications, Brussels; *Sinfonia concertante* for clarinet and 24 strings, 1963, EMB; other version of it with 24 string and 12 wind instruments, 1964, EMB; *Concerto semplice* per violino e orchestra (Ricordanze II.), 1973, EMB.

SONGS WITH ORCHESTRA ACCOMPANIMENT: *Egy ismeretlen istennek* (For a God Unknown), (J. Steinbeck – M. Benedek), bass solo, 1946; *Munkások* (Workers), (R. M. Rilke – E. Várhelyi), bass solo, 1947; *Vörös Rébék* (Red Rebecca), (Poem by J. Arany), ballad, mezzosoprano solo, 1947; *Szivárvány havasán...* (On the Snowcapped Mountain), 17 folk song arrangements, 1948; *Two Rumanian, Two Greek, Two Bosnian and Two Macedonian Folk Songs,* 1949; *Twelve Balkan Folk Songs* for soprano solo and chamber orchestra, 1949.

SONGS WITH PIANO ACCOMPANIMENT: *Three Songs to French Poems* (Poems by P. Verlaine – L. Szabó; J. Richepin, Ch. Baudelaire – M. Babits), 1947; *Two Hungarian Folk Songs* (From "Virágim, virágim"), 1953, EMB; *Four Hungarian Folk Songs,* 1955, Tankönyvkiadó; *Two songs* (Poems by W. Vogelweide, W. Blake – M. Babits), 1956; *Four Songs* (Poems by A. József), 1957; *Színészdal* (Actor's Song), (Poem by S. Petőfi), 1963; *Ballad and Three Songs* (Poems by A. Mezei), 1968; *Sok gondom közt* (In all my Worries), (Poem by A. József), 21 Songs, 1972; *Öt dal* (Five Songs), (Poems by G. Hajnal), with guitar accompaniment, 1974.

INSTRUMENTAL PIECES: *Twelve Variations* for piano, 1945; *Two Piano Pieces,* 1947; *Sonatina* for piano duet, 1950, EMB; *Sonata da camera* for flute and piano, 1964, EMB; *Ciaccona* for violoncello, 1967, EMB; *Chamber Sonata* for clarinet and piano, 1969, EMB; *Quatuor pour instruments de bois* (Psaume et jeu), 1970, EMB; *Four Etudes* for clarinet solo, 1972, EMB; *Quartetto* per archi (Ricordanze III.), 1977, EMB.

In addition, numerous a cappella choral works, folk dance plays, pieces of incidental music, etc.

LÁSZLÓ SÁRY

(b. Győr, 1 Jan. 1940.) He studied first at the Conservatory in Győr, subsequently at the Academy of Music, Budapest, where he was pupil of Endre Szervánszky. Graduated in 1966.

VOCAL MUSIC: *Lamento 65* for vocal quintet, 1965; *Three Madrigals* for vocal quintet, 1966; *Cantata No. 1* for soprano, chamber chorus and chamber ensemble, 1967–68; *Hommage aux ancêtres* for vocal sextet, 1969; *Incanto* for vocal quintet, 1969; *Improvisations '69* for vocal sextet and chamber ensemble, 1969; *Psalmus* for any kind of solo voice and two string instruments plucked with a plectrum, 1972; *Pentagram* for five instrumental ensembles (with male and female voices) and six articulators, 1972.

ORCHESTRAL MUSIC: *Canzone solenne* for full orchestra, 1971, EMB; *Immaginario No. 1* for full orchestra, 1971, EMB.

INSTRUMENTAL MUSIC: *Variations* for clarinet and piano, 1966, EMB + BH; *Catacoustics* for two pianos, 1967, EMB; *Musica da camera* for flute and percussion, 1968; *Fluttuazioni* for violin and piano, 1968–69, EMB + BH; *Versetti* for organ, 1966–69, EMB + BH; *Pezzo concertato* for flute and piano, 1969–70, EMB + BH; *Sonanti No. 1* for cembalo solo, 1970, EMB + BH; *Sonanti No. 2* for flute and percussion, 1970, EMB + BH; *Sonanti No. 3* for dulcimer solo, 1970; ᵢ*Versetti nuovi* for organ, 1971; *Trio* for flute, piano and gongs, 1972; *Image* for clarinet, violoncello, and piano, 1972; *Sounds* for any instrumental or vocal soloists, or any kind of chamber ensembles or orchestras (instruments, soloists), 1972–73; *String* for one or more keyboard instruments or chamber ensemble, 1973.

JÓZSEF SOPRONI

(b. Sopron, 4 Oct. 1930.) He started his music studies at his native town, then continued at the Academy of Music, Budapest as a pupil of János Viski. In 1958 he was appointed professor of the Béla Bartók Conservatory. Since 1963 he has been professor at the Academy of Music.

STAGE WORK: *Antigone,* opera in three acts, to text by Sophokles, 1968–74.

WORKS FOR CHORUS AND ORCHESTRA: *Requiem egy költő halálára* (Requiem to the Death of a Poet), oratorio, 1960; *Carmina polinaesiana,* cantata for female choir and chamber ensemble, 1963; *Ovidii metamorphoses,* cantata for soprano solo, mixed choir and orchestra, to a poem by Ovid, 1965; *De aetatibus mundi carmina,* cantata, soprano and baritone solo, mixed choir and orchestra, to poems by Ovid, 1968.

SYMPHONIC MUSIC: *Concerto* for string orchestra, 1953, EMB; *Concerto for Viola and Orchestra,* 1967, EMB + BH; *Concerto for Violoncello and Orchestra,* 1967, EMB; *Symphony,* 1964; *Eklypsis* for orchestra, 1969, EMB; *Symphony No. 1,* 1975, EMB; *Concertino* for flute, clarinet, cimbalom and orchestra, 1976; *Symphony No. 2* (The Seasons), 1977.

CHAMBER MUSIC: *Sonatina* for viola and piano, 1958; *String Quartet* No. 1, 1958; *String Quartet* No. 2, 1960, EMB; *Musica da camera* for piano trio, 1963, EMB;

String Quartet No. 3, 1965, EMB; *String Quartet* No. 4, 1973, EMB; *Sonate pour flûte et piano,* 1971, EMB; *Concerto da camera* for chamber ensemble, 1972; *Sonata* for horn and piano, 1976, EMB; *Musica da camera No. 2,* for violin, clarinet, violoncello and piano, 1976, EMB; *Three Pieces* for flute and cimbalom, 1977; *Six Bagatelles* for wind quintet, 1977.

INSTRUMENTAL PIECES: *Four Bagatelles* for piano, 1957, EMB; *Partita* for harpsichord, 1957; *Meditatio con toccata* for organ, 1959, EMB; *Seven Piano Pieces,* 1963, EMB; *Incrustations pour piano,* 1970; *Invenzioni sul B-A-C-H pour piano,* 1971, EMB; *Jegyzetlapok* (Notes), volumes I, II, III, for piano, 1974–77, EMB; *Four Interludes* for piano, 1976.

SONGS: *Three Songs* to poems by M. Radnóti, 1962, EMB; *Three Songs* to poems by P. Verlaine, 1966.

DISCOGRAPHY:
Ovidii metamorphoses
Erika Sziklay (soprano), Tibor Ney (violin)
Choir and Orchestra of the Hungarian Radio and Television,
conductor: Miklós Erdélyi
LPX 1298

Invenzioni sul B-A-C-H
Ádám Fellegi (piano)
SLPX 11692

Three Songs to poems by M. Radnóti
Erika Sziklay (soprano), Loránt Szűcs (piano)
.SLPX 11713

Eklypsis; Concerto for Violoncello; String Quartet No. 4; Sonata for Flute and Piano
Orchestra of the Hungarian Radio and Television, conductor: György Lehel
László Mező (violoncello),
Kodály Quartet
Erzsébet Csik (flute), Zoltán Kocsis (piano)
SLPX 11743

REZSŐ SUGÁR

(b. Budapest, 9 Oct. 1910.) He graduated in composition at the Academy of Music, Budapest in 1942 as a pupil of Zoltán Kodály. From 1946 to 1949 he was teaching at the Municipal Higher Music School, since 1949 he has been professor at the Béla Bartók Conservatory, Budapest. Since 1968 he has been professor of composition at the Academy of Music. He was winner of the Erkel Prize (1953) and the Kossuth Prize (1954), holder of the "Merited Artist of the Hungarian People's Republic" title (1976).

STAGE WORK: *A tenger lánya* (The Daughter of the Sea), ballet, 1961.

WORKS FOR CHORUS AND ORCHESTRA: *Hunyadi* (Heroic song), oratorio, 1951, EMB; *Kőműves Kelemen* (Kelemen, the Mason), cantata, 1958, EMB; *Paraszti háború* (Peasant War), oratorio, 1976.

ORCHESTRAL MUSIC: *Divertimento* for string orchestra, 1948; Cooperative Society of Hungarian Librettists, Composers and Publishers; *Suite,* 1954, EMB; *Concerto in Memoriam B. Bartók,* 1962, EMB; *Metamorfosi* per orchestra, 1966, EMB; *Partita* for string orchestra, 1967, EMB; *Sinfonia a variazione* per orchestra, 1970, EMB; *Epilógus* (Epilogue), for orchestra, 1974, EMB; *Concertino* per orchestra da camera, 1976, EMB.

CHAMBER MUSIC: *Serenade* for two violins and viola, 1943, EMB; *Sonata* for violin and piano, 1946, EMB; *String Quartet* No. 2, 1950, EMB; *Frammenti musicali* sextet for piano and quintet of wind instruments, 1958, EMB; *Rhapsody* for violoncello and piano, 1959, EMB; *String Quartet* No. 3, 1969, EMB.

PIANO PIECES: *Baroque Sonatina,* 1943–46, Arts Council.

SONGS: *Six Songs,* 1954, EMB; *Chinese Songs,* 1954.

Choral works.

DISCOGRAPHY:

Hunyadi (Heroic Song)

Gabriella Déry, Erzsébet Komlóssy, József Simándy, György Melis (soloists)

Budapest Choir, Hungarian State Concert Orchestra, conductor: Miklós Forrai

LPX 11418

IMRE SULYOK

(b. Budapest, 30 March 1912.) He studied composition at the Academy of Music, Budapest with Zoltán Kodály and organ with Aladár Zalánfy. From 1939 to 1951 he was on the staff of the Hungarian Radio, then he joined Editio Musica, Budapest. Since his retirement in 1972, Sulyok has been active as editor of the new edition of the collected works of F. Liszt. He has been functioning as organist and conductor in Lutheran churches since 1936.

WORKS FOR CHORUS AND ORCHESTRA: *130. zsoltár* (Psalm No. 130), 1947; *28. zsoltár* (Psalm No. 28), 1954; *Óda a gyorsasághoz* (Ode to Speed), for six solo voices and chamber ensemble, 1963; *A tudomány dícsérete* (In Praise of Science), cantata, 1967; *Cantata on Dedication of an Organ* for mixed choir, string orchestra and organ, 1971; *Expulsio* motet for mixed voices, 1977.

ORCHESTRAL MUSIC: *Suite,* 1944–52; *Concerto for Organ,* 1956; *Ode,* 1958; *Concertino da Camera* for piano and chamber ensemble, 1963; *Dal és Körtánc* (Song and Roundelay), four youth orchestra, 1963, EMB; *Five Orchestral Miniatures,* 1964; *Chaconne,* 1968.

CHAMBER MUSIC: *Serenade* for string trio, 1939; *Clarinet Quintet,* 1950; *Flute Trio,* 1954, EMB; *String Quartet,* 1955, EMB; *Andante* for violin and piano, 1958,

EMB; *Introduzione e Rondo* for violin and piano, 1958, EMB; *Dal és Körtánc* (Song and Roundelay), for quintet of wind instruments, 1962; *Musica arcaica* for wind quintet, 1968, Schott, EMB.

INSTRUMENTAL WORKS: *Te Deum,* 1940, EMB; *Prelude, Adagio and Fugue* for organ, 1942, Nordiska Musikförlaget, Uppsala; *Invocation* for organ, 1946, EMB; *Prelude* for organ, 1948, EMB; *Four Easy Violin Pieces,* 1951–54, EMB; *Variations on a Folk Song* for violin and piano, 1955, EMB; *Sonata for Organ,* 1957, EMB + BH; *Two Organ Preludes,* 1958; *Seven Little Organ Preludes manualiter,* 1968; *Tema con variazioni* per tromba e pianoforte, 1971, EMB; *Andante sostenuto* per corno e pianoforte, 1971, EMB; *Kakas* (Cock), variations for violin and piano, 1972, EMB; *Passacaglia con fuga* for organ, 1973; *Partita on Theme of an Early Hungarian Song* for organ, 1975.

Songs, folk song arrangements, sacred and secular choral works, incidental music to radio and theatre plays.

DISCOGRAPHY:
Te Deum Phantasy
Gábor Lehotka (organ)
SLPX 11808

FERENC SZABÓ

(b. Budapest, 27 Dec. 1902; d. Budapest, 4 Nov. 1969.) Studied at the Academy of Music, Budapest under Leo Weiner, Zoltán Kodály and Albert Siklós. In 1926 he made contact with the labour movement; having been engaged in illegal party-work, he had to emigrate from Hungary in 1932. He was living first in Berlin, then in the Soviet Union. In 1945 he was appointed professor of composition at the Academy of Music, Budapest, from 1958 to 1967 he was director-general of this institution and from 1949 to 1951 president of the Association of Hungarian Musicians. Kossuth Prize laureate (1951 and 1954), "Merited Artist of the Hungarian People's Republic" (1952), "Outstanding Artist of the Hungarian People's Republic" (1962).

STAGE WORKS: *Lúdas Matyi,* ballet, 1960, EMB; *Légy jó mindhalálig* (Be Faithful onto Death), opera in three acts, based on the novel by Zs. Móricz.

WORKS FOR CHORUS AND ORCHESTRA: *Meghalt Lenin* (Lenin Died), cantata for mixed choir and orchestra, 1933; Muzgiz, Moscow; *Nótaszó* (Melodies), 1960, EMB; *Föltámadott a tenger* (In Fury Rose the Ocean), oratorio, 1955, EMB.

CHORAL WORKS: *Farkasok dala* (Song of the Wolves), 1929, EMB; *Munkát, kenyeret!* (Work and Bread!), 1930; *Szabadság legyen a jelszó* (Liberty Be the Watchword), 1932; *November 7,* chorus suite, 1932; *Three Small Choruses* to poems by

A. József, 1948, EMB; *Hajnali nóta* (Song at Dawn), 1942; *Vallomás* (Declaration), for mixed choir, brass instruments and percussion, 1967, EMB.

SYMPHONIC MUSIC: *Sinfonietta,* 1938; *Lyrical Suite* for string orchestra, 1936, Muzgiz, Moscow, EMB; *Moldovan Rhapsody,* 1940, EMB; *Concerto – "Hazatérés"* (Homecoming), 1948, EMB; *Számadás* (Summary), 1949; *Felszabadult melódiák* (Free Melodies), an orchestral version of seven movements of the piano cycle, 1955, EMB; *Lúdas Matyi,* suite, 1950, EMB; *Emlékeztető* (Memento), symphony, 1952, EMB; *Bal-. let Music* (Lúdas Matyi – Suite No. 2), 1961, EMB; *Elfelejtett szerenád* (Serenade Oubliée), 1964, EMB.

CHAMBER MUSIC: *String Quartet* No. 1, 1926, EMB; *String Trio* for two violins and viola, 1927, EMB; *Air* for violin, viola or violoncello with piano accompaniment, 1953, EMB; *String Quartet* No. 2, 1962.

INSTRUMENTAL PIECES: *Piano Toccata,* 1928, EMB; *Sonata* for solo violoncello, 1929, EMB; *Two Sonatas* for solo violin, 1930, Korda, EMB; *Two Piano Pieces – All'Concerto, Sonatina,* 1933, EMB; *Eight Easy Piano Pieces,* 1933; *Five Small Piano Pieces,* 1933; *Piano Sonata No. 1,* 1940, EMB; *Piano Sonata No. 2,* 1947, EMB; *Felszabadult melódiák* (Free Melodies), for piano, 1949, EMB; *Piano Sonata No. 3,* 1957– 61, EMB; *Sonata* (alla rapsodia), for clarinet and piano, 1964, EMB.

SONGS: *Three Songs* with piano accompaniment, to poems by M. Radnóti, 1965, EMB.

A great number of mass songs, rallying marches and folk song arrangements. Music to films.

DISCOGRAPHY:
Song of the Wolves – Declaration – Three Little Choruses (Poor Man, Vers Chronicle, Dúduoló)
Choir and Orchestra of the Hungarian Radio and Television,
conductor: Zoltán Vásárhelyi
LPX 11330

In Fury Rose the Ocean (Oratorio)
Róbert Ilosfalvy (tenor)
Budapest Choir, Hungarian State Concert Orchestra, conductor: Gyula Németh
LPX 11386

ENDRE SZÉKELY

(b. Budaest, 6 Apr. 1912.) He studied at the Academy of Music, Budapest as a pupil of Albert Siklós. Until 1945 he conducted workers' choirs, subsequently performed various functions in Hungarian musical life: he was secretary general of the Union of Hungarian Musicians, and of the Béla Bartók Association, conductor of the Choir of the Hungarian Radio and director of several other choirs, professor at the Teachers' Training College in Budapest. At present he is manager of the Budapest Chamber Ensemble. He was awarded the Erkel Prize in 1954 and 1974.

WORKS FOR CHORUS AND ORCHESTRA: *Petőfi Cantata*, 1952; *György Dózsa*, oratorio, 1959; *Nenia*, oratorio, 1968–69.

ORCHESTRAL MUSIC: *Suite No. 1*, 1948, Association of Hungarian Musicians; *Symphony*, 1956, EMB; *Partita* for strings, 1957, EMB; *Partita* for orchestra, 1965; *Fantasma* for orchestra, 1969, EMB; *Humanisation* for chamber orchestra and electronic tapes, 1974; *Sonores nascentes et morientes*, 1975, EMB.

CONCERTOS: *Concerto* for piano, percussion and strings, 1958, EMB; *Sinfonia concertante* for piano, violin and orchestra, 1960–61, EMB; *Concerto* for eight solo instruments and orchestra, 1964, EMB; *Concerto* per tromba and orchestra, 1971, EMB;

Riflessioni for cello and orchestra, 1972; *Concerto* for piano and stereo tape, 1975, EMB; *Concerto* in memoriam Webern for horn and orchestra, 1976, EMB.

CHAMBER MUSIC: *Vörös Rébék* (Red Rebecca), ballad for mezzosoprano and piano, 1946–47; *Wind Quintet No. 1,* 1952, Mills; *Sonata* for piano, 1952, EMB; *String Quartet No. 2,* 1959, EMB; *Wind Quintet No. 2,* 1961, EMB; *Chamber Music for Eight,* 1963; *Chamber Music for Six,* 1965; *Wind Quintet No. 3,* 1966; *Three Sketches* for soprano and guitar, 1967; *Musica notturna for Eleven,* 1968, EMB; *Trio* for percussion, piano and violoncello, 1968–69, EMB; *Maqamat* for soprano solo and chamber ensemble, 1970, EMB; *String Quartet No. 4,* 1972; *Solokantate* for soprano solo and chamber ensemble, 1972, EMB; *Capriccio* for flute and piano, 1964, EMB; *Sextet* for clarinet, piano and string quartet, 1971; *Trio* for cimbalom, violin and viola, 1974; *Duos* for flute and cimbalom, 1974, EMB; *Kammerkantate* for soprano, flute, cello and stereo tape, 1977; *Chamber Music* for contrabass concertante, flute, percussion and keyboard instruments (1 player), 1977; *Song between Heaven and Earth,* 1977, EMB.

PIANO PIECES: *Three Sonatas,* 1954, 1962, 1972, EMB.

Choral works, songs, educational music.

DISCOGRAPHY:

Fantasma; Concerto for trumpet and orchestra; Trio for percussion, piano and cello; String Quartet No. 4
Choir and Orchestra of the Hungarian Radio and Television
conductor: György Lehel
Kodály String Quartet
György Gergely (trumpet), Ferenc Petz (percussion), Ádám Fellegi (piano), László Mező (violoncello)
SLPX 11666

Sonata No. 3 for piano
Ádám Fellegi (piano)
SLPX 11692

Trio for cimbalom, violin and viola
Márta Fábián (cimbalom), András Kiss (violin), Tivadar Popa (viola)
SLPX 11899

IVÁN SZÉKELY

(b. Budapest, 14 Febr. 1950.) He started studying music at the age of five and soon appeared at concerts. Subsequently he studied composition at the Béla Bartók Conservatory under Rezső Sugár, then at the Academy of Music under Ferenc Farkas. He attended several courses abroad, among others spent as holder of fellowship half a year in Warsaw. While cultivating passive and active forms of music making alike he is especially concerned with the theory and practice of some fields like the music of the Middle Ages, jazz, electro-acoustics as well as Hungarian and foreign folklore. He makes animation experiments with old and present-day music; leads courses, writes, gives lectures. Member of several international and national musical societies. At present he is professor at the Academy of Film and Dramatic Art in Budapest.

STAGE WORKS: *La guapa testaidua,* comedy with dance and music, 1972; *Pinocchio,* musical play for children, 1973; *Les trois mousquetaires,* musical chase in two parts, 1974; *A ballada folytatása* (The Ballad is Going On), dance play, 1975; *A három kövér* (The Three Fat Ones) musical play for children, 1977; *Electronic Ballet* (provisional title), 1978.

SYMPHONIC MUSIC: *Symphonic Music,* 1976.

SOLO AND CHAMBER MUSIC: *Piece for Clarinet,* 1971; *Lamento* (for piano),

1972; *Ballade, Virelai et Rondeau,* 1973; *Ballade, Virelai et Rondeau, avec interludes* (both: to Machaut's poems; Hungarian and original text versions), for soprano, viola, horn and flute, 1975; *Rondeau-Fragment,* for tenor, viola, horn and flute, 1971; *Görög ének* (Greek Song), Greek text for smaller mixed choir and percussion, 1976.

LIVE-ELECTRONIC MUSIC: *Variations on Themes of the Author's "Symphonic Music",* for violoncello, two pianos or piano duet and five electronic performers, 1974; *For Alrun* for female voice and a live-electronic performer, 1975; *"For Alrun's Reflection* (as above), 1978.

MUSIC FOR THEATRE (including separate instrumental, vocal and dance pieces): *among them: Alcestis, Hekabe, Electra, Troilus and Cressida, Thespis' Hand-Cart, Ivanov, Geschichten aus dem Wiener Wald*

OTHER WORKS: incidental music (incl. also silent films, songs, jazz compositions, treatments (early music; musical plays – incl. *Raisin* 1977), music for animated cartoons, musical radio-dramas (incl. *Amalfi* 1977), instrumentations and settings, open-air music experiments (incl. works for church-bells), acoustic experiments

WRITINGS: several studies and articles e.g. acoustics, electro-acoustics, musical animation

ISTVÁN SZELÉNYI

(b. Zólyom, 8 Aug. 1904; d. Budapest, 31 Jan. 1972.) He studied at the Academy of Music, Budapest with Zoltán Kodály (composition) and István Laub (piano). From 1926 to 1930 he taught at the Fodor Music School. In 1930—1932 he lived in Paris. In the period 1945 to 1949 he was professor at the National Conservatory and the State Musical High School, later he became the director of the High School. Between 1951 and 1956 he edited the periodical Új Zenei Szemle (New Musical Review). He was professor of theory and history of the musical styles at the Academy of Music, Budapest. He won the Erkel Prize in 1969.

STAGE WORKS: *A tékozló fiú* (The Prodigal Son), pantomime, 1931; *Babiloni vásár* (Fair at Babylon), pantomime, 1931.

WORKS FOR CHORUS AND ORCHESTRA: *Virata,* oratorio, 1935; *A gyász órájában* (In the Hour of Mourning), cantata, 1936; *Ádám indult el így* (Adam Set Out Thus), cantata, 1936; *Spartacus,* oratorio, 1960; *Tíz nap, amely megrengette a világot* (Ten Days That Shook the World), oratorio, 1964; *Pro Pace,* oratorio, 1968; Orchestral Songs.

ORCHESTRAL MUSIC: *Symphony No. 1,* 1926; *Ouverture activiste,* 1931; *Géptánc – Munkatánc* (Machine Dance – Work Dance), 1942; *Egy gyár szimfóniája*

(Symphony of a Factory), 1946; *Hommage à Bartók,* 1947, Arts Council, Leeds, New York; *Suite* for string orchestra, 1952; *Concerto da Camera,* 1963; *Dance Suite* for string orchestra, 1964.

CONCERTOS: *Concerto for Violin,* 1930; *Triple Concerto,* 1933; *Summa vitae* for piano and orchestra, 1956, EMB; *Concertino* for piano, 1964; *Variations concertants* for piano and orchestra, 1965; *Concerto for Piano,* 1969.

CHAMBER MUSIC: *Sonata* for flute and piano, 1926; *Piano Trio,* 1934; *Two Duets* for violin and violoncello; *Four String Quartets,* No. 1, 1927; No. 2, 1928; No. 3, 1929; No. 4, 1964, EMB; *Sonata* for four violins, 1946; *Piano Trio,* 1962, EMB; *Tre dialoghi,* for violin and violoncello, 1965; *Chamber Music* for brass winds, 1966, EMB, Schott; *Little Suite* for a choir of violins in four parts, 1963, EMB, Schott.

PIANO PIECES: *Seven Sonatas* VI: EMB; *Sonatina,* 1960, EMB; *Two Recitatives,* 1926, published by the composer; *Three Sketches,* 1926, published by the composer; *Forty Easy Piano Pieces,* 1957, EMB, BH; *Colorit* for piano duet, 1932, Hansen, Copenhagen; *Toccata,* 1964, EMB; *Musical Picture Book* for piano, 1967, EMB, Schott.

VIOLIN PIECES: *Solo Sonata* No. 1, 1925, EMB; *Solo Sonata* No. 2, 1934; *Improvisations,* 1946, R; *Twenty-four Small Pieces,* 1963, EMB, BH; *Eight Small Duets and Sonatina* for two violins, 1963, EMB, Schott, BH; *Sinfonietta a tre* for three violins, 1964, EMB, Schott, BH; *Children's World* on four strings, 1967, EMB, Schott.

Choral works, songs, pedagogical works.

WRITINGS: *Rendszeres modulációtan* (Methodic Theory of Modulation), 1927, 1960, Budapest; *A zenetörténet és bölcselettörténet kapcsolatai* (The Interrelations of the History of Music and the History of Philosophy), 1944, Budapest; *Liszt élete képekben* (Liszt's Life in Pictures), 1956, EMB; *A magyar zene története* (The History of Hungarian Music), 1959, EMB; *A romantikus zene harmóniavilága* (The Harmonic Realm of Romantic Music), 1965, EMB; *A népdalharmonizálás alapelvei* (Principles of Folk Song Harmonization), 1967, Tankönyvkiadó.

ENDRE SZERVÁNSZKY

(b. Kistétény, 27 Dec. 1911; d. Budapest, 25 June 1977.) Studied composition at the Academy of Music, Budapest, under Albert Siklós. From 1942 to 1948 he was teaching at the National Conservatory, from 1948 until the end of his life he was professor of composition at the Academy of Music. He was winner of the Erkel Prize in 1953 and 1954, and of the Kossuth Prize in 1951 and 1955. In 1972 he was awarded the title "Merited Artist of the Hungarian People's Republic" and in 1977 "Outstanding Artist of the Hungarian People's Republic".

STAGE WORKS: *Napkeleti mese* (Oriental Tale), dance play, 1948–49, EMB; *Vasból való vár* (The Iron Castle), musical play for children, 1950; *Az ezernevű lány* (The Girl of Thousand Names), musical play for children, 1962.

WORKS FOR CHORUS AND ORCHESTRA: *Honvéd Cantata,* 1949, EMB; *Tavaszi szél* (Spring Breeze), cantata, 1950; *Requiem,* 1963; *Az Éj* (The Night), cantata to a poem by Petőfi, 1974–75; *Folk Song Cantata,* 1975.

CHORAL WORKS: *Folk Song Suite* for male choir, 1947; *Three Petőfi Choruses* (Song of Dogs, River Flowed Over, Manacles) for mixed choir, 1953, EMB; *Three Male Choruses* to ancient Chinese poems (The Road, Village-sunset, Rain), 1958, EMB.

SYMPHONIC MUSIC: *Divertimento No. 1* for string orchestra, 1939, MK, EMB; *Divertimento No. 2,* 1942; *Divertimento No. 3* for string orchestra, 1943; *Suite,* 1945, MK; *Serenade* for string orchestra, 1947, Cs, EMB; *Symphony,* 1946–48; *Merry March,* 1949, EMB; *Rhapsody,* 1950, EMB; *Serenade for Clarinet,* 1950, EMB; *Concerto for Flute,* 1952–54, EMB; *Concerto* in memory of Attila József, 1954, EMB; *Six Orchestral Pieces,* 1959, EMB; *Concertino for Recorder,* 1961; *Variations for Orchestra,* 1964, EMB; *Concerto for Clarinet,* 1965, EMB.

CHAMBER MUSIC: *String Quartet No. 1,* 1936–37, Arts Council, EMB; *Twenty Small Duets* for two violins, 1941, Cs, EMB; *Sonata* for violin and piano, 1945, Arts Concil, EMB; *Eight Small Pieces* for violoncello and piano, 1945; *Twenty-five Duos* for two violins, 1946, EMB; *Trio* for oboe, clarinet and bassoon, 1950; *Trio* for flute, violin and viola, 1951, EMB; *Sonatina* for flute and piano, 1952, EMB; *Népdal-Vonósnégyes* (String Quartet on Hungarian Folk Songs), 1952; *Quintet for Wind Instruments No. 1,* 1953, EMB; *Two pieces* for two violins and piano on Lithuanian and Czech folk songs, 1953; *Ten Easy Pieces* for violin and piano, 1955, EMB; *Five Concert Etudes* for flute, 1956, EMB; *Suite* for two flutes, 1956, EMB; *Quintet for Wind Instruments No. 2,* 1957, EMB; *String Quartet No. 2,* 1956–57, EMB; *Two Duos* for flute, 1972, EMB; *Three Spiritual Songs* for soprano, flute and piano, 1972; *Seven Etudes* for flute, 1974–75.

PIANO PIECES: *Folk Song Suite* for piano duet, 1935, MK, EMB; *Small Suite,* 1939, MK; *Sonatina,* 1940, Cs, EMB; *Seven Jewish Folk Songs,* 1945–46; *Sonatina* for piano duet, 1950, EMB.

SONGS: *Eight Petőfi Songs* for voice and piano, 1951 EMB; *Three Songs* for voice and piano to poems by Á. Tóth and Gy. Juhász, 1956–57, EMB; *Búsulnak a virágok* (Grieving Flowers) for soprano solo and orchestra, 1957; *Six solfeggios* for voice with piano accompaniment, 1957–58.

Incidental music to theatre and radio plays: Shakespeare's Macbeth, Zrinyi's Szigeti Veszedelem (Thre Disaster at Sziget Castle), Racine's Berenice, Calevala; incidental music to several films; minor divertimentos for orchestra and string orchestra; folk song arrangements for male, female and mixed choruses; studies and educational music for voice, piano, violin and wind instruments; orchestrations and instrumentations for works by Frescobaldi, Mozart, Moussorgsky and Bartók.

DISCOGRAPHY:
Concerto in memory of Attila József
Hungarian State Concert Orchestra, conductor: Gyula Borbély
LPX 1213

Serenade for Clarinet – Song of Dogs – Concerto for Clarinet – Variations for Orchestra
Béla Kovács (clarinet)
Orchestra of the Hungarian Radio and Television, Mixed Choir of Veszprém City
Conductors: Ádám Medveczky, István Zámbó
SLPX 11716

SÁNDOR SZOKOLAY

(b. Kunágota, 30 March 1931.) He received his first musical education at the music school of Békéstarhos, then continued at the Academy of Music, Budapest, studying composition under Ferenc Szabó, later under Ferenc Farkas. From 1951 to 1957 he was teaching solfeggio at the Municipal Music School Organization. From 1957 to 1961 he was employed at the Music Department of the Hungarian Radio. Since then he has devoted himself to composition. Since 1966 he has taught at the Ferenc Liszt Academy of Music in Budapest (prosody, composition, counterpoint); since 1977, he has acted as music advisor to Hungarian Television. He was prize winner of the Composers' Section at the Wieniawski Competition in 1956 and of the World Youth Festival in 1955, 1957 and 1959. He was awarded the Erkel Prize in 1960 and 1965, the Kossuth Prize in 1966. In 1976 the title "Merited Artist of the Hungarian People's Republic" was conferred on him.

STAGE WORKS *Orbán és az ördög* (Urban and the Devil), ballet, 1958; *Az iszonyat balladája* (The Ballad of Horror), ballet, 1960; *Vérnász* (Blood Wedding), opera, 1962–64, Artisjus, Budapest; *Hamlet,* opera, 1966–68, Artisjus, Budapest; *Sámson,* opera, 1973; *Az áldozat* (The Victim), one-act oratoric ballet, first performed at the Budapest State Opera House in 1971; *Csalóka Péter* (Delusive Peter), tale-opera in one act to a libretto by Sándor Weöres, first performed and relayed by the Hungarian Radio in 1978.

WORKS FOR CHORUS AND ORCHESTRA: *Karácsonyi dalok* (Christmas Songs), 1955; *Vízimesék* (Children's cantata), 1957; *Mesteremberek* (Artisans), 1958; *A tűz márciusa* (Fiery March), oratorio, 1958; *Világok vetélkedése* (Rivalry of Worlds), cantata, 1959; *Istár pokoljárása* (Isthar's Descent to Hell), oratorio, 1960; *Néger kantáta* (Negro cantata), 1962, L; *Déploration* in memory of F. Poulenc, 1964; *Révélation,* to a poem by A. Musset, 1966, L; *A zene hatalma* (The Power of Music), chorus fantasy for mixed choir, children's choir and orchestra, to poems by M. Babits, 1969; *Musza Dag,* oratorical incidental music to Werfel's Musa Dagh, for mixed choir and orchestra, 1969; *Hungarian Choral Symphony* to poems by E. Ady, 1970; *Vitézi ének* (Song of Heroes), to a poem by B. Balassi, cantata, 1970; *Christmas Pastorale* to biblical texts, cantata, 1970; *Whitsun Song* after biblical texts, cantata, 1972; *Apocalypse Cantata* inspired by Dürer's woodcuts, to biblical texts, cantata, 1971; *Ancient Song,* cantata to poems by I. Csanády, 1971; *Hommage à Kodály,* cantata to poem by Gy. Illyés, 1975; *Musica Notturna,* cantata for female voices, to poems by M. Babits, 1975; *Cantata in Memory of the Galley-Slaves* (to codex texts), 1975; *Ady Cantata,* 1975–76.

CHORAL WORKS: *Two Ballads* for mixed choir, two pianos and percussion, 1957, EMB; *Two Motets,* 1962; *Musica Notturna* for female voices, to poems by M. Babits, 1975; *Three Epigrams to poems by J. Pannonius,* 1976; *Hymn Fragment,* to a poem by F. Juhász, for mixed voices, 1976; *Aphorisms to One-Line Poems* by S. Weöres, for mixed voices, 1977; *Ten Attila József Fragments* for mixed voices, 1978; *A zengő csuda-erdő balladája* (The Ballad of the Ringing Miraculous Forest), after folk texts, for mixed voices, 1978; children's choruses, mass songs.

CONCERTOS: *Concert Rondo* for piano and string orchestra, 1955; *Concerto* for violin, 1956; *Concerto* for piano, 1958, transcribed: 1960, EMB; *Concerto* for trumpet, 1969.

CHAMBER MUSIC: *String Quartet,* 1973; *Sestetto d'ottoni,* 1975; *Dirge and Cult Dance* for cimbalom and chamber ensemble, 1974; *Miniatures* for brass sextet, 1976; *Alliterations* for brass quintet, 1976; *A Minden-Titkok Titka* (The Secret of All Secrets), solo cantata to poems by E. Ady, for soprano solo and chamber ensemble, 1976.

INSTRUMENTAL MUSIC: *Three Piano Pieces,* 1949; *Tréfás szvit* (Jolly Suite), for piano, 1953; *Children's Miniatures* for piano, 1954; *Sonatina* for piano, 1955; *Sonata* for violin solo, 1956, EMB; *Small suite for Children,* for violoncello and piano, 1959, EMB; *Portraits* for piano, 1975; *Flute Solo Sonata,* 1976; *Organ Fantasia for Two Performers,* 1976; *Miniatures* for organ, 1976; *Al fresco,* five organ pieces, 1976; *Lamenti* for cimbalom solo, 1976.

SONGS: *Indian songs* for soprano and chamber ensemble, 1960; *Three Miniature Ballads* for soprano and chamber ensemble, 1960; *Dalok imádság helyett* (Songs in Place of Pràyer) for soprano solo and piano, to poems by L. Nagy, 1974; *Anacreontic Songs,* 1976.

Incidental music to films, theatre and radio plays, educational music.

DISCOGRAPHY:
Nocturne and Capriccio
Ferenc Ferencsér, József Szalay (cimbalom)
LPX 1306

Gipsy Suite
Choir and Orchestra of the Hungarian State Folk Ensemble
LPX 1281

Blood Wedding (Opera in three acts)
Erzsébet Komlóssy, Ferenc Szőnyi, András Faragó, Stefánia Moldován, Erzsébet Házy, Sándor Palcsó, Zsuzsa Barlay (soloists)
Children's Choir of the Hungarian Radio and Television, Choir and Orchestra of the Hungarian State Opera House, conductor: András Kórodi
LPX 1262/3

ANDRÁS SZŐLLŐSY

(b. Transylvania, 27 Febr. 1921.) He studied composition at the Academy of Music, Budapest under Zoltán Kodály and János Viski, later at the Accademia di Santa Cecilia in Rome with Goffredo Petrassi. Simultaneously with his musical studies he took also his Doctor's degree in philosophy. Since 1950 he has been teaching history and theory of music at the Academy of Music.

STAGE WORKS: *Oly korban éltem* (Improvisations on the Fear), ballet, 1963; *Pantomime* – ballet, 1965; *A tűz fiai* (Sons of Fire), ballet, 1977.

VOCAL MUSIC: *Nyugtalan ősz* (Restless Autumn), cantata for baritone solo with piano accompaniment, 1955, EMB; *Kolozsvári éjjel* (Night at Kolozsvár), elegy for voice and wind quintet, 1955.

ORCHESTRAL MUSIC: *Concerto* No. 1 for strings, brass instruments, piano and percussion, 1957; *Concerto* No. 3 for sixteen strings, 1968, EMB; *Concerto* No. 4 for small orchestra, 1970, EMB; *Trasfigurazioni* for orchestra, 1972, EMB; *Musica per orchestra,* 1972, EMB; *Musica concertante* for small orchestra, 1973, EMB; *Preludio, Adagio e Fuga* for orchestra, 1973, EMB; *Sonorità* for orchestra, 1974, EMB; *Lehellet* (Concerto No. 5) for orchestra, 1975, EMB; *Concerto per clavicembalo ed archi,* 1978, EMB.

INSTRUMENTAL PIECES: *Tre pezzi per flauto e pianoforte,* 1964, EMB; *Musiche per ottoni,* 1975, EMB.

Choral works, songs, incidental music to plays and films.

WRITINGS: *Kodály művészete* (Kodály's Art), Budapest, 1943; *Bartók Béla válogatott zenei írásaì* (Selected Musical Writings of Béla Bartók), Budapest, 1948; *Bartók Béla válogatott írásai* (Selected Writings of Béla Bartók), Budapestg, 1956; *Arthur Honegger,* Budapest, 1960; *Bartók Béla összegyűjtött írásai I.* (Collected Writings of Béla Bartók, I), 1967, EMB.

DISCOGRAPHY:
Concerto No. 3 – Concerto No. 4
Ferenc Liszt Chamber Orchestra, Győr Philharmonic Orchestra
conductors: Frigyes Sándor, János Sándor
LPX 11525

Trasfigurazioni; Musica per orchestra
Orchestra of the Hungarian Radio and Television,
conductor: György Lehel
SLPX 11733

Sonorità; Lehellet (Concerto No. 5); Tre pezzi per flauto e pianoforte; Musica concertante
Budapest Symphony Orchestra, conductor: György Lehel
Budapest Chamber Ensemble, conductor: András Mihály
Severius Gazzelloni, András Schiff
SLPX 11805

ERZSÉBET SZŐNYI

(b. Budapest, 25 Apr. 1924.) She studied composition with János Viski and piano at the Academy of Music, Budapest, where she obtained a teacher's diploma in singing for secondary schools. In 1947 she studied in Paris with Tony Aubin, Olivier Messiaen and Nadia Boulanger. She was awarded Prix de Composition at Conservatoire de Paris in 1948. Since 1948 she has been professor of solfeggio and theory at the Academy of Music. Since 1960 head at the Department for Teacher Training and Choir Conducting. She worked in close cooperation with Prof. Zoltán Kodály, and played an important part in implementing Kodály's ideas for music education in Hungarian schools and abroad. In 1964 she became member of the Board of Directors of the International Society of Music Education (ISME), where she held the post of vice president in 1970–74. She was awarded the Erkel Prize in 1959.

STAGE WORKS: *Dalma,* opera, 1952; *Makrancos királylány* (The Stubborn Princess), children's opera, 1955, Artisjus; *Firenzei tragédia* (Florentine Tragedy), one-act opera, 1957; *Képzelt beteg* (The Hypochondriac), musical comedy, 1961; *Kis rongyos* (The Small Ragged One), musical play, 1962; *100 cifra ködmön* (A Hundred Fancy Jerkins), musical comedy, 1965; *Az aranyszárnyú méhecske* (The Little Bee with the Golden Wing), children's one-act opera, 1974.

WORKS FOR CHORUS AND ORCHESTRA: *A didergő király* (The Shĭvering King), children's oratorio, 1959, EMB; *A hazug katona* (The Mendacious Soldier), oratorio, 1960; *Tinódi egri summája* (Tinódi's Song about Eger), youth oratorio, 1963, EMB; *Cantata Attila József,* 1968; *Cantata Miklós Radnóti,* 1975.

VOCAL COMPOSITIONS: Choral works, among them: *Új várak épültek* (New Forts Have Been Built), 1947, Cs, Workers' Music Association, London; *Balatoni képek* (Sketches of Lake Balaton), 1953, EMB; *Canticum Sponsae,* 1956, L; *Two Sonnets by Petrarca* with harp and clarinet accompaniment, 1960, EMB; *Lament,* 1967, EMB; *Thirty-three Light Small Choruses,* 1967, EMB; *Anacreon,* 1969, EMB; *Two Mixed Choruses* (Poem by L. Benjámin), 1970; *Japanese Songs* (Sai-gyo, Niko Horiguchi, Tsa-ra-yu-ki, Ishikawa, translation by D. Kosztolányi), 1970, NPI, EMB; *Fifty Bicinia* to Japanese, American and Canadian folk songs, 1971, EMB; *Something has Spoken to Me in the Night* (Poem by Th. Wolfe), for mixed choir, 1972; *The Ink-Bottle* (Poem by S. Petőfi), for children's choir, 1970, EMB; *Holiday-Song* (Poem by L. Szabó), for children's choir, 1970, EMB; *Running to the Meadow* (Poem by G. Devecseri), for mixed choir, 1970, EMB; *For St.Dominic's Day* (Poem by J. Arany), canon for children'choir, 1970, EMB; *Sicut Cervus* for male choir, 1976, Ed. Arezzo International Choir Festival; *Ad Aristium Fuscum,* Ode by Horace for soprano or tenor, two pianos and percussion, 1965.

ORCHESTRAL MUSIC: *Parlando and giusto,* 1947, Artisjus; *Divertimento No. 1,* 1948; *Divertimento No. 2,* 1951, EMB; *Musica festiva,* 1964, EMB; *Prelude and Fugue,* 1969; *Allegro,* 1969, EMB + BH.

CONCERTOS: *Concerto for Organ,* 1958, EMB; *Trio Concertino,* pedagogical work, 1958, EMB.

CHAMBER MUSIC: *21 énekesjáték* (Twenty-one Vocal Plays), for two sopranos and chamber ensemble, 1948, MK; *Duet* for violin and viola, 1955, EMB; *Trio* for wind instruments, 1958, EMB + BH; *Youth Piano Trio,* 1962, EMB; *Trio Sonata,* 1964, EMB + BH.

INSTRUMENTAL PIECES: *Two Piano Sonatinas,* 1944, 1946; *Play,* for piano duet, 1946; *Colours* suite for piano, 1947; *Five Songs* for violin and piano, 1948; *Fantasy and Fugue* for piano, 1948; *Piano Sonata,* 1953; *Air* for violin and piano, 1954, EMB; *Six Organ Pieces,* 1955, EMB; *Serenade and Dance at Dawn* for violin and piano, 1954, EMB; *Play* for violoncello and piano, 1954, EMB; *Prelude* for violin and piano, 1958; *Five Preludes* for piano, 1963, EMB; *Sonatina* for violin and piano, 1963, EMB; *Introduction, Passacaglia and Fugue* for organ, 1965, EMB.

WRITINGS: *A zenei írás-olvasás módszertana* I, II, III (Musical Reading and Writing I, II, III), 1954, EMB, in English: BH, 1972, in Japanese: Zen-On, 1971; *A zenei írás-olvasás módszertana* IV. La formation musicale par l'éducation de l'oreille, 1965, Éditions Beauchemin, Montréal; *Kodály's Principles in Practice,* 1973, Corvina, Budapest + BH, Diesterweg, (in English, French, German, Spanish, Japanese, Russian); *Sol-Fa Teaching in Musical Education* (in Musical Education in Hungary, edited by Frigyes Sándor), EMB, Corvina, Budapest (in English, German, Japanese,

French, Russian, Hebraic). *Musical Education for Children from the Age of Three to Ten in Hungary,* 1968, Panton Ed. Prague; *Utazások öt kontinensen* (Travels to five Continents), 1978, Gondolat.

DISCOGRAPHY:
Six Pieces for Organ (Praeambulum, Flying Harmonies, Quasi Dance)
Sebestyén Pécsi (organ)
LPX 1222

Piccola Ouvertura
Orchestra of the Budapest Municipal Music School,
conductor: Margit Kutassy
LPX 1188

concerto for Organ
Gábor Lehotka (organ)
Hungarian State Orchestra, conductor: Gyula Németh
SLPX 11808

Six Pieces for Organ
Sebestyén Pécsi (organ)
"Da camera" Schallplattenedition SM 93267

BALÁZS SZUNYOGH

(b. Budapest, 5 Febr. 1954.) He started his musical studies with piano then he continued to study composition at the Béla Bartók Conservatory under József Soproni from 1968–72. From 1972 to 1977 he attended the Academy of Music, Budapest where his professor for composition was Emil Petrovics and his studies for chamber music were with György Kurtág. At present he teaches chamber music at the Academy of Music and acts as an assistant professor for composition.

In 1973 he won the first prize at the composers' competition held at the Academy to commemorate the Petőfi anniversary. In 1974 the prize founded by Renée Zippser for young composers was conferred on him. In 1975 he won first prize in the contest of composers organised on the occasion of the centenary of foundation of the Academy of Music. In 1976 won second prize in the artistic category of the *Creative Youth* contest organized by the Ministry of Cultural Affairs, and in 1977 he was awarded the prize founded by Albert Szirmai for composer graduates of the Academy of Music.

PIANO WORKS: *Three Piano Pieces,* 1972; *Prelude for Piano,* 1974; *Hommage à Stravinsky,* 1975.

VIOLIN MUSIC: *Three Movements for Solo Violin,* 1977–78.

CHAMBER MUSIC: *Six Pieces* for flute and piano, 1971–72; *Four Duos* for cello and piano, 1976, EMB 1977; *Variations* for chamber ensemble, 1976–77.

VOCAL MUSIC: *Two Songs* to poems by S. Petőfi, 1973; *Kalendárium* (Calendar), a song cycle to poems by S. Weöres and A. Károlyi, 1975, EMB 1977; *Keserédes* (Bittersweet), a cantata to poems by M. Radnóti, 1977–78.

BÉLA TARDOS

(b. Budapest, 21 June 1910; d. 18 Nov. 1966.) He studied composition at the Academy of Music, Budapest as a pupil of Zoltán Kodály. Up to 1945 he was conducting worker's choruses, later he was musical editor of Szikra Publishing House, then director general of the National Philharmony Concert Bureau. From 1955 to his death he was director of Editio Musica, Budapest. He was prize-winner at the Béla Bartók Competition for Composers in 1948, and was awarded the Erkel Prize in 1960 and 1966.

STAGE WORK: *Laura,* opera, 1958, revised: 1964, Artisjus.

WORKS FOR CHORUS AND ORCHESTRA: *Májusi kantáta* (May Cantata), 1950; *A város peremén* (At the Outskirts of the City), cantata, 1958, EMB; *Dózsa feje* (Dózsa's Head), 1958, EMB; *Szabadság született* (Liberty has been Born), 1960; *Az új Isten* (The New God), cantata after A. Tóth's poem, 1966.

ORCHESTRAL MUSIC: *Overture,* 1949; *Suite,* 1950; *Mesejáték – nyitány* (Overture to a Fairy Tale), 1955; *Symphony,* 1960, EMB; *Evocatio,* 1964, EMB.

CONCERTOS: *Concerto for Piano,* 1954, Mills, London; *Fantasy* for piano and orchestra, 1961, EMB; *Concerto for Violin,* 1962, EMB.

CHAMBER MUSIC: *Octet* for wind instruments, 1935; *Piano Quartet,* 1941; *String Quartet* No. 1, 1947, EMB; *String Quartet* No. 2, 1949; *String Quartet* No. 3, 1963,

196

EMB; *Quartettino, Divertimento* for quartet of wind instruments, 1963; *Cassazione* for harp trio, 1964; *Sonata* for violin and piano, 1965, EMB.

INSTRUMENTAL MUSIC:

PIANO: *Five Bagatelles,* 1955, EMB; *Szivárvány* (Rainbow), seven small pieces, 1957, EMB, BH; *Two Small Pieces,* 1960, EMB; *Miniatures,* 1961, EMB; *Suite,* 1961, EMB; *Sonatina,* 1961, EMB + BH; *Six Small Studies,* 1963.

OTHER INSTRUMENTS: *Improvisations* for clarinet and piano, 1960, EMB; *Prelude and Rondo* for flute and piano, 1962, EMB, BH.

Songs, choral works—without or with accompaniment—among them: *Muzsikásláda* (Music Box), 1954, BH; *Keserű esztendők* (Hard Years), 1959, author; *Five Michelangelo-Sonnets,* 1966; mass songs, educational music, incidental music to plays and films.

DISCOGRAPHY:

Evocatio
Hungarian State Concert Orchestra, conductor: Miklós Erdélyi
LPX 1297

Hard Years (Suite)
Choir of the Hungarian Radio and Television, conductor: Zoltán Vásárhelyi
LPX 11330

The New God
György Radnai (baritone)
Budapest Choir, Hungarian State Concert Orchestra, conductor: Miklós Erdélyi
LPX 11352

Divertimento for Wood-wind Instruments – Sonata for Violin and Piano – String Quartet No. 3 – Five Bagatelles for Piano
Zoltán Jeney (flute), Tibor Szeszler (oboe), Ferenc Meizl (clarinet), László Hara (bassoon), André Gertler (violin), Diane Andersen, Dezső Ránki (piano)
Tátrai String Quartet
LPX 11487

JÁNOS VAJDA

(b. Miskolc, 8 Oct. 1949.) He studied composition under Emil Petrovics and graduated in 1975.

His opera *Barabbas* was first performed by the Hungarian Television in 1977; it was awarded a quality prize, and the special prize of the international jury at the Salzburg Television Opera Festival. His chamber music works and the choral work *Black Glory* have been performed by the Hungarian Radio and also included in concert programmes. In 1974 he was awarded the Albert Szirmai Prize, and in 1977 the René Zippser Prize.

STAGE WORK: *Barabbas,* one-act opera, 1976.

SYMPHONIC WORKS: *Musica Antiqua 1—2,* 1974–76.

CHAMBER MUSIC AND VOCAL CHAMBER MUSIC: *Brass Suite,* 1975; *Two Tests,* 1976, EMB; *Three Duets* to poems by L. Kassák, 1975; *Chanson Royal* in memory of Machaut, 1977.

CHORAL WORKS: *Tenebrae factae sunt* for mixed choir, 1972; *Six Little Madrigals* to poems by Miklós Radnóti, 1974; *Fekete Glória* (Black Glory) to poem by L. Nagy, 1977, EMB.

ISTVÁN VÁNTUS

(b. Vaja, 1935.) He started studying music in the music department of the Grammar School of Debrecen Reformed College, and went on to study composition at the Conservatory of Debrecen under Emil Szabó. He graduated in composition from the Academy of Music, Budapest as a pupil of Ferenc szabó in 1960. He lives in Szeged. He first joined the staff of the Szeged Conservatory, then became assistant professor at the Szeged Faculty of the Ferenc Liszt Academy of Music, a post which he also holds at present. In addition to his activities as composer and teacher he has given performances to several outstanding early works using his own instrumentation (Monteverdi's *Orfeo;* Bach's *Art of Fugue;* Bach's *Musical Offering*). His artistic awards include the prize given to creative artists by the city of Szeged (1967, 1975) and the Erkel Prize (1976).

STAGE WORKS: *A három vándor* (The Three Wanderers), one-act opera after an Old Indian-Persian tale, libretto by I. Cserhalmi: first performed at the National Theatre, Szeged, 1967; *Aranykoporsó* (Golden Coffin), opera in three acts based on the novel by Ferenc Móra: first performed at National Theatre, Szeged, 1975. It was also given performance during the Budapest Art Weeks in 1976.

CHORAL WORKS: *Madrigal* for female choir, 1960; *Jöjj, vihar!* (Come, Tempest!) for mixed voices (Poem by Á. Tóth), 1961; *Jön a vonat* (The Train is Coming) for mixed voices (Poem by Gy. Juhász), 1962; *Vörös szekér a tengeren* (Red Cart on the Sea) for mixed voices, to a poem by E. Ady, 1963; *A bánat* (Grief) for female choir (Poem by A. József), 1964; *Testament* for mixed voices (Poem by Gy. Juhász), 1967; *Inventio poetica* for double choir (Poem by B. Balassi), 1975, EMB; *Tűz* (Fire) for male choir, to a poem by L. Nagy, 1977.

SONGS: *Két őszi dal* (Two Autumn Songs) for mezzosoprano and piano, to poems by F. Lődi, 1961; *Kvá király szerelme* (King Kva's Love) for baritone and piano, to a poem by F. Németh, 1964; *Coolie* for brass and piano, to a poem by S. Weöres, 1969.

CANTATAS: *Vadrózsák* (Wild Roses) for female choir and orchestra, to folk texts, 1958; *Himnusz az emberhez* (Hymn to Man) for mixed voices and orchestra, to a poem by Gy. Juhász, 1970.

CHAMBER WORKS: *Children's Music* for flute, violins, cello and piano, 1958; *Parabola* for cello and piano, 1960; *Suite for Solo Violin,* 1961, EMB; *Rézdomborítás* (Brass Embossing) for trumpets, trombones and cymbals, 1969; *Burlesca* for trumpets, bassoon, double bass and percussion, 1970; *Dithyrambs* for piano, 1976.

ORCHESTRAL WORKS: *Musica terrena* for organ and full orchestra, 1960; *Elegy* for full orchestra, 1961; *Visszaverődések* (Reverberations) for chamber orchestra, 1976, EMB; *Naenia* for string orchestra, 1977.

FERENC VÁRY

(b. Gyula, 29 Nov. 1928.) He studied composition at the Academy of Music, as a pupil of Ferenc Szabó. Since 1960 he has been professor at the Béla Bartók Conservatory, Budapest. In 1957 he won a Gold Medal at the Composer's Competition at Vercelli, was prize-winner at the World Youth Festival in 1957, and was awarded the Erkel Prize in 1958.

STAGE WORKS: *Tékozló fiatalok* (The Prodigal Young), musical play, 1955; *Eve, The Mannequin,* musical, 1963; *Lysistrate,* ballet, 1963; *Mese a tűzpiros virágról* (Tale about the Fire-Red flower), musical, 1965; *Macskazene* (Catcall), allegorical musical, 1969.

MUSIC TO FAIRY TALES: *Sündisznócska lovagol* (The Little Hedgehog Rides), 1958; *Toppantó királykisasszony* (The Stamping Princess), 1958; *A húsvéti tojások* (Easter Eggs), 1958; *Philemon és Baucis* (Philemon and Baucis), 1959; *Boncidai kalamajka* (Tizzy at Boncida), 1964; *Jácint úrfi* (Master Jácint), 1966; *Hétszínpiros ünneplő* (Holiday Attire of Seven Red Colours), 1972; *Buci királyfi* (Prince Buci), 1972.

CHORAL WORKS: *Csikós Dani* (Danny Rider), 1953, EMB; *Chorus Suite,* 1958, EMB; *Ten Choruses* for equal voices, 1958; *A csillagok csillaga* (The Star of Stars),

1959; *Cinege-csacsogás* (Twittering), 1964; *Az elűzött könnyek* (Tears Driven Away), 1964; *Kórusballada* (Chorus Ballad), for mixed choir, with piano accompaniment, 1968; *Suite* (Poem by O. Demény), in seven movements, 1971, EMB; *Madrigali di Alberi e di Fiori* (Poem by Á. Dutka), for mixed choir in eight movements, 1972.

ORCHESTRAL MUSIC: *Symphony No. 1*, 1951–55; *A gyulai vár regéje* (The Legend of the Fortress at Gyula), 1957; *Május* (May), rhapsody, 1958; *Hommage à Bihari* for two flutes, clarinet, kettle drum and string orchestra, 1976, EMB.

INSTRUMENTAL MUSIC: *Pezzi scelti* per due trombe, 1972, EMB; *Conversazione* per clarinetto, viola e pianoforte, 1976.

·SONGS: *Rózsadalok* (Rose Songs), 1955; *Bóbita* (Bow), 1957, EMB; *Dalok messzi tájakról* (Songs from Far Away Regions), 1957, EMB; *Ballad*, 1960; *Könyörgés Budapestért* (Prayer for Budapest), for soprano solo, with piano accompaniment, to a poem by L. Gereblyés, 1969.

LAJOS VASS

(b. Poroszló, 5 Apr. 1927.) He studied composition at the Academy of Music, Budapest, as a pupil of Sándor Veress and Ferenc Farkas. During his studies he was conductor of several choirs, from 1949 to 1957 he was conductor of the Male Choir of the Army Ensemble, of which he was also artistic director for some time. From 1957 to 1958 he was conductor of the State Male Choir. Since 1960 he has been leader of several choirs, including the mixed choir of the Central Art Ensemble of the Iron Workers' Trade Union. He was awarded the Erkel Prize in 1952.

STAGE WORKS: *A kiskakas gyémánt félkrajcárja* (Diamond Half Penny of the Little Cock), opera for children, 1960; *Lúdas Matyi* (Matty the Gooseboy), music to a drama, 1972; *Babszemjankó* (Tom Thumb) 1973; *A kismalac és a farkasok* (The Little Pig and the Wolves), 1974; *Terülj, terülj asztalkám!* (Magic Table), 1976; *Csacsi történet* (Silly Story), 1977, Children's operas; *Világszépe* (World's Beauty), 1972; *Rózsa and Ibolya,* 1977, Puppet theatre incidental music.

WORKS FOR CHORUS AND ORCHESTRA: *Mese az esztendőről* (Tale About the Year), oratorio, 1959; *A fény köszöntése* (To Light), 1960; *Vasmunkások dicsérete* (Praise of the Iron Workers) 1962; *Requiem a hősök emlékére* (Requiem in Memory of the Heroes), 1963; *Matthias Rex,* oratorio for solo voices, narrators, mixed and children's choirs, symphonic orchestra, 1971; *Risponde la notte,* madrigal to poems by Strozzi and Michelangelo, 1962; *Firenze* for female or male choir in three parts, to poem by D. Campana, 1966, NPI; *Borúra derű* (After Rain Comes Sunshine), 1970, EMB; *Rózsa, szőlő, eső, majoránna* (Rose, Grape, Rain, Majorine), 1972, NPI; *Music of the Bodrogköz,* folk-song suite in 5 movements for mixed choir and symphony orchesra, 1978.

CHORAL WORKS: *Három betyár* (Three Outlaws), 1956, EMB; *Nocturne,* 1969, EMB; *Varázsének* (Magic Song), 1969, EMB; *Az esztendő* (The Year), twelve choruses for children's or female choir, 1969, EMB; *De summo bono,* cantata to a text by Albert Szenczi Molnár, for mixed choir, tenor solo and organ, 1974; *Furor bestiae,* cantata in memory of the release of the galley-slaves, for mixed choir and organ, 1975.

ORCHESTRAL MUSIC: *Sinfonietta,* 1949; *Este a táborban* (Evening in the Camp), 1951; *Partita,* 1954; *Tre fantasie libere,* 1960; *Diákélet* (Students' Life), 1961; *Partita concertante,* 1968.

INSTRUMENTAL PIECES: *Prelude and Fugue* for piano, 1958; *Toccata* for cimbalom (dulcimer), 1958; *Suite per 2 clarinetti,* 1967.

SONGS: *Egy gondolat bánt engemet* (One Thought Torments Me), 1952; *Két fonódal* (Two Spinning Songs), 1955, EMB; *Lebegő táj* (Floating Landscape), 1963, EMB; *Fehér liliomszál* (White Lily), four children's songs for soprano solo and chamber ensemble, 1971; *Mit játsszunk, lányok?* (What Shall We Play, Girls?), four children's songs for soprano solo and chamber ensemble, 1971.

BÉLA VAVRINECZ

(b. Budapest, 18 Nov. 1925.) At the Academy of Music, Budapest, he studied under Rezső Kókai (composition), János Ferencsik and László Somogyi (conducting). He was artistic director of various folk ensembles. From 1957 to 1958 he was conductor of the Philharmonic Orchestra at Győr. From 1961 to 1973 he was the principal conductor of the Symphony Orchestra of the Ministry of Home Affairs, and since 1974 the musical leader of the Budapest Dance Ensemble. He was prize winner at the World Youth Festival in 1957.

STAGE WORKS: *Magyar képeskönyv* (Hungarian Picture Book), ballet, 1952; *Szivárvány havasán* (In the Snow-Capped Rainbow Mountains), ballet, 1965; *Dance Rhapsody,* ballet, 1965; *Mese* (Tale), ballet, 1966; *Az ördög nem alszik* (You Can Never Be Too Careful), ballet, 1966; *Élet-szerelem* (Love of Life), ballet, 1966; *A zsák* (The Bag), ballet, 1967; *Üzenet* (Message), ballet, 1967; *Ballada a szerelemről* (Ballad of Love), ballet, 1968; *Örvény* (Whirlpool), ballet, 1967; *A nagyidai cigányok* (Gypsies from Nagyida), ballet, 1968; *Erzsi Szöllősi,* dance ballad, 1976; *Fölmelegít a láng* (Flame Warms Up), in memory of Petőfi, ballet, 1977; *Szüret* (Vintage), ballet in two acts, 1977.

INCIDENTAL MUSIC: *Varázslámpa* (Magic Lamp), (Egerszegi), 1951; *Aranylako-dalom* (Golden Wedding), (Örsi), 1962; *Jones császár* (Emperor Jones), (O'Neill), 1968; *Faluvégen* (At the End of the Village), incidental music to a television play, 1968; *Four One-Act Folk Song Plays,* 1969.

WORKS FOR CHORUS AND ORCHESTRA: *Honvédeskü* (Soldier's Oath), canta-ta, 1950; *Széles a Balaton* (Wide Waters of Balaton), poem by S. Weöres, 1959; *In 1848,* 1959; *A kisdobos* (The Drummer-Boy), 1955; *Ünnepi bokréta* (Festive Bouquet), 1960; *Emlékezz!* (Remember!), 1962; *Harc és győzelem* (Fight and Victory), dramatic cantata, 1963; *Visszapillantás* (In Retrospect), chamber oratorio, 1965; *Véreink* (Our Bloods), dramatic cantata, 1969; *Kata Kádár,* stage oratorio, 1976.

ORCHESTRAL MUSIC: *Suite* No. 1, 1950; *Symphony,* 1955; *Two Orchestral Pieces,* 1955; *Andrew Overture,* 1957; *Considerazioni,* 1959; *Passacaglia,* 1962; *Festive Music,* 1964; *Dance Suite,* 1964; *Concert Rhapsody* for violin and orchestra, 1966; *Variazioni per '19,* 1968; *Concert Variations* for cimbalom and chamber ensemble, 1953–71; *A nagyidai cigányok* (Gypsies from Nagyida), overture, 1971; *Symphony,* 1955 (rev. 1973); Liszt: *Csárdás macabre* (arrang.), 1972; *Hajsza* (Chase) for chamber orchestra, 1976; *Three Orchestral Songs,* 1974.

CHAMBER MUSIC: *Scherzo* for violin and piano, 1947; *Rhapsody No. 1,* for violin and piano, 1958; *20 Duos for Shepherd's Pipe (Flute) and Cimbalom,* 1967; *Duo concertante* for violoncello and cimbalom, 1970; *Three Pieces for two Cimbaloms,* 1971; *Ten Háfiz-gházál* (translated by G. Képes), for solo voice and chamber ensemble, 1973; *Gyermekjátékdalok* (Songs for Children's Games), trio for flute, violoncello and cimbalom, 1973; *Three Songs,* to poems by K. Bejatli, G. Eminescu and B. Michelangelo, for voice and piano, 1973; *Swineherd's Dance* for cimbalom and chamber orchestra, 1973; *Dirge* for cimbalom, 1976.

CHORAL WORKS: *Bagpipe Songs,* 1950, EMB; *Széles a Balaton* (Wide Waters of Balaton), 1951, EMB; *Julcsa Varga,* 1951; *Ha kérdez a gyermek* (When the Child Asks), (words by Zs. Gál), 1960; *Balatonparton* (On the Shores of Balaton), (words by Gy. Takáts), 1974; *Four Folk-Songs of Szebény,* 1975.

Numerous folk song arrangements and other pieces for folk ensembles, for sym-phonic or popular orchestra, with or without chorus; music to dance play for folk en-sembles, songs, choral works, arrangements for popular orchestra.

DISCOGRAPHY:
Old Verbunk from the Ipoly Region
Orchestra of the Hungarian State Folk Ensemble, conductor: Gábor Baross
IPX 1028

Girl's Dance of Tardona
Choir and Orchestra of the Hungarian State Folk Ensemble
conductor: Gábor Baross
HIP NK 1530/a, Audio-International Air 204.
SLPX 18020

Sárköz, Székely, Békés, Somogy, Csongrád, Kunság, Csángó and Palots Folk-Songs
Éva Kürthy, Erzsi Török, Imre Bojtor, Sándor Tekeres (soloists), Duna Art Ensemble
Orchestra, conductor: Béla Vavrinecz
SLPX 1114; WST 17.008; L XWN 19.008.

*Hungarian Picture-Book; Wide Waters of Balaton; Rhapsody No. 1; Verbunk and
Csárdás of Kapuvár; Transdanubian Leaping Dance; Pictures of the Mezőség*
Mátyás Jónás (violin), Choir of the Hungarian State Folk Ensemble, Budapest Dance
Ensemble Orchestra, conductor: Béla Vavrinecz
LPX 18.006

*Karád Swineherd's Dance; Leaping Dance; Wallachian; Tomtit; Lad's Dance; Somogy
Ring Dance; Sárköz Ring Dance; Cumanian Verbunk; Kapuvár Verbunk; Hungarian
Verbunk; Somogy Csárdás; Szatmár Csárdás; Poor Csárdás; Turning Dance; Gipsy
Dance; Stick Dance; Palots Csárdás; Mátra Verbunk*
Mátyás Jónás and his orchestra, Girl's Choir of the Bartók Ensemble,
László Maácz (soloist)
LPX 18.007

Hungarian Rhapsody No. 19 (Liszt—Vavrinecz); *Csárdás macabre* (Liszt—Vavrinecz)
Orchestra of the Hungarian State Folk Ensemble, conductor: László Berki
LPX 10.104

Opre moy, gipsy suite (jointly with S. Szokolay)
Choir and Orchestra of the Hungarian State Folk Ensemble,
conductor: Rezső Lantos
LPX 1281

Brahmsiana; Marosszék Songs; Fireworks Csárdás; Dance Rhapsody
Duna Art Ensemble Orchestra, conductor: Tivadar Mészáros, Tavasz '67 Choir, Judit
Szücs (solo)
LPX 18.017

Slipper Dance; Spurred Verbunk; Kalocsa Csárdás
Orchestra of the Iron Workers' Art Ensemble, conductor: Béla András
PM 25 043 S

In the Green Forest of Szamosszeg; You See, Mother
Mrs József Simon (solo) 'Fly, Peacock' Folk Orchestra, conductor: Árpád Kovács
SP 60014-a

Death Dance Csárdás (Liszt—Vavrinecz), Orchestra of the Budapest Dance Ensemble, Mátyás Jónás (violin)
30 CV 1120 Musidisc

Hungarian Picture Book; Wide Waters of Balaton
Choir of the Hungarian State Folk Ensemble;
Orchestra of the Budapest Dance Ensemble
conductor: Béla Vavrinecz
LPX 10112

Wedding Songs; Doboz Csárdás
Orchestra of the Budapest Dance Ensemble, Mátyás Jónás (violin)
Visages du monde 6836 D-s + d

Three Dances; Two Duos for flute and cimbalom; *Children's Songs of Kalocsa; Children's Game Songs; Gencs Verbunk; Swineherd's Dance; Lament; Duo concertante; Concert Variations*
Márta Fábián (cimbalom), József Bige (shepherd's pipe), Tihamér Elek (flute), Jolán Fábián (cimbalom), Ferenc Belej, Csaba Onczay (cello), Éva Kádas (contrabass), Júlia Kádas (viola), Duna Art Ensemble Orchestra,
conductor: Béla Vavrinecz
SLPX 10140

Csárdás-Stroke; Gipsy Stick Dance from the Upper Tisza Region; Girls Along the Galga; Türe Lad's Dance; Miller's Danger and Horse-Herd's Csárdás; Happy Love; Csárdás Concerto
Zoltán Barcsay (cello), László Fehér (clarinet), Oszkár Ökrös (cimbalom), Gyula Tóki (violin), Budapest Dance Ensemble Orchestra, conductor: Béla Vavrinecz
SLPX 18034

JENŐ VÉCSEY

(b. Felsőcéce, 19 July 1909; d. Budapest, 18 Nov. 1966.) He started his studies simulta-neously at the University of Sciences and for composition with Zoltán Kodály at the Academy of Music in 1935. In 1942 he joined the staff of the National Széchényi Libra-ry where he was appointed to the Music Department. In addition to his compositions, he made significant contributions to musico-historical and -bibliographical literature, mostly relative to the material preserved in the Music Collection of the National Széchényi Library. He was on the editorial board of RISM and of the AIBM; edited the Hungarian section of the bibliographical part of "Fontes Artis Musicae". He initiated and directed the editorial work of the series "Musica Rinata" until his death. He was collaborator in the preparatory work of the new Haydn Collected Edition, and was member of the Musicological Committee of the Hungarian Academy of Sciences.

STAGE WORK: *Scholar Kele,* ballet, 1943.

ORCHESTRAL MUSIC: *Divertimento,* 1939–40; *Intermezzi per archi,* 1942; *Rhap-sody,* 1940–41; *Two Symphonic Dances,* 1945; *Castle Boldogkő,* symphonic poem, 1951, revised version: *Prelude, Notturno and Scherzo,* 1958; *Concerto Symphonique in Memoriam Gyula Krúdy,* 1958.

CONCERTOS: *Concertino* for piano and orchestra, 1953–56; *Concertino* for double-bass and orchestra, 1954; *Rhapsody* for harp and orchestra, 1954.

CHAMBER MUSIC: *String Quartet,* 1942; *String Sextet,* 1956, EMB; *Bagatelles* for two pianos, 1962.

PIANO PIECES: *Rhapsody,* 1939 (i.e. first version of Rhapsody for orchestra); Bagatelles, 1942.

SONGS: *Two Songs* for contralto or mezzosoprano and piano, 1943.

ARRANGEMENTS of works by the two Haydns, Erkel, Mosonyi, Doppler, Liszt, Arnold, Joseph Ruzitska, Barta, Császár, Aggházy, Bartha, Füredi, Mátray, Hubay, Nyizsnyai. Twelve Songs for voice and chamber orchestra (music of Egressy, Szentirmay, Simonffy, Szénfy).

WRITINGS: *Library Short-listing of Music* (in Hungarian), 1958; *Joseph Haydn's Works in the Music Collection of the National Széchényi Library* (in Hungarian, German and English), 1959; *Illustrated History of Hungarian Music* (in collaboration with Dezső Keresztury and Zoltán Falvy) (in Hungarian), 1960; *Accessions of the Last Fifteen Years to the Music Collection of the National Széchényi Library* (in Hungarian), 1958; *Welcoming the Haydn Year* (in Hungarian), 1958; *We Celebrate Haydn* (in Hungarian, German, English and French), 1959; *The Haydn Autographs of the National Széchényi Library* (in Hungarian), 1960.

LÁSZLÓ VIDOVSZKY

(b. Békéscsaba, 25 Febr. 1944.) Studied composition under Géza Szatmári at Szeged from 1959 to 1962, and from 1962 at the Academy of Music, Budapest under Ferenc Farkas. He graduated in composition in 1967. 1970–71 he studied in Paris (GRM and Olivier Messiaen). He is one of the founders of the New Music Studio (1970), and since 1972 he has been teaching at the Teachers' Training College of the Academy of Music.

WORKS: *Song to a Poem by Horace,* for soprano solo, flute, violin, cello and harpsichord, 1965; *Versus No. 2* for flute, 1965–69; *Fragment* for full orchestra, 1970; *Music for Győr* for orchestra, 1971; *Double* for two prepared pianos, 1968–72, EMB; *Autoconcert,* audio-visual, 1972; *405* for prepared piano, chamber ensemble and tape, 1972; *C + A + G + E Music Nos 1 and 2,* 1972, 1973; *Undisturbed* (with Z. Jeney and L. Sáry) for chamber ensemble and tape, 1974; *Circus* for 3 electric organs, 9 performers, 1974; *Schroeder's Death* for piano, a pianist and 3 assistants, 1972–75; *Fine Tuning* for 5 sound sources, 1975; *Hommage à Kurtág* (with P. Eötvös, Z. Jeney, Z. Kocsis and L. Sáry), 1975; *Gaga* for clarinet, cello and piano, 1976; *RENORAND* for 2 performers, 1976; *The Prince's Message,* audio-visual, 1976; *Souvenir de J.* for 55, 66, 78 or 91 performers, 1977; *Hommage à Dohnányi* for 12 performers (with B. Dukay, Z. Jeney, Z. Kocsis and L. Sáry), 1977.

IMRE VINCZE

(b. Kocs, 26 Sept. 1926; d. Budapest, 3 May 1969.) He studied composition as a pupil of Ferenc Szabó at the Academy of Music, Budapest, where he became later on professor. He was awarded the Erkel Prize in 1952 and in 1956.

CHORAL WORKS: *Szerelem, szerelem* (Love, Love), 1955, EMB; *Persian Songs,* 1967, EMB.

ORCHESTRAL MUSIC: *Symphony No. 1,* 1951; *Symphony No. 2,* 1953; *Köszöntő* (Felicitation), overture, 1954; *Movimento Sinfonico,* 1957, EMB; *Aforismo,* 1959, EMB; *Cantata senza parole,* 1960; *Concertino,* 1961, EMB; *Symphony No. 3,* 1967; *Rapsodia concertante* for piano and orchestra, 1966, EMB.

CHAMBER MUSIC: *String Quartet No. 1,* 1954; *Sonata* for violin and piano, 1956; *String Quartet No. 2,* 1958; *String Quartet No. 3,* 1961; *Divertimento* for wind quintet, 1962, EMB; *Sonata* for bassoon and piano, 1964, EMB; *String Quartet No. 4,* 1965, EMB; *Choral and Fugue,* 1968.

ORGAN COMPOSITION: *Fantasy and Fugue,* 1960.

Music to films, and choral works.

JÁNOS VISKI

(b. Kolozsvár, 10 June 1906; d. Budapest, 16 Jan. 1961.) He studied the violin already in his early years and composition under Zoltán Kodály at the Academy of Music, Budapest. He was professor of the National Conservatory, Budapest, in 1940, then director of the Conservatory at Kolozsvár (Cluj) in 1941. From 1942 until his death he was active as professor of composition at the Academy of Music, Budapest. He was awarded the Greguss Medal in 1942, the Erkel Prize in 1954, the "Merited Artist of the Hungarian People's Republic" title in 1955 and the Kossuth Prize in 1956.

WORK FOR SOLO AND ORCHESTRA: *Az irisórai szarvas* (The Deer of Irisóra), for baritone solo and orchestra, 1958.

CHORAL WORKS: *Hozsánna* (Hosanna), 1932, MK; *Fohászkodás* (Supplication), 1937, MK; *Virág és pillangó* (Flower and Butterfly), 1937, MK; *The Rákóczi March,* 1938, MK; transcribed: 1960; *Folk Song Suite,* 1950; *Csuklyában jár a barát* (The Monk Wears a Hood), 1950.

ORCHESTRAL MUSIC: *Symphonic Suite,* 1953, UE, Associated Music Publishers, New York; *Two Hungarian Dances,* 1938, UE, Associated Music Publishers, New York; *Enigma,* 1940, UE, Associated Music Publishers, New York; *Concerto for Vio-*

213

lin, 1947, Arts Council, EMB, BH; *Concerto for Piano, 1953, EMB, BH; Concerto for Violoncello,* 1955, EMB, BH.

INSTRUMENTAL MUSIC: *String Trio,* 1930, lost; *Five Small Piano Pieces,* 1948, R; *Epitaph for Anton Webern,* for piano, 1960, EMB.

SONGS: *Ave Maria,* 1927–32, MS, lost; *Ősz* (Autumn), 1928, MS, lost; *Testvérem, ilyen legyen a szíved* (My Brother, May You Have Such a Heart!), 1931, MS, lost; *Jaj annak a fának* (Oh, for that tree...), 1931, MS, lost; *A haldokló* (The Dying), 1945; *Aki meghalt* (The Dead), 1945; *Tavaszodik* (Spring is Coming), 1950; *Március* (March), 1951; *Terv* (Plan), 1952.

LEO WEINER

(b. Budapest, 16 Apr. 1885; d. 13 Nov. 1960.) He studied composition at the Academy of Music, Budapest from 1901 to 1906 as a pupil of János Koessler. For a while he was engaged as répétiteur at the Vígopera (Comic Opera). From 1908 to his death he was professor at the Academy of Music (theory of music, chamber music). He acquired world-wide reputation as a teacher of chamber music, bringing up a whole generation of well-known artists. He was awarded the Francis Joseph Prize in 1907, the Coolidge Prize in 1922, the Kossuth Prize in 1950 and 1960, the "Outstanding Artist of the Hungarian Peoples's Republic" title in 1953.

STAGE WORK: Incidental music for "Csongor és Tünde" by Vörösmarty, 1913, R.

ORCHESTRAL MUSIC: *Serenade,* 1906, Bote und Bock, Berlin; *Farsang* (Carnival-time), 1907, Bote und Bock, Berlin; *Csongor és az ördögfiak* (Csongor and the Devil's Sons), 1913, Hansen, Copenhagen; *Csongor and Tünde,* suite, 1913, R, EMB; *Divertimento No. 1,* 1923, R, EMB; *Katonásdi* (Playing at Soldiers), 1924, UE; *Suite,* Hungarian Folk Dances, 1931, R, EMB; *Pastorale, Fantasy and Fugue,* 1938, R, EMB; *Divertimento No. 2,* 1938, R, EMB; *Divertimento No. 3,* 1948, R, EMB; *Variations on a Hungarian Folk Song,* 1950, R; *Prélude, nocturne et scherzo diabolico,*

1950, EMB; *Divertimento No. 4,* 1951, EMB; *Divertimento No. 5,* 1951; *Ünnepi han-gok* (Festive Sounds), overture, 1951; *Toldi,* symphonic poem, 1952.

TRANSCRIPTIONS FOR ORCHESTRA: J. S. Bach: *Toccata, Adagio and Fugue in C major,* two versions, 1928, UE, 1934, UE; J. S. Bach: *Andante from Sonata for Solo Violin No. 3,* 1936, R; Bach: *Prelude from the Sonata for Solo Violin No. 4,* 1936, R; Beethoven: *Wut über den verlorenen Groschen,* Op. 129, 1959; Liszt: *Weinen, Kla-gen...,* 1933, R, EMB; Liszt: *Feux follets,* 1933, R, EMB; Liszt: *Sonata in B minor,* 1955; Schubert: *Grand Rondeau in A major,* Op. 107, 1934, R; Bartók: *Two Ruma-nian Dances,* 1938, R, EMB; Bartók: *Ten Pieces from "For Children",* 1952, EMB.

CONCERTOS: *Concertino* for piano and orchestra, 1923, UE; *Ballad* for clarinet and orchestra, 1949, R; *Romance* for violoncello, harp and orchestra, 1949, R, EMB; *Concerto for Violin* in D major (transcription of the sonata for violin and piano No. 1, 1950); *Concerto for Violin* in F sharp minor (transcription of the sonata for violin and piano No. 2, 1957), Mills, London.

CHAMBER MUSIC: *String Quartet* No. 1, 1906, Bote und Bock, Berlin; *String Trio,* 1908, Bote und Bock, Berlin; *Sonata for Violin and Piano No. 1,* 1911, R; *Sonata for Violin and Piano No. 2,* 1918, Bárd, Budapest, EMB; *String Quartet No. 2,* 1921, Bárd, Budapest; *String Quartet No. 3* (Pastorale, Fantasy and Fugue), 1938, R.

INSTRUMENTAL PIECES:

PIANO: *Three Pieces,* 1910, Rahter, Leipzig; *Miniature Sketches,* 1917, Bárd, Bu-dapest; *Katonásdi* (Playing at Soldiers), 1924, UE; *Passacaglia,* 1936, R, EMB; *Hun-garian Peasant Songs,* five series, 1932–50, R, EMB; *Three Dances* (from Divertimento No. 1), 1941, R, EMB; *Lakodalmas* (Wedding Dance), 1936, R, EMB; *Twenty Easy Pieces for the Youth,* 1948, R, EMB; *Cadences to Beethoven's Concertos* No. 1, No. 2, No. 3 and No. 4, 1949, Suvini-Zerboni, Milan; *Thirty Easy and Moderately Difficult Short Pieces for the Youth,* 1952, EMB.

VIOLIN AND PIANO: *Lakodalmas* (Wedding Dance), 1936, R, EMB.

VIOLONCELLO AND PIANO: *Romance,* 1921, Bárd, Budapest.

CLARINET AND PIANO: *Ballad,* 1911, R.

FOR OTHER INSTRUMENTS: *Peregi Verbunk* (Recruiting Dance from Pereg), for violin, viola or clarinet and piano, 1951, EMB.

WRITINGS: *A zenei formák vázlatos ismertetése* (Outline of Musical Forms), 1911, R; *Összhangzattanra előkészítő jegyzetek* (Preparatory Notes to Harmony), 1911, R; *Az összhangzattan előkészítő iskolája* (Preparatory Course of Harmony), 1917, R; *Elemző összhangzattan* (Analytical Harmony – Functions), 1943, R; *A hangszeres zene formái* (The Forms of Instrumental Music), 1954, EMB.

DISCOGRAPHY:
String Quartet No. 3
Sebestyén String Quartet
LPX 11396

Csongor and Tünde, Op. 10 (Suite) – *Suite Op. 18*
Budapest Philharmonic Society Orchestra, conductor: Tamás Breitner
LPX 11526

Recruiting Dance from Pereg, Op. 40
László Horváth (clarinet), Mária Steinert (piano)
LPX 11534

WORKS OF HUNGARIAN COMPOSERS
PUBLISHED BY EDITIO MUSICA BUDAPEST
AS WELL AS ORCHESTRAL HIRE MATERIAL
ARE AVAILABLE FROM:

KULTURA

Hungarian Foreign Trading Company for Books and Newspapers
Budapest 62. P.O.B. 149. Tel.: 159—450
Telex: 22—4441

For particulars and catalogues please contact the above address.

Our representatives abroad:

ARGENTINA
Juan Horváth
Lavalle 361 Entrepiso 5.
Buenos Aires

AUSTRALIA
Boosey and Hawkes (Pty.Ltd.)*
26/28 Whiting Street
Artarmon N.S.W.2064

AUSTRIA
Universal Edition A.G.* *
Karlsplatz 6
Wien I.

Hofmeister-Figaro Musikverlag
Brucknerstrasse 6
Wien I

BELGIUM
Metropolis P.v.b.a.
Van Ertbornstraat 5
B-2000 Antwerpen

BRAZIL
Livraria Bródy, Ltda.
Rua Cons.Crispiniano 404—30.
Sao Paolo

Livraria D.Landy
Rua 7 de Abril 252 5s S/31.
Sao Paolo

CANADA
Boosey and Hawkes Ltd.*
279 Yorkland Blvd.
Willowdale M2J 157
Ontario

218

CZECHOSLOVAKIA
Ceský Hudební Fond**
Staré Mésto
Parizská 13
110 00 Praha 1

DENMARK
Wilhelm Hansen Musikforlag*
Gothersgade 9/11
DK-1123 København

Engstrøm and Sødring Musikforlag
Palaisgade 6
DK-1261 København

FINLAND
Music Fazer Musiikkikauppa*
Aleksanterinkatu 1
Helsinki

FRANCE
Boosey and Hawkes, Sagem*
4 rue Drouot
Paris 9e

GERMAN DEMOCRATIC REPUBLIC
Internationale Musikleihbibliothek
Leipziger Strasse 26
108 Berlin

GERMAN FEDERAL REPUBLIC
Boosey and Hawkes GmbH.*
Prinz-Albert-Strasse 26
53 Bonn 1

ISRAEL
From Music Supply
2 Brenner Street
Tel Aviv

ITALY
Carisch S.p.A.
Via General Fara 39
20124 Milano

G.Ricordi e.C.**
Via Berchet 2
20121 Milano

JAPAN
Nippon Gakki Co.Ltd.*
Tokyo Branch
1, Ginza 7-chome,
Chou-ku Tokyo

THE NETHERLANDS
Ed.Broekmans and Van Poppel*
Van Baerlestraat 92-94
Amsterdam Z

NORWAY
Musik Huset
Karl Johansgatan 45
Oslo

Norsk Musikforlag**
Karl Johansgatan 39
Oslo

POLAND
Polskie Wydawnictwo Muzyczne**
Centralna Biblioteka Nutowa
ul. Senatorska 13/15
Warszawa

SPAIN
Real Musical Madrid
c.Carlos III.No.1
Madrid 13

SWEDEN
Boosey and Hawkes Svenska AB
Kryptongatan 7
S-431 22 Mölndal 1

SWITZERLAND
Ed.Eulenburg GmbH.*
Grütstr.28
8134 Adliswil-Zürich

UNITED KINGDOM
Boosey and Hawkes*
Music Publishers Ltd.
295 Regent Street
London W1A 1BR

UNITED STATES
Boosey and Hawkes Inc.*
30 West 57th Str.
New York 10019, N.Y.

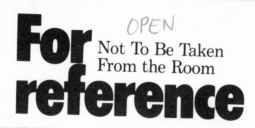
*   = For Orchestral Hire Material too
** = Just for Orchestral Hire Material

2297